CALIFORNIA CHROME
OUR STORY

California Chrome
Our Story

Perry Martin

Lisa Groothedde, Rommy Faversham

McCarran Media

Library of Congress Control Number: 2021925629

First Printing, 2022

Dedicated to my loving wife

Denise Maria Martin
May 28, 1960 – June 14, 2021

We shared our lives for 35 years, experiencing work and play, joy and sorrow, victory and defeat; and through it all, our love grew greater every day. I miss you!

Preface

On the first Saturday in May of 2014, the lives of my wife, Denise, and I were changed forever.

Surrounded by our friends and family under the famous twin spires of Churchill Downs, we watched with tremendous pride as our home-bred chestnut colt California Chrome, the first horse we had ever bred, raced into the history books as just the fourth California-bred in history—and the first in 52 years—to win the Kentucky Derby (G1), our sport's most coveted treasure. As it turns out, that was just the beginning of the ride of a lifetime that has been our gift from California Chrome.

From his early days as a lanky foal at Harris Farms in California's verdant Central Valley to his current home at Arrow Stud on the beautiful island of Hokkaido, Japan, California Chrome took us on a worldwide journey. We marveled at unforgettable vistas on three continents outside our own, from the sandy deserts of Dubai to the undulating green grass gallops of England and the mountain-laced pastures of Chile. We were planning a trip to visit him in Japan when the COVID-19 pandemic brought worldwide travel to a screeching halt in early 2020.

In between these sojourns, we were greatly honored to accept Eclipse Awards, racing's highest accolades, alongside two sets of former partners for his Horse of the Year titles in 2014 and 2016, as well as numerous awards from the California Thoroughbred Breeders Association, including a pair of California Horse of the Year trophies, in regard for his many athletic accomplishments. Our wildly popular colt also distinguished himself as the first and only two-time winner of racing's unique Vox Populi Award, an annual honor that is voted upon by the general public and bestowed by the connections of the original "America's Horse," Secretariat.

California Chrome's talent, charisma and longevity garnered him legions of fans and granted him household name status during his racing days, which came to an end in January 2017 when he retired as a healthy 6-year-old with $14,752,650 in career earnings, the most money won by any Thoroughbred to ever run a race in North America.

But that was not the end of our horse's saga, as his second career begat as much intrigue as his first.

My wife and I were the only people who could write this story, as we were there from the very beginning. We planned the breeding which resulted in California Chrome, remained loyal to him through ownership changes, heavily supported him as a stallion throughout his North American breeding career and continued to contribute toward his legacy by securing lifetime breeding rights to him in Japan. Denise and I were all-in on Chrome; you might even say we "Let it ride!"

This book is an effort to clear the social media and internet fog surrounding California Chrome and to dispel the salacious gossip which in today's world passes as journalism. It is a clear-eyed look at the business of breeding and racing a champion racehorse and all the thrills and heartaches that go along with it.

Enjoy!

- Perry Martin

Foreward By Rommy Faversham

It's always fun to think about California Chrome. His magic lifts our spirits. Thank goodness he couldn't be classified an intoxicant. Otherwise, he would have surely been rendered illegal.

Chrome's heroics sparked his enormous fan base (the indefatigable "Chromies") into a unique state of mass euphoria that no one dare attempt to rein in. Columns of normally mild-mannered adults would start to swarm the winner's circle well before he passed them at the finish line. Hundreds of perfectly rational adults, all convinced Chrome was really "their horse," were completely incapable of standing on ceremony. The owners never seemed to mind, so the trackside ushers all ran for cover, wishing to avoid being trampled by the revved-up throng and their new lease on life. To avoid the claustrophobic conditions, despite being a graciously welcomed friend of his owners, I liked to position myself alongside the professional camera corps and just soak it all in.

The fact is, California Chrome checks all the boxes. His modest origins and unsung connections only made for some of his best stories. He entered the walking ring with the radiance and charisma of a matinee idol. And then he would run, usually leaving the rest of the racing world in his wake.

California Chrome came to epitomize "equipoise," a wonderful term that goes back to the mid-17th century. It suggests the combined heightened state of equilibrium (balance) and poise—the only two qualities capable of overcoming that menacing slipped saddle while competing in, and then winning, the world's richest horse race in 2016. Equipoise also became the namesake of the most celebrated racehorse during the early years of the Depression. Indeed, Chrome carries three of his pedigree strains.

Chrome's good-natured, history-making trainer, Art Sherman, provided his own unique background that weaved perfectly into the Chrome Experience. For Art, who conditioned Chrome while in his late 70s, it all goes back to his formative years, when he was an exercise rider and boxcar companion to the great Swaps. Together, they traveled to Louisville and the Run for the Roses, where the "California Comet" outran mighty Nashua. Kentucky Derby-winning California-bred Hall of Famers (to be) are extremely hard to come by, and Art can claim an intimate relationship with both of them.

Swaps also served as an integral part within the pedigree of Love the Chase, the dam of California Chrome. Her ancestry's defining feature was the close (3X3) and auspicious inbreeding pattern to 1971 Champion 2-Year-Old Filly Numbered Account, whose broodmare sire was, quite suitably, Swaps. For good measure, it is also quite remarkable that Swaps and California Chrome both descend from the same distinctly American female family.

Bottom line: Chrome's often maligned pedigree was remarkably similar to that of his fourth generation tail-male sire, the great Triple Crown champion Seattle Slew. Same sire line, obviously. And dams who were both closely inbred to key descendants of La Troienne, 20th century America's greatest matriarch.

As Chrome began reeling off triumphs of increasing prestige, I knew I had to find out for myself if his breeder was aware of the powers from crossing all of the different strains of La Troienne. To my delight, Chrome's co-breeder, majority owner and exceptionally quick study, Perry Martin, was quite cognizant of the fact La Troienne was baked into his charge's DNA.

It turns out, pedigrees are a great way of starting up a friendship. Perry and his wonderful wife, Denise, were side-by-side career scientists, which I think only complemented their appreciation of pedigree theory. It was nice. We had a lot to talk about from the get-go.

We have all been diminished by Denise's recent passing. For myself, I will always remember her own special equipoise. For as Chrome became more and more of a legend, Denise countered with a heightened sense of gratitude and humility.

In 1999, Perry published what has been described as the definitive book on the subject of electronics testing: "Electronic Failure Analysis Handbook." And so, I thought it to be wonderfully sublime when Chrome captured the $143,000 Trans Gulf Electromechanical Trophy Handicap at Meydan Racecourse in preparation for that unforgettable 2016 Dubai World Cup. With California Chrome around, there was never a shortage of electricity.

This horse became a veritable cornucopia of superlatives. My two favorites are "richest Kentucky Derby winner" and "richest tail-male descendant of Seattle Slew," in light of the remarkable parallels within their pedigrees. But there are so many more.

He is also the first and only multiple winner of the annual Secretariat Vox Populi Award, more than sufficient proof (as if he needed it) he is one of the most popular horses of the modern era.

How good was California Chrome? I would harken back to maybe his best-ever performance: the Pacific Classic. It turns out the 2016 edition marked the first time in the 79-year history of Del Mar that a pair of future Hall of Famers, both of them ridden by Hall of Famers, had ever met.

Perennial champion distaffer Beholder was back for more, having become the marquee venue's first female Pacific Classic winner in near record-breaking fashion 12 months earlier. Nothing really mattered though, once Chrome burst out of the gate and took total control. Cruising home by five lengths, he made the mighty mare appear almost ordinary while she easily bested the rest of the field. But then, it was the jockeys who had the final word.

Beholder's rider, Gary Stevens, just shook his head.

"What a horse," he marveled. "California Chrome is as good as I've ridden against."

Chrome's regular pilot, Victor Espinoza, left even less to the imagination.

"I'm going to say this now—this is the best horse I've ever ridden," said the rider of American Pharoah, the sensational Triple Crown ("Grand Slam") winner from just a year earlier.

Ever since the importation of their country's greatest stallion, Sunday Silence, Japanese farms have demonstrated a very healthy demand for Kentucky Derby winners. The offer for California Chrome in 2019 was simply too good to refuse. Add in the generous breeding rights and terms for his eventual return to the U.S., and it was just good business. As Perry put it, "It's hard to say no to everything we asked for."

Prior to his move to Arrow Stud on the northern island of Hokkaido, Chrome shuttled for two seasons to Haras Sumaya in Chile while doing three at Taylor Made Farm in Kentucky. Early returns show his daughters to be outperforming his sons. His runners generally seem to have a liking of grass, which is a bit unusual for the A.P. Indy line. So far, Chrome has done particularly well with broodmares carrying complementary strains from the female families that appear in his own pedigree. The family of Numbered Account. The family of Pulpit and Lucky Pulpit. Just as the maxims of female family inbreeding would predict.

California Chrome's only full brother was foaled during his 4-year old campaign. From the beginning, the resemblance was unmistakable. Halfway through the weanling's first summer, I was completely bowled over when the Martins asked if they could name him Faversham. It was a gift I will always treasure.

Not a big surprise, Faversham's racing career was nothing like his older brother's. After a most promising debut, he was soon worse for wear, having survived a violent incident in deep stretch, never really recapturing that initial spark. He did look like a shooting star on the Santa Anita turf one delightful afternoon, when he put away a nice field of maiden special weight horses at better than 17-1.

Now it's time to follow his career as a stallion up at Daehling Ranch in Northern California. Obviously, with identical pedigrees, the hope is for Faversham to have some mates carrying the same family strains that already seem to work well with Chrome.

Our hero may have always had the look of a new, shiny penny, but California Chrome has always been very much of a throwback. Pedigree-wise, he is a throwback to Seattle Slew. There was also a durability about him that was more akin to the tough horses of yesteryear. Chrome is the only Kentucky Derby winner to be voted Horse of the Year at age 5 or older. In fact, he is the only non-gelding to ever be voted Horse of the Year in non-consecutive years.

Chrome also proved to be a consistently fast horse. He didn't set a lot of track records (two), but his winning times were often some of the fastest in the history of those fixtures.

Chrome was as versatile as was ever the need. He won at seven different distances, from 4 1/2 furlongs to 1 1/4 miles, and joins Secretariat as the only Kentucky Derby winners to win a Grade 1 stakes race on the grass.

Always good to travel, California Chrome is the only horse to win or place in two Breeders' Cup Classics and two Dubai World Cups. The international jet-setter has now raced, trained or resided on four different continents. Chalk a lot of this up to his superior temperament, as well as the steady hand of the Sherman team, particularly Art's son Alan Sherman and Chrome's devoted groom, Raul Rodriguez.

We're also charmed by a great horse whose moniker couldn't have been more perfect. In this case, a five-syllable official name that highlights his origins, much like Seattle Slew. Most of the time, though, it's just Chrome, a wonderful, single-syllable name that has never been associated with a famous runner or progenitor before.

We now get to enjoy the very clever names a good number of his offspring are (and will be) sporting. You can do a lot of rhyming with Chrome. Oh, give me some Chrome, where the buffalo roam.

Wait, I think that's too many letters.

— *Rommy Faversham*
Thoroughbred Pedigree Analyst & Author
equicross.com

About the front cover photo

This book's cover image of California Chrome in the winner's circle at the 2014 Kentucky Derby was taken by my friend and doctor, Jon Overholt, M.D.

In 2013, I began seeing Dr. Overholt to treat a case of cellulitis I had contracted on both of my ankles. Cellulitis is a common bacterial skin infection that causes redness, swelling and pain in the infected area of the skin. I had been fishing—one of my favorite pastimes—and got hundreds of irritating chigger bites around my ankles. I treated the bites with antiseptic and lidocaine ointment, which seemed to work well as the swelling and redness subsided quickly; but, several months later, the cellulitis appeared.

This diagnosis required monthly doctor visits, as the circulation in these areas was poor and oral antibiotic treatment was slow to work. The treatment would take many months to finally eliminate the infection. We rotated treatment between oral and topical antibiotics, with some periods of using both. This was done to not let the oral antibiotics overstress my digestive tract.

With us thereby seeing each other on a regular basis, Dr. Overholt and I developed a good rapport. During one visit, I remember him asking me how life was treating me. I told him that it couldn't be better, as I had a 2-year-old Thoroughbred colt who was going to win the Kentucky Derby (G1) the following May. In return for my seemingly outrageous prediction, I got that raised eyebrow look, then we carried on with the regular examination and other innocuous small talk.

The next month, I brought my doctor a gift: an 8" x 10" photo of California Chrome in the winner's circle after my colt's first big career victory in the $100,000 Graduation Stakes at Del Mar. That news precipitated a five-minute discussion about Chrome and the plans for his future.

From that day forward, the first five minutes of every doctor's visit was spent catching up on California Chrome. I had created a "Chromie," and there were always new racing accomplishments and next-level goals to share with him during the rapid build-up to the 2014 Triple Crown series. Dr. Overholt even called to congratulate me after our colt's emphatic win in the $1 million Santa Anita Derby (G1), Chrome's fourth consecutive victory and final prep race for the big dance.

On Kentucky Derby day, my late wife, Denise, and I ran into Jon, who had brought his granddaughter, Cyan, all the way from California to Churchill Downs to take part in the festivities. We invited them to join us in the famed winner's circle if we were lucky enough to emerge victorious. We were, and they did, after I cleared them through the security pile-up.

Once clear of the security line, the crowd of people in the enclosure kept pushing them forward. When they could finally stop, Jon turned to watch security organize the media photographers about ten yards back from where Chrome would be positioned for pictures. The first row were on one knee, the second row was standing and the third row was on ladders for that special angle. Just then Cyan said, "Grandpa watch out, Chrome is right behind you!" Jon turned and quickly snapped that photo with maybe the best angle of all before being ushered out of camera view for the Pro's.

And that is the origin of our cover photo—a magical moment in time captured by one of the first of what would eventually become an immeasurable number of people whose lives were positively impacted by one very special horse, and none more significantly than our own.

— *Perry Martin*

About the back cover photo

Approaching the Derby stretch run.
Photo Courtesy of Dan Dry

Photo of California Chrome photographed as he is on his way to winning the 2014 Kentucky Derby at Churchill Downs in Louisville, Ky. The photo was originally taken for Churchill Downs website Kentuckyderby.com

The photo is included as part of a photo exhibit and display of iconic Louisville photos in a new (lower level) Walking Tunnel at Muhammad Ali International Airport in Louisville, KY (the Walking Tunnel is scheduled to open in early 2022)

Dan Dry, PriceWeber's image consultant extraordinaire, has won over 400 national and international photography, advertising, and design awards. A member of the *Louisville Courier-Journal's* Pulitzer Prize-winning photography staff from 1976 until 1982, Dan then went on to travel the world shooting for *National Geographic.* Dan also served as director of the Kentucky Derby photo team for 30 years and director of photography for the Breeders' Cup for 31 years—no, don't ask him for tickets!—and is the sole author of over 20 coffee table books and (famous foodie that he is) cookbooks.

Contents

Dedication — v
Preface — vi
Foreward By Rommy Faversham — viii
About The Front Cover Photo — xiv
About The Back Cover Photo — xvi

1 THE HORSE BUSINESS IS VERY INEFFICIENT — 1

2 FOOTBALL, MINIMUM WAGE AND ISAAC ASIMOV — 6

3 CALIFORNIA, HERE WE COME! — 23

4 OUR FIRST HORSE — 43

5 DUMB ASS PARTNERS — 49

6 IT'S A BOY! — 57

7 AN AUSPICIOUS START — 70

8 THE BIG LEAGUES — 79

9 DREAM SEASON — 87

10 OUR RUN FOR THE ROSES — 96

11 THE SECOND JEWEL — 104

12 TRIPLE CROWN LETDOWN — 109

13 THE EYE OF THE STORM — 115

Kentucky Derby Rings — 123

14 DEL MAR DUST-UP   124

15 THREE RACES: MORE THAN $6 MILLION ON THE LINE   128

16 THE LOST YEAR   136

17 CALIFORNIA CHROME LLC   158

18 BACK ON TRACK   163

Photo Insert   189

Photo Insert   190

19 THE LAST RACE   191

20 THE BUSINESS OF BREEDING   197

9 PHOTOS FROM A MAGICAL DAY IN SEPTEMBER 2019   217

Photo Insert   218

Photo Insert   219

Photo Insert   220

Photo Insert   221

Photo Insert   222

Photo Insert   223

Photo Insert   224

Photo Insert   225

21 SELLING TO JAPAN   226

Komorebi No Omoide   235

22 THE NEXT GENERATION   236

23 LOVE, AND LOSS   240

24 EPILOGUE   243

About The Author 246

Acknowledgements 249

CALIFORNIA CHROME: CAREER
ACCOMPLISHMENTS 251

1

THE HORSE BUSINESS
IS VERY INEFFICIENT

There is an old joke that eventually finds its way to anyone who is either courageous or foolish enough to dabble in Thoroughbreds: "What is the easiest way to become a millionaire in the horse racing business? Start out as a billionaire."

My wife, Denise, and I did not start out in the racing business as billionaires. Quite the opposite, in fact.

Family Values

We both grew up in Chicago, living about four miles away from each other as the crow flies. But our paths did not cross until fate simply brought us together when we were in our 20s.

Denise and I were both children produced by "The Greatest Generation," so called because of the extraordinary sacrifices required to win World War II.

Denise's mom and dad were both born in Poland and immigrated to the United States after the war. Her father left Poland after the Nazi invasion and joined the British Expeditionary Force to fight the Nazis. He learned English while training in England and shook the hand of a young Queen Elizabeth II upon her visit to their base.

My father was accepted into Massachusetts Institute of Technology for his college studies, but he joined the Army in the middle of the war instead. He was first stationed in North Africa, where he saw limited fighting with his company, and later transferred to Europe to replace front-line troops as they marched into Germany for the first time near the end of the war. The fighting was intense, as the Germans were defending their home territory for the first time. My father was wounded in the clearing of a small German village, and received a Purple Heart.

Denise and I were stuck with the outmoded values of truth, honor, self-reliance and self-sacrifice passed on by our parents, and apparently were too ignorant to learn the new values of self-righteousness and self-indulgence taught by our schools, politicians and media. We were taught that the best place to look for a hand up was the end of your own arm! It is very hard to live in today's world with these outdated values, but that is how we were raised.

I firmly believe that our upbringing contributed to our later success in business, as well as the horse racing industry. We were self-starters and risk-takers who, despite our middle-class roots, created and campaigned the highest-earning Thoroughbred racehorse in history, all while sticking to the values that had been instilled into us at an early age.

If I hadn't lived it, I might not have believed it myself. To borrow a term from horse racing, what are the odds?

Risk Management

Being successful in horse racing is all about managing risk.

The day of a race, every horse owner experiences that "sick" feeling in the pit of their stomach, which inescapably persists until the race is safely over. The knowledge that one bad step can end a horse's career, and possibly its life, is probably one of the most difficult feelings I have ever had to deal with. It is very much like watching your kids perform on a gymnastics balance beam, except if your child breaks their leg, they are not put down. This "hazard" risk is always in the back of every horseperson's mind. You can help to protect the financial side of things with insurance, but that can never make you whole again!

Managing risk comes in many forms.

For the well-heeled, who enter the game to experience the spotlight, purchasing into an established champion at 2 or 3 years old eliminates all of the inherent risks from breeding through on-track performance and leaves only the hazard risk. This reduction of risk comes at a price, for, at this stage, the cost will be in the millions of dollars. This may be small change to big players, but it represents life-changing money to many small owners and breeders, and thus is good for the sport. For the small owners and breeders, taking some, or all, of the risk off the table is often a wise move, as a horse's development may take an unexpected turn.

The 2-year-old in training sales, conceptualized in North America during the 1950s and today a prominent source for acquiring racehorses, are the next rung down the risk ladder. These young horses have had foundation training (been broke to the saddle and ridden, typically for a period of 60 to 90 days) and usually put in an eighth of a mile or quarter-mile timed work just prior to the sale so potential purchasers can see how they move on the track. The horses are shown on-site for a few days leading up to the sale, allowing close-up inspection of their conformation and walk. At a 2-year-old auction, it is standard procedure for X-rays of each horse to be placed in a repository for review by licensed veterinarians hired by prospective buyers. The vets can also scope a horse's throat to look for breathing issues.

The next rung down the Thoroughbred risk ladder is the yearling sales, the "beauty pageants" among horse auctions. For yearlings, it is all about their looks. In most cases, these horses have not been broke or ridden, but have been put through a physical development program based mostly on walking. They have been X-rayed during their development, with surgeries often performed to correct any deficiencies. Sale-bound yearlings usually get two to three months of conditioning and training to learn how to stand and walk properly for potential buyers. As some of the bigger sales are conducted for up to 10 days or more, the yearlings are typically evaluated by sales company personnel for placement in their catalogs, with the "better" (i.e., better-looking) horses getting earlier placement.

Another rung lower on the risk ladder is purchasing weanlings (young horses recently separated from their mothers, or dams) at mixed-age sales. Here, with so little development on the table, the risk is high, but it is not the highest.

The highest risk of all is breeding your own horse for sales or racing purposes. Breeding is not exactly cheap, with access fees for top stallions reaching into hundreds of thousands of dollars. The absolute best mares sell at auction for millions of dollars. Foaling, boarding, veterinary fees, farrier visits, transportation, insurance and other expenses can easily add up to thousands of dollars each month for a mare and her foal. These costs accumulate over time, which explains the high sale prices. High-priced mares matched with high-priced stallions are supposed to generate high-priced offspring. Yet many breeders do not recoup the stud fees they have paid, while others enjoy a return of 20 times or more the stud fee!

What do I mean when I say the horse business is very inefficient?

A buyer is extremely dependent on his or her available knowledge base when purchasing a horse. Many owners simply depend on their hired trainers to select the best. Others prefer to be involved in the process.

Several racetracks in the U.S. have owner-oriented groups that offer seminars for how to buy a racehorse. They will gather at a designated trainer's barn on the backside of the track, where the trainer will bring out horses to point out various conformation "issues." The session will usually end with the trainer showing a horse with "perfect" conformation. Warning: Do not go to the Equibase website to look up that "perfect" horse's race record; you will probably be disappointed!

Conformation of a horse is an evaluation of a horse's size, alignment, proportions in leg and body and other physical traits. It is interesting what constitutes "good" conformation for trainers. I have attended several of these seminars, and each trainer has a slightly different opinion of what "good" conformation is, and the importance of each feature. Still, American trainers overall have a similar view of this issue. It is interesting that I have had discussions with a Ph.D. in equine biomechanics and his description of perfect horse conformation is much different from that of American trainers.

I reconcile this discord within the framework of this inefficient equine marketplace. It explains how Seattle Slew—California Chrome's great-great-grandsire—could be purchased at auction as a yearling in 1975 for just $17,500 because he had "poor" conformation, yet go on to become a Triple Crown winner, Racing Hall of Fame inductee and important sire of sires. It also helps me understand how The Green Monkey could be purchased as a 2-year-old in 2006 for a record $16 million, then only manage to earn $10,440 with just a single third-place finish from three starts before he retired from racing with a physical ailment.

There is opportunity in the horse racing world, but you must tread carefully. This is the basis of what we understood to be true when Denise and I entered these dangerous deep waters.

2

FOOTBALL, MINIMUM WAGE AND ISAAC ASIMOV

Before we venture too far into our journey, you're probably asking yourself, "Who are these people, and how did they get to this point?"

For me, it would be best to start with high school, where I learned some important life lessons starting at the age of 14.

Making The Team

I was on the football team for most of my first two years in high school in 1970 and 1971. Lane Technical High School in Chicago, Illinois is a perennial football powerhouse in the city, although the team seldom does well at the state level. Still, many Lane Tech players have been recruited to major college teams over the years.

Making the freshman and sophomore ("frosh-soph") football team was simply a matter of toughness.

On day one of practice, the coach told us that he wasn't going to cut anybody, as there were no limits to how many players would be allowed on the frosh-soph team. There was only so much equipment to issue, however, so we would have to cut ourselves down to the right number before they issued equipment.

The coach made a roster and took attendance every day. He made it clear that if you missed football practice, you were off the team. The only way to miss practice without eliminating yourself from the team was to present a doctor's note as your excuse.

First off, this was really the freshman team, as all of the sophomore players had been issued equipment and were off on the other side of the football field, practicing. As incoming freshmen, my group comprised about 400 guys who didn't have a clue what we were in for!

The coach knew exactly what to do to wean out the wannabes quickly. The first exercise he assigned us was "Run 'til you puke."

Football practice lasted for three hours after school. For our first practice, all we did was run for the entire three hours. Circle the football field, then keep going. Only about 10 guys dropped out and went home during this initial three-hour run. Those were the lucky ones.

I made it until the end of practice, then walked the 2 1/2 miles home. I walked both to and from school every day; of course, I now tell my children it was uphill both ways! The daily trek to and from high school was not a hardship in the long run, because it probably gave me some conditioning in my legs. But, despite that regular exercise I had built into my daily routine, I was not prepared for the rigors of trying out for the football team.

When I woke up the day after our first three-hour run during practice, I could hardly walk. My feet had blisters and my legs were sore and cramped. I got dressed, had breakfast, then started my long walk to school which, on this particular day, seemed longer than it had ever been before. I wore two pairs of sweat socks to provide a little more padding. It was slow going at first, but I eventually began to loosen up and move faster.

By the time I made it to school, I was feeling much better; still hurt, but it was acceptable. I made it through my classes and then off again to the gridiron. There were only about 200 guys on day two.

After attendance was taken, we were off and running again. Three more hours of running, to be precise.

At the end of practice, the coach dismissed us, saying, "You had better get used to this; it's all we are going to do the first two weeks!"

As we broke up and headed home, I heard someone grumbling, "If I wanted to run, I would have gone out for track!"

By the time those two grueling weeks were over, we were down to 60 potential freshman players from the inaugural field of about 400, so they congratulated those of us who had survived the process and issued equipment.

For some reason, I was happy I had lasted and been rewarded with my equipment. I thought that made me tough, or at least special. Then I learned that when you were issued equipment, the hitting started.

I was assigned to the line coach, and I quickly found out that linemen were all about hitting. We learned how to block and hit and be hit. It was that last part that had me going home every night to take an hour-long soak in a hot bathtub. Every morning, I would wake up black and blue, and go off and do it all over again. It was not enjoyable.

I should have quit, but I didn't want to be called a quitter. So, I stuck it out through my entire freshman season.

After football season was over, there was a short period of time where all I had to worry about was classwork. That was actually nice.

Summer came. Usually, teenage summers meant time off to goof around, but not if you were on the Lane Tech football team.

The school district made it clear that there could not be organized practice during the summer months. They didn't say anything about unorganized practices.

It was made clear to us as football players that we were expected to show up for summer practices under the direction of the team captains. The practices could not be held on school property, so they were conducted instead at a city park.

Workouts were bad in the fall during football season, but they were brutal during the hot Chicago summer. Once again, I did not enjoy it.

I stuck it out through about half of my sophomore football season. It was then that I came to a decision. This was not the football I played in grade school. That football was fun. It was running, throwing and catching, and playing every down on both sides of the ball. But at the high school level, they had somehow found a way to take all the fun out of the game. As a bonus, I got to hurt all the time while taking a lot of precious hours away from studying.

It was the hardest decision I made during my high school years, because I did not want to be called a quitter. I finally decided that I had to do what was right for me and not worry about the names people might call me.

I grew up at that moment and decided to quit the football team. I was turning 16 soon, and could get a job. I probably would not like it, but at least I would be paid for my time and efforts, and not have to ask my parents for money all the time.

My First Job

The Mayflower grocery store, which was one block away from my home, was torn down and a new neighborhood grocery store, Kohl's, was scheduled to open in about four weeks. I went in, filled out a job application and got a call to return for an interview the next week.

When I showed up for the appointment, there were about 20 guys and two girls there. The district manager for Kohl's was there to do the hiring. He had us all stand in a straight line. He walked down the line and looked us over.

There was a guy with long hair, and the manager said to him, "You need a haircut."

The guy said he was not cutting his hair, so the manager pointed to the door. The guy left the store.

The manager looked at us, then pointed to the door again.

"This is a customer-focused business, and you are all going to be interacting with customers and representing the store," he said. "We want a clean-cut appearance. You need to bathe every day and wear clean clothes—black slacks and a white shirt. You will be given a name tag that you will wear. Anyone who cannot do this should leave now."

Nobody did.

He smiled and said, "You're all hired."

I started working at Kohl's grocery store in 1972 for $1.65 per hour, which was minimum wage at the time. I had to join a union, AFL-CIO, as I recall.

I remember thinking what a shrewd bunch of negotiators I had working for me. It must have been a long, hard contract negotiation to get them all the way up to the minimum required by law. But, then again, there were the benefits.

If you worked full time for three months, they would give you health insurance. That is a great benefit, but I never met any employee who wasn't in management who got it. After one full year of employment, you were entitled to a week of vacation and an automatic raise of 15 cents per hour.

I guess I just didn't know how lucky I was, only having to work 10 hours a month (considering taxes) just to pay my $15 monthly union dues. What a waste of money!

I'll never forget my first day at work, but I should tell you about the night before.

My parents went out of town to visit one of my mom's sisters. This happened all the time, as my mom wanted to encourage family ties.

This trip, I got to stay home alone, because I was a big boy now; I had a job. So, on Friday afternoon, they loaded my little brother in the car and took off to Kalamazoo, Michigan.

My first day of work was to be for the grand opening of the grocery store on a Saturday. The managers had placed an ad in the newspaper with tons of specials that savvy shoppers just could not miss. But this was Friday night, I was a teenager and I was home alone. Not only that, but my dad had forgotten to lock up the bar before he left.

I called my friends, and two of them came over. I showed them the booze we had and asked what they wanted. They didn't know, and I could not provide any guidance.

We decided to make a punch. I grabbed a large half-gallon pitcher and brought it over to the bar. I didn't want to use a lot from any one bottle of alcohol and risk getting caught when my parents got home, so I poured about one-third of a bottle from each. Whiskey, gin, vodka, rum, tequila and, for some reason, scotch went into the pitcher. That should be enough for the three of us! I'll add a little orange juice, and we should be good to go. It tasted like crap, but that didn't stop us from drinking it.

I turned up the radio, tuned in to Chicago's WLS AM rock station and we drank and talked. At some point, we didn't notice the taste anymore, and it started to go down pretty easy.

The next morning, we all woke up on the floor. Wow, my first hangover on my first day of work—and it was a doozy. I made it through the day somehow, head pounding and sweating, but, I must say, all-in-all, it was not as bad as football practice!

Arlington Park

I made some new friends at my first job. One guy, Tony, told me about the fun he had when his dad took him to the racetrack on weekends. I got invited along. So, on one weekend day that we both had off work, we went out to Arlington Park for the Thoroughbred races.

It was a wonderful experience. Fresh air, with a hint of hay and horses. Then there were the strange characters at the track: the guy who would smack his racing form against his leg during races, a bunch that talked to themselves and there was always one guy who would cheer every winner like he bet $1 million on it, but, somehow, he never cashed any tickets. If the people were not a little off one way, they went off in another direction, dressing like they were at a formal wedding, rather than a casual sporting event. I fit right in.

A very new experience for me was gambling. I believe you were supposed to be 18 years old before you could wager, but I was already more than 6 feet tall, had considerable football conditioning and had grown a mustache. I had no problem placing bets.

My friend had given me a five-minute handicapping lesson, so I was good to go. Actually, I took the information he had furnished me, sifted out the stuff that made sense, then added some of my own analysis. I also added the need to view the horses in the paddock before the race.

Statistics are great, but you need to ground your opinions in reality, and knowing the condition of the horse before the race is very important. Is the horse sweating heavily? Is it acting nervous? What is its coat condition? These are all physical projections that very much affect the outcome.

Over time, I would learn that you can refine this reality check by getting to know the horses as individuals. If you watch a horse run multiple races, you will learn if that horse is always nervous before a race or always sweating, for example. This knowledge allows you to discount factors.

My friend cautioned me that there were other opinions and other ways to try and figure the race results. He introduced me to tip sheets. His favorite was the "green sheet." I noticed there was also the "red sheet," which made me wonder if there was any difference between the two guides, other than one was printed with green ink and the other with red ink.

One day, I purchased both and compared them to each other. Basically, they both picked all the same horses, but ordered them a bit differently. From that day forward, I would rely on my own judgment and only purchase the racing form in order to handicap races myself.

During my first day at the track, I think I picked three winners out of the 10-race card, but none of them were favorites. Thirty percent at the track is a good average, just like batting .300 in baseball.

In those days, I usually bet $2 per race. I had only brought $20 with me on my first day at Arlington Park, and there were other expenses: entry fee, parking, racing form, a hot dog and a Coke. I went home with $36.

Sixteen dollars to the plus-side might not seem like much now, but you have to remember that I was only earning $1.65 per hour at my grocery store job. Do the math! Those initial racetrack winnings were more than I would make for a full eight-hour workday. AND, NO UNION DUES!

After I got my driver's license, I was able to borrow the family car and drive myself to the races. Sometimes I would drive across town after the Thoroughbred races were over at Arlington to attend the night-time Standardbred or harness races. I liked the harness races; they were easier to handicap, since all the races were conducted at the same distance. I used to call going to daytime and nighttime races all in one day "the daily double."

At that time, the Chicago-area harness races were held at Maywood Park, Sportsman's Park, Hawthorne Race Course, Washington Park and Balmoral Park. Only Hawthorne still exists. All of those Standardbred tracks except Maywood applied for Thoroughbred racing dates from time to time.

Funny story later in life. On one of my flights to Dubai during California Chrome's racing career, I sat in the first class lounge with Scott Hazelton, a TVG host whose father, Richard, was a top trainer on the Chicago circuit, back when Chicago had a circuit.

Sportsman's Park and Hawthorne were right next to each other, located between the major streets of Cicero Avenue and Laramie Avenue. Scott's family lived in one of the nearby apartment buildings on Laramie. He told me he hated it when one of the tracks was running because jerks would park in front of his place, and he would have to park four blocks down and walk home. I told him I was one of those jerks! I didn't want to pay the $2 for parking, as I would rather bet it.

Horse racing became a big part of my life in the 1970s. It never has been the end-all, however. Some people do get sucked in, and that's too bad. For me as a teenager, family, school and work always needed to come first. Those priorities are still with me today.

College: Constructive Laziness

After graduating from high school, I attended Michigan Technological University (MTU) in Houghton, Michigan, which is located in the Upper Peninsula portion of the state, just a stone's throw across Lake Superior from the Canadian border.

To say MTU students are isolated up in the northern woods is not an understatement. The school mascot is a husky. I remember the university bookstore sold a T-shirt that featured a picture of a country road with a sign that read, "End of World – 18 miles. Michigan Tech – 20 miles."

I enrolled in applied physics so I could substitute 18 hours of electives for the language requirement that was necessary for a physics degree. I have a hard time with foreign languages, so I took 18 hours of metallurgy courses to check the language boxes and another eight hours of metallurgy courses as free electives. Twenty-six college undergraduate hours of metallurgy is pretty substantial, as I would find out later in life.

MTU adhered to the quarter system when I was a student: 10 weeks of classes per quarter, a break of about two weeks between quarters and the rest of the time in the year allotted to holidays. I loved the quarter system; it seemed to move at the right speed for me.

One quarter, I had a nuclear engineering class and a metallurgy class in using the Scanning Electron Microscope (SEM) and related methods. Both of these classes required a paper to be written for a significant part of the grade. I thought, why not look at a nuclear fuel pellet with the SEM, and slightly tailor my paper for each class. Two birds, one stone.

A problem the nuclear industry had was the inspection of fuel pellets for "hot spots." Hot spots were uranium-rich volumes in pellets which would locally heat when inside a reactor. The pellets were inspected using neutron radiography which, at the time, was a very specialized type of work. Because only a few companies did this type of work, it was expensive and a bottleneck to the supply chain.

My paper proposed that a SEM could be used to inspect the pellets in two ways. The first way was using backscatter electrons. The outside of the pellet could be imaged using only backscatter electrons and the uranium intersecting the surface of the pellet would appear brighter because it was much heavier than the matrix material. By mapping the total area of the bright regions and comparing that to the area which should be presented if we assume a uniform distribution of uranium, we could, using statistics, calculate the probability of the pellet being uniform. Using a related SEM technique called Energy Dispersive Spectroscopy (EDS), we could use characteristic X-ray maps to do the same thing and double-check our work.

This method would not be foolproof, but I proposed that 20%-25% of the pellets could be inspected in this manner if the pellet use was limited to the outward-most reactor regions where the neutron flux was less sensitive. This would address the bottleneck and possibly force inspection price reductions.

I wrote two very similar papers and submitted them to the appropriate class.

I received a B+ in my metallurgy class. The instructor thought I could have done more to refine my techniques.

I received an A+ in my nuclear engineering class. My instructor, Professor Don Daavettila, was very impressed. In fact, he was so impressed, he had the department secretaries re-type the paper in a slightly modified format that he provided and then he submitted the paper, without my knowledge, to be presented at the American Nuclear Society annual meeting, which was to be held at the University of Michigan that year. My paper was accepted for presentation.

I was informed about this development along with the whole class at the end of the quarter. I was called to the front of the class to receive the acceptance letter. There I was, a junior in college, and I had only two months to prepare a presentation which would be given to professional nuclear engineers from all over the world, many at the Ph.D. level. Talk about butterflies!

Two months later, I was ready. I had been given department resources and made about 10 overhead projector slides for the presentation. I had notecards explaining each one of the slides which introduced the observer to electron-material interactions and how that was used to ascertain useful data. The final slides covered the statistical analysis, which should have been straight-forward for this audience.

I circulated a letter from the head of the physics department to all of my course instructors, asking them to give me an allowance for time off in order to represent the university at the conference. I got extra time to submit my homework and even got a pass on one test, with the instructor informing me he would simply give me the average score of all my other tests.

Professor Daavettila drove me and several other students to the conference using an official State of Michigan car. We stopped at state police stations along the way to fill the gas tank. It was a nice drive over the Mackinac Bridge to Ann Arbor, Michigan.

As MTU was part of the university system, our instructor and all the students got discount preferred pricing to stay at the University of Michigan's school union. MTU paid for the rooms, and we got tickets to eat for free in the cafeteria.

The presentation went very well. The attendees were very attentive, and I was peppered with a lot of good questions from the group after my talk. Since the material was a little out of their field, I think no one wanted to stray too far out of their comfort zone and risk being made to look stupid by an undergraduate student.

A few people walked up to the podium afterward to ask questions in a more one-on-one environment. We were asked to move our group out to the lobby so the next speaker could start.

Out in the lobby, a Ph.D. professor from Penn State told me how much he enjoyed my little joke. I said, "What joke?"

It seems when I was explaining Auger electrons, I pronounced it ['ôgər] rather than (AW-zhər). Auger electrons are named after their discoverer and are electrons that are emitted when an electron from a higher energy level falls into a vacancy in an inner shell. I thought maybe they bored into the atom like an auger. My bad.

At the end of the conference, the host professor congratulated me on my presentation, and said it was the talk of the conference. He told me that it was second in the voting for the conference's best paper. He also said he was sure the only reason it wasn't voted as best paper was because some of the judges were a little intimidated by a college junior even presenting at the conference. He said they believed if an undergraduate student received the best paper award, it would reflect poorly on the other conference speakers.

I felt a warm glow inside and thanked him. When I got back to MTU, there was an article about me in the school newspaper, and I was a bigwig for a whole week.

See what being lazy can do for you?

After I graduated from MTU in 1978 with a Bachelor of Science degree in applied physics, I was recruited by the Idaho National Engineering Laboratory outside of Idaho Falls, Idaho. They had an opening for an investigator to examine components from the 1979 Three Mile Island accident using an automated SEM. At the time, there were not a lot of SEM people with nuclear experience, and a LexisNexis database search had uncovered my paper.

Once again, I came in second to a Ph.D.; first on my conference paper and now on the job offer. But ultimately, I am grateful for not being selected for this position. It would have changed my life immensely if I had moved to Idaho, rather than attending graduate school at the University of Illinois Chicago. I would not have met the love of my life.

Denise

In grad school, the costs for my first year and a half were covered by a teaching assistantship. The assistantship covered my tuition and paid me a monthly stipend of about $600 in exchange for teaching three physics labs per semester.

After the third semester of working under this arrangement, I was called into the office of the head of the physics department. I was informed that I was losing my assistantship because I was a resident of Illinois. Huh?

The professor explained that the university was losing funding and had to reduce the number of assistantships. Because I was an Illinois resident, I was one of the logical choices to rescind an assistantship, because I would only need to pay the resident rate of tuition, which was less than the non-resident tuition rate. He explained further that I could go to work to earn tuition money, while foreign students only had student visas and could not work.

It hit me; foreign students were getting preference over U.S. resident students for funding that was sourced from state taxes paid by residents of Illinois. The fact that the department head was once a foreign student did not escape me, so I said a few choice things that would hinder my school career going forward. Enough said.

After I lost the assistantship, I ended up getting three jobs. The first was for UPS, making $15 per hour for part-time work at night, loading and unloading trucks at a distribution center. UPS offered medical insurance as if working full time. These benefits were acquired by the Teamsters Union, which was in this case a useful union. I went to school during the day and worked three to four hours at night, or five to six hours at night in the months leading up to Christmas.

After one more semester, I earned my Master of Science degree in physics and dropped out of the doctorate program for this field of study. Instead, I transferred over to the metallurgy department to take part-time graduate courses.

With my master's degree, I was able to get two part-time teaching jobs in physics: one at Loyola University Chicago and another at North Park College. My weekdays were very busy. On Mondays, Wednesdays and Fridays, I would teach mornings at Loyola, and on Tuesdays and Thursdays, I would teach mornings at North Park. On weekday afternoons, I would take one or two metallurgy courses; at night, I would work at UPS. For weekend activity, I joined a billiards league and represented the Sit N Bull bar by playing 8-ball in bars around the city.

One Saturday, I went into the Sit N Bull a couple hours early to warm up before we headed across town. I had no idea on that seemingly normal day in 1985 that my entire life was about to change, and for the better.

A beautiful girl was sitting alone at the bar. She was reading the book "Foundation," by Isaac Asimov.

Intrigued, I sat down next to her and told her she was reading one of my favorite books. We talked, and I found out her name was Denise, and she was waiting for her girlfriend.

For about 20 minutes, we discussed some of Asimov's other books. Then her friend arrived. I asked the bartender for a pen and wrote my name and phone number on a small napkin. I handed it to her, and asked her to call me the following Saturday before I excused myself.

Usually, the man asks for the woman's number, but I had found that was a mistake. That road can waste a lot of time. Either she was interested and would call, or she wasn't and would not.

I did get a call the next Saturday, and we made a date to go to the races. Denise had never been to a racetrack, and she seemed very excited to try it out.

I felt this girl was special and I would need to find out quickly if we were compatible. Where most men make their mistake is in trying to become the man a woman is looking for. That method may get you short-term success, but it invariably results in long-term disappointment. I would be myself and just see what happened.

Our first date went well. I explained about handicapping and betting the horses, but I could see that Denise was just being polite and wasn't really interested in betting.

The horses, however, were a different story. We started spending more time around the Arlington Park walking ring before each race and I explained what I would look for in each horse. I could see the utter joy in Denise's eyes as we viewed the horses. One of the horses raised its tail and defecated. I pointed at the horse and joked that one is lighter now and would have an advantage. We both smiled.

By the last race, I was ahead about $10. As was my tradition, I made a $10 win bet on a 6-1 shot that I liked. The horse lost, so we left for dinner after breaking even for the day.

We had a very nice dinner and got to know more about each other. I was intrigued by her background.

Denise was a first-generation naturalized U.S. citizen, as her parents were legal immigrants from Poland. Her dad learned English while serving in the military overseas, and her mom learned after arriving in the states. Denise's mom told me that just being immersed in the language allowed her to learn to speak English quickly; she taught herself to read English by grocery shopping.

Every time Denise's mom would go to a store, she would look at the cans and boxes. The pictures on the outside would tell her what was inside. She would assume that the words matched the contents which matched the pictures. So, for example, if there was a picture of a tomato on a can, there would be tomatoes inside the can. She would learn the meaning of the words whole, diced or stewed after opening the cans.

Denise's father was the main wage-earner for the family, and made a good living as a machinist in the days when products were still made in the USA. Her family was able to save some money and purchase a two-story brick apartment building with an apartment on each floor. Renting out the upstairs apartment allowed them to pay off the mortgage faster.

Chicago is a city of immigrants, groups of whom tend to cluster and reside in neighborhoods with values and cultures similar to their own. Neighborhoods do bump up against each other and there is spillover, mixing and turnover.

Denise's neighborhood began to get rough when she was a child. She went to Chicago public schools for the first few years, but after she was attacked one day while going to the store for her mom, she transferred to a Catholic elementary school and convent in rural Indiana. She later attended Madonna High School, an all-girls Catholic school in Chicago.

After graduation, she worked at Mitsubishi and attended classes part-time at Northwestern University.

During our first dinner conversation, I explained my work situation and noted that I only had weekends available to see her. We agreed to spend the next weekend together down by the lakefront, where the city's museums are clustered.

The bustling Chicago lakefront would become a staple of our dating routine. We would attend a Bears game at Soldier Field or visit one of the city's wonderful museums, or the Shedd Aquarium, the Adler Planetarium or Lincoln Park Zoo. After a year of dating, I proposed to her outside the planetarium.

We agreed on a two-month engagement, and decided we would elope to Las Vegas to be married at the end of May. This was very practical, as all of my schools would be out for summer by then. I had several weeks of vacation available with UPS, so I would schedule some time off and make our travel plans.

At that time, Denise was living in her parents' apartment building , and directly above them, but she didn't want us to live there. So she decided to take some time off from her office job during our engagement in order to find us an apartment to live in together.

In 1986, we were married in our shorts at the Chapel of the Stars in Las Vegas. A purple limousine picked us up in front of the historic Desert Inn, where we spent our honeymoon. Perhaps the limo color was an omen for the future.

At the hotel, we had a quiet suite in the back complex next to the golf course. It was perfect!

On special anniversaries in later years, we would return when we could to the Desert Inn to celebrate; that is, until the Desert Inn was closed in 2000 and demolished so the new Wynn Las Vegas could be constructed on its former site. After that, we would return to the Wynn.

As newlyweds, we lived for a few months in the apartment Denise had found for us. She went back to her office job, while I sent out job resumes during the days and worked at UPS during most evenings. I did get a few interviews, but I never seemed to get the right fit for a professional job where I could apply my education.

One of the potential employers to whom I submitted an application was the U.S. Office of Personnel Management (OPM). The application contained all of my university transcripts. The OPM staff reviewed and classified me, then sent my review to me and several government organizations that had openings which fit my professional qualifications.

I immediately received letters requesting first-stage phone interviews from three military bases, all in California. Two of these invitations were from the U.S. Navy: the Naval Air Weapons Station China Lake in Southern California and the Naval Air Station Alameda in Northern California. The third invitation was from the U.S. Air Force's McClellan Air Force Base outside Sacramento.

Upon discussion, Denise and I agreed California would be an interesting place to live for a short time. Neither of us had ever even visited the state. We thought China Lake was too isolated and we did not care for its desert climate, so we nixed that one. Alameda was interesting, but the Bay Area has a big downside; it's quite expensive to live there.

We decided it was McClellan, or nothing.

3

CALIFORNIA, HERE WE COME!

I arranged the phone interview, and it went pretty smoothly. The OPM had classified me as being qualified for a metallurgist position that they had open, with the primary job function being to perform failure analysis. I had actually taken several collegiate courses in using the Scanning Electron Microscope for use in failure analysis, which really helped with the interview.

I was offered the job but, before the call ended, I asked if I could fly out to Sacramento on my own dime to tour the facility and meet the people. The representative agreed and we arranged a date for my tour.

I had a written job offer in my hands before I flew out to California, so I took it with me. I arranged a quick two-day trip, and stayed at a La Quinta Inn near the Air Force base.

The day of our meeting, I drove my rental car to the main gate of McClellan, where a nice airman holding a M16 rifle directed me to the gate parking lot. I parked there and walked back to the guardhouse, where I provided my base contact's information and filled out a visitor pass form. Someone from the lab where I would be working drove out, signed me in and drove me back to the lab.

I spent the morning meeting my immediate supervisors and colleagues and touring the facilities. At the end of the morning, I officially accepted the job.

My new boss took me to lunch in the cafeteria, then walked me over to the personnel office, which was near the main gate. The personnel workers pulled my file and began processing my employee paperwork while my supervisor excused himself and went back to work.

Before I left the base that day, I had an employee badge/base pass, a sticker for the front bumper of our car so I could enter the base, travel orders which would pay our mileage and per diem for our road trip from Chicago to Sacramento and a relocation package to move our simple furnishings as well. I was asked to report for work six weeks later, in December 1986.

On the second day of my scouting trip, I visited a few apartment complexes, and ultimately settled for one nearest the base. The billboard above the complex read, "If you lived here, you would be home now." Made sense to me! I planned on walking to work in the mornings from time to time, but leaving our Jeep Wrangler for Denise to use was not the reason; she could not drive a stick shift.

I signed a one-year lease for our new home and paid the first month's rent and cleaning deposit. The one-bedroom apartment would be repainted and recarpeted before we moved in. I took two keys for the apartment with me, and flew back to Chicago the next day.

We were renting our apartment in Chicago on a month-to-month basis, so we gave our lease termination notice upon my return.

We scheduled a moving company that had been recommended by the Air Force, and they picked up our belongings. As newlyweds, we didn't have much stuff, so our meager belongings got loaded in the back of a 40-foot trailer and a partition was erected. The moving company then loaded another Chicago family's things inside the trailer for their move to Denver, Colorado. They would deliver their haul to Denver first, then go on to Sacramento, where we would meet them at our new apartment.

Denise and I drove out to California in our Jeep Wrangler, stopping in several hotels along the way to break up the long journey. It was December 1986—probably not the wisest time of year to be traveling through some of the northern states.

I remember we took Interstate 80 all the way. One stop was in Cheyenne, Wyoming, where the temperature was 30 degrees below zero. A 20 mph wind was howling through the night, and even with the baseboard heat turned all the way up, the thin hotel walls kept our room very chilly. We cuddled under the covers all night to keep warm.

In the morning, the Jeep would not start. The entire vehicle was frozen. Luckily, I had bought the Jeep when I lived up in Northern Michigan, and it came equipped with an engine block heater. I always carried an extension cord under the back seat, so I pulled it out and plugged it into the engine block, then ran the cord through the hotel room door to plug it into an outlet. The door would not completely close with the cord holding it open, so as we shivered and waited for the Jeep to warm, our wait got colder.

After 45 minutes, I was able to get the Jeep started. I turned the heater to full blast, then stowed the extension cord and waited in the room with the door now fully closed. Another 15 minutes later, the Jeep was warm enough for us to continue our trip west.

After we finally arrived at our new apartment, we slept in a sleeping bag on the floor for two nights until our bed and furnishings caught up to us. But at least it was warm.

With the big move to California completed, we settled into our new routines.

Two Becomes Four

Soon after arriving in Sacramento, Denise and I spent a weekend evening enjoying the harness races at Cal Expo, the home of the annual California State Fair.

Denise did not have a job at this point, so our visit to Cal Expo, combined with her love of horses, inspired her to shadow a harness trainer, Mr. Jenkins, in the mornings. She volunteered to help around his barn by walking horses, mucking stalls and doing whatever needed to be done. This was fun for her, and she enjoyed it until, after a few months, she had put on some weight in places that allowed Mr. Jenkins to guess that she was with child. He told her she could not work around the horses anymore.

Denise was disappointed, but soon she was able to get a civilian job with the Air Force at McClellan in the supply and warehousing group. I would drop her off on the other side of the base in the mornings before I went to the lab, and pick her up before going home in the evenings. This was perfect.

After we welcomed our first child—our daughter, Kelly—in August 1987, our one-bedroom apartment suddenly felt very cramped. Who knew that such tiny humans came with so many necessary accessories?

We moved into a nice neighborhood about seven miles away from the base. We rented a very sunny apartment with two bedrooms, two baths and an open floor plan. It would not be long until our son, Perry Martin Jr., would help us fill up this new space as our second child; he was born in August 1989.

We knew we would want to purchase a house of our own someday, so we started a savings account to accrue enough for a down payment. We could not add very much money each month. We were putting the maximum amount allowed into my 401(k) retirement savings plan provided by the Air Force.

As the mother of two very young children, Denise did what she could to supplement our household income.

Making The Grade

I had taken employment with the Air Force as a GS-9 metallurgist. By the time our second child arrived in August 1989, I had progressed to a GS-11.

My initial work was all metallurgical in nature: analyzing metal failures. But, in time, I was also analyzing plastic aircraft canopy failures, composite material failures and even a ceramic failure. Most of the other people in the lab doing this work were GS-12 materials engineers.

In fact, I was the only metallurgist at McClellan Air Force Base, so I had some business cards printed that featured my name with "Base Chief Metallurgist" underneath it. Some of the guys who had been working there longer than me took exception, but they got their revenge by making much more money than me.

You see, a metallurgist is classified as a scientist, while a materials engineer is classified as an engineer. Engineers were in higher demand at that time, and the OPM had justified higher pay rates for engineers. Engineers even had a higher target grade (12) than scientists, who only rated a grade 11. I was topped out!

Under the guidance of my supervisor, I started filling out Air Force Standard Form 172 (SF 172) on a monthly basis. This form allows you to update your federal work experience; it is reviewed for accuracy and signed off by your supervisor, then placed in your personnel folder. I would be comprehensive when I filled out these forms, but I really focused on non-metal projects I was doing to emphasize I was working on all types of materials and not just metals. After a year of such updates, I requested my first desk audit.

A desk audit is part of the Federal Personnel System. The U.S. government realizes that a federal worker's duties can grow out of the specific position description under which one is working. In my case, after being assigned projects for a year that really were GS-12 materials engineer jobs, I was basically saying the government was screwing me by paying me as a GS-11 metallurgist.

The lady from the personnel office pulled and reviewed my file. There was just over one year of appropriate experience documented in the file. She then interviewed me and followed up with my supervisor. She concluded that the government had me working in a position beyond my pay level. She authorized my supervisor to reclassify my position as a GS-12 materials engineer and promote me into it. I threw out my "Base Chief Metallurgist" cards!

With the bump in pay, Denise and I were able to save money a little quicker for a down payment on a house.

This is an example of how the desk audit system works when management is on board and wants it to work properly. Our section chief called an all-hands meeting and announced my promotion to the section. There were cheers all around, as I had finally made it to journeyman level.

During this meeting, our supervisor also told us that the lab was in trouble, as there was not enough work coming in via Air Force Standard Form 206 (SF 206) to fund us. This document was used to transfer funds between USAF entities; as such, it included the purpose of the funding and authorization signatures.

Our supervisor encouraged us to go out and promote the lab to the various engineering groups in order to bring in funding. I would turn out to be very effective at this.

With extra money going into the bank, Denise and I tried to get pre-qualified for a home loan. It took some time, but we finally found a bank that would work with us.

Now having the power of a pre-qualification letter in hand, we would pack the kids in the car and spend our weekends house hunting. Everything that we liked was out of our price range. That big backyard for the kids was looking like something that would break the budget.

The "Homes" section of the Sunday newspaper was our guide, as all of the new housing developments would be advertised in it.

There was a new development that was approximately a 45-minute drive north of Sacramento, and which promised large backyards at an affordable price. We decided that I would take a day off from work in mid-week and we would travel during rush hours in order to determine how this added encumbrance would affect my potential daily commute to and from McClellan. It would certainly be a significant lifestyle change for someone such as myself, who took pleasure in walking to school as a youngster and to work during my early days at McClellan.

We found that area of Sacramento had not really been developed yet, and the commute to Yuba City was very reasonable. The housing development did have larger lot sizes and the homes did seem to give you more for the money. We liked the medium-sized model, but we didn't make a decision during that first visit, preferring instead to search a bit more first.

After a couple more weekends of hunting, we returned to Yuba City to look one more time at the model home we liked. We found the right lot for us and signed a letter of intent that day.

Our house still needed to be built, so we would frequently return to the development to select our decorative options, such as countertop materials and types of flooring for the kitchen and bathrooms, and to finalize the contract with the builder. Our lender was in the loop at every junction, so the loan would process with the final sign-off by the county building inspector.

Fighting The System

At work, I specialized in failure analysis and crash investigation, starting out mostly with airplanes, then expanding my scope to include missiles, drones, satellites, radar systems and other highly confidential areas as I developed the electronics failure lab. Through this crash investigation, I started working on projects that involved electronic failures.

At the time, light-bulb analysis was about the only electronic analysis being done in crash investigations. This was fairly straightforward stuff. Investigators wanted to know what warning lights were on during a crash, and this could be determined by examining the bulbs or bulb fragments after a crash.

A bulb filament is a very brittle material at room temperature. So, if a bulb is off, you would have a brittle failure when the plane impacted. On the other hand, when a bulb is on, the filament becomes very hot and very ductile, not unlike a blacksmith heating the metal of a horseshoe so it becomes more ductile and easily formed to a horse's hoof. Therefore, if a warning light's bulb filament had a ductile failure from impact, the bulb was determined to have been on at the time of the crash.

I was working a more complex level of electronic failures, not just from projects derived from our base, but from all over the entire Air Force. I even was allocated several million dollars from our aircraft management directorate to develop a specialized laboratory in order to do this type of work.

Several very important projects I had done on aircraft electrical power systems and high-power radar systems were getting high-level attention, and I was required to brief these projects all the way up to the Air Force chief of staff. I was becoming a recognized expert in this field and was asked to participate in a project directed by the Air Force laboratory at Wright-Patterson Air Force Base in Ohio. This project was to develop an Air Force guide or manual on using electronic failure analysis techniques in crash investigation.

The Air Force published this work as WL-TR-95-4004, "Aircraft Mishap Investigation Handbook for Electronic Hardware." I was given an acknowledgement for my participation in the introduction. However, I was not happy with how this guide turned out; I thought there was much more that could have been done. That inspired me to write my first book, "The Electronic Failure Analysis Handbook," published after three years of hard work by McGraw Hill in 1999.

I continued to update my personnel folder every month. After three years of input, I noticed that my folder had its own file cabinet drawer in the personnel office.

Once a month, I would sit down with my supervisor and show him the work I was doing to verify my SF 172 updates, and he would validate the forms and submit them to personnel. I went a step further and wrote a position description that detailed everything that I was currently doing. I even included copies of travel orders issued at the headquarters level that stated my specific expertise in electronic failure analysis was required to address projects deemed crucial by the U.S. Air Force. I requested my second desk audit.

This audit was not supported by management; however, per the regulations, it does not have to be. The higher-ups decided to just sit back and let the system collapse on me. They felt that, without their support, the inertia of the federal government would be enough to stop me in my tracks. But the desk audit exists for a reason.

A very serious-minded personnel representative who did her job by the rules was assigned my case. She started by conducting a 45-minute interview with me. I had pre-prepared a list of senior people with whom I had worked at the Air Force laboratories and command levels, including their phone numbers, and gave that to her before the end of our interview. I included a copy of the position description I had written that detailed what I was really doing. I also offered to give her a tour of the specialized laboratory I had built to support work coming in via SF 206 for other directorates. She left, then called me to schedule a second interview after about three weeks.

The second interview was very positive. The personnel representative told me she first pulled my file and needed help moving it to her desk. I just smiled, and said I like to stay on top of my updates!

She explained that she had gone through my file and pulled out some of the updates which dealt with high-level Air Force management. She then matched the file with the contact people I had provided and called them individually. She said she was very uncomfortable dealing with management levels that high in the chain of command, but she was able to talk to each commander or director provided. Every one of them not only validated my updates, but said they believed the updates were understated.

She also told me that the position description I had provided to her could not be used, because she classified it as a high GS-14 level. We would need to down scope the position description to a GS-13, because a desk audit can only promote one GS level and I was a 12.

She then asked for a tour of my lab, which I was happy to provide. I also introduced her to the five people working with me who were covered, budget-wise, by the 206 hours I was generating from projects.

About two weeks later, the desk audit paperwork came down to my supervisor, who signed off on the new GS-13 position description detailing my electronic failure analysis duties, as well as the paperwork promoting me into the position. Two weeks after that, the paperwork came down with my promotion.

No one but me in our section was happy. Several people ran to the branch chief's office to complain, since they had been promised a promotion. They were very upset that their long-time brown-nosing had not produced anything fruitful.

The branch chief subsequently ran to my supervisor's office to figure out what was going on. I just stayed in my lab and worked, waiting for the storm to blow over. What I didn't know was that my promotion for merit was putting the entire brown-nose political structure in jeopardy and could not be allowed to stand!

Six weeks later, I received paperwork for a demotion back to GS-12. When I went to my supervisor and asked what this was about, he surprised me by telling me the truth. He said the branch chief had promised a promotion to someone else, so they were demoting me to give the spot to this other person. I actually thought the other person deserved a promotion, just not my promotion.

I looked up the federal regulations and filed an official protest against the government's actions. The paperwork simply said I was promoted by mistake and the mistake was being rectified. My protest simply stated the truth; it was my belief that the promotion was not a mistake, and I had been offered no opportunity to present evidence to the contrary. I motioned that the government's demotion should be reversed, since I had been denied all rights of due process.

It took six weeks for my protest paperwork to be processed, and a date was assigned to an administrative judge another eight weeks out. The hearing would be conducted by telephone at the date and time assigned.

The telephone hearing was very brief. The administrative judge introduced all the players, then simply asked the lawyer for the government if she could prove there was a hearing over the demotion. The lawyer kept repeating that no hearing was required. The judge suggested that the lawyer should re-read the 14th Amendment to the U.S. Constitution, which covers due process. He then ruled in my favor and ordered the government to reinstate me with back pay and interest.

I received a copy of the ruling in the mail the following week; the week after that, I got the promotion paperwork and back pay. During this battle, there had been a number of jerks in the lab who would look me in the face and laugh, "Ha ha, you got demoted." After the matter was settled, I made sure to look them up to tell them I was promoted again, and this time with back pay and interest!

Management in the lab was evaluated by the work production numbers produced by the laboratory. With the direction of my supervisor, I went out and got funding for specialized equipment, negotiated for space to set up the lab and acquired funding to cover a total of six personnel. We were working these jobs with five people, so were generating excess production to cover at least one slacker. I felt they needed the production, so they would leave me alone.

They did need the production, and my supervisor continued to encourage me to grow the work to cover even more workers, but the petty upper management just could not let things stand. It was a control issue, and only those supported by management could be promoted.

The government scheduled a hearing to demote me, which would be held at the division level. The notice I received stated the same premise as the previous position: that my promotion had been a mistake. Management believed a hearing would cover the due process requirement and they could do anything they wanted. By bumping it up to the division level, a new and higher ranking, supposedly unprejudiced authority figures could rubber-stamp the pre-ordained findings.

The division level meeting was quite succinct. The division chief led the meeting, which was attended by my supervisor, my branch chief, a court reporter, an Air Force lawyer and me.

The division chief read a statement that indicated the purpose of the meeting was to correct a mistake made by personnel. Then he asked me if I had anything to say. I did.

"Isn't the purpose of this meeting to gather evidence to determine if a mistake has been made?" I asked.

To my surprise, he said, "No, personnel has informed us a mistake has been made. Do you have anything to add?"

I asked if he had reviewed my personnel folder, and he said no. I asked if he had any plans to review my personnel folder, and he said, "Son, I have people that do that."

I replied, "I see, then I have probably taken up too much of your time already."

He dismissed the meeting, and I walked back to my office to start working on the protest appeal to the demotion that I knew was coming.

Base Closure

Around this time, in 1995, the U.S. military was conducting its third round of base closures.

In the previous two rounds, during the early 1990s, they had closed the Sacramento Army Depot and Mather Air Force Base, both located near Sacramento. These closures had hit the local community very hard with the loss of a combined 35,000 jobs. Conventional wisdom said they wouldn't hit the same community again, as losing another 30,000 jobs at McClellan Air Force Base could not be absorbed. Conventional wisdom was wrong, and McClellan was selected for closure.

It would not simply vanish overnight though; there was a five-year draw-down plan being put into place. The nightly news broadcasts and daily newspapers would hammer the military at every opportunity as uncaring SOB's. Air Force public relations specialists were slow to react, probably because there was no way to defend the actions. Eventually, civilian personnel started to implement new base closure rules allowing for personnel leave to accumulate beyond the six-week maximum, as well as job relocation programs and a buyout program to help workers transition to the private sector.

In confusion, there is opportunity.

During my tenure at McClellan, I had worked the reliability side of many programs for the Air Force, and occasionally I had been sent as an observer to test programs conducted at private laboratories. One of these private labs was National Technical Systems (NTS) in Saugus, California, where, during one visit, I had the opportunity to meet Jack Lin, the company president. In fact, he had given me his business card. When the base closure calamity began to materialize, I dug his card out of my desk and decided to call him one day after work.

I started our conversation by telling him I thought there was an opportunity for a large contract at McClellan to privatize the laboratory I was working in. I explained the public relations problem the Air Force was having, and gave him the name and phone number of a lawyer who served on the Sacramento City Council as a liaison to the Air Force.

Within a week, the lawyer had arranged for Jack to meet with the base commander and his public relations specialists. The plan worked. Jack offered them a public relations lifeline: they could demonstrate they were promoting the privatization of jobs at the base by starting with the privatization of the lab.

There was a non-committal agreement to explore this opportunity. They scheduled another meeting, which would include high-level people from the funding and contracting groups. The city council member would keep the pressure on by leaking his involvement to the media, thereby bringing a focus to the effort and increasing public expectations for progress. If the Air Force stepped back from this tentative agreement, it would be perceived as again not caring about the community.

As the effort gained traction in the media, I had the hardest time listening to the gossip from my co-workers in the lab and pretending I didn't know anything about the situation. I also had to watch the progress unfold ever so slowly.

Jack had assigned a division manager to oversee the effort, and I would talk to him from time to time to get an inside update. It was excruciating waiting, but I had other things to occupy my time.

The demotion paperwork had finally come down and I had a long protest/appeal letter ready to submit in a more than timely fashion. I'm not a lawyer, but I was pretty sure that whatever that second hearing was, it was not due process. Still, I decided to proceed another way.

I stated that the hearing showed that the Air Force was not interested in due process, though I was sure they would be able to cobble together a management group that would eventually put on a show that could pass for due process. I offered to waive my rights to due process under the Air Force personnel system so we could proceed to a hearing based simply on the merits of the Air Force's claim that my promotion had been a mistake. I stated that I did not want to draw out the process, as the whole episode was adding to the stress being put upon my family by the pending base closure.

I received the initial ruling in the mail about four weeks later. There was a long dissertation about how there was a good possibility that the demotion would have been again reversed and sent back to the Air Force to handle within their system. The judge talked about how the preferred outcome would be for the two parties to settle between themselves. He concluded the notice by accepting my waiver of rights and set a hearing with witnesses by telephone conference call in 10 weeks.

I was asked to provide a discovery list and witness list to both the judge and the Air Force's lawyer within two weeks. I sent them these requests by certified mail in two days.

The Air Force's list of witnesses was very short: only the director of personnel for the base, who would provide a written statement about the case. I was given two weeks to review the statement and prepare any questions for the director to be answered by phone.

My discovery list was short as well, and included a copy of the demotion hearing transcript. I wasn't going to use it, having already waived my rights, but I wanted my opposition to spend time worrying about it. I also listed a copy of my personnel record and a copy of the Air Force personnel regulations that dealt with desk audits. My witness list included the personnel specialist who conducted the desk audit and my supervisor. That's all I needed.

The personnel director's statement basically said that the big mistake in the process was not having upper management sign off on the promotion. I had reviewed the regulations. There was not a requirement for upper management approval; the regulation clearly stated that the employee's direct supervisor must approve the promotion, as that person has the required knowledge of the employee's work.

During the telephone hearing, I was able to get the director to admit that there was no regulation requiring upper management approval, although he said it was a courtesy that was followed. The personnel specialist stated that she had followed the regulations and had done everything properly. My supervisor stated that he had signed off on the promotion because he agreed with the personnel specialist's analysis of the work level. He also stated that the lab had a responsibility to perform the electronic failure analysis work as funded by multiple Forms 206, and that he had continued to assign me this work through demotion and promotion and demotion because I was the only qualified person to do it.

I was not surprised when the ruling reversing my demotion came down six weeks later. I again would receive back pay and interest.

If the Air Force was going to be my career, I was sure I would be haunted by this episode. Although the closure of McClellan was now a certainty, what would happen to the laboratory was still very much in the air.

Working For NTS

It was a long, drawn-out, nine-month process for the NTS lab operation contract to be implemented, but it finally was issued in mid-1997. I got a call telling me about it the day it happened, but I could not say anything about it, except to a few special colleagues, until the Air Force announced it a week later. Then it was another five weeks to implementation, as there was a lot to do on both sides.

NTS offered everyone in the lab a position if they wanted it, as the new Air Force contract was cost plus fixed fee. The Air Force had always been able to justify having the amount of people they did working in the lab, so NTS subsequently hiring up to that number of workers was pre-justified.

The lab conference room was taken over by NTS management so they could schedule interviews with each McClellan employee who wanted to investigate the opportunity. I signed up right away, and was the fourth person interviewed.

Of the 82 people who worked in the Air Force base's lab, only 18 would sign on to work for NTS. The others preferred to be reassigned to other positions on the base in order to collect as many benefits as they could during the closure process. Some were already retired in place, and just putting extra time toward their retirement pensions. Some waited for a position to open at another base, and others just could never perform in a real job where you were expected to do something.

NTS brought in six additional workers to Sacramento from the 15 other labs the company had around the country.

After my interview, I was sent a job offer. If I took the position with NTS, I would receive a 20% raise in salary from my GS-13 pay rate and a promotion to co-lab manager. They were bringing Jim Freeman, a former NTS division manager, out of retirement to operate the new McClellan division for a two-year term, and I would shadow him until I was ready to take on the full load.

The generous offer included a $15,000 signing bonus. Being in management, I would receive an annual NTS stock option package as well. NTS was a public company at the time, trading on the Nasdaq.

They also had a full health insurance plan along with a college tuition reimbursement plan. I would take advantage of the tuition reimbursement right away, as I thought it would be a good idea to get a Master of Business Administration (MBA) if I was going into management.

I accepted the NTS offer immediately and turned in my paperwork to leave the Air Force under their buy-out program. With 13 years of government service, I would receive two weeks' pay for each year of service for a total of 26 weeks of pay. I had also saved 11 weeks of vacation time, for which I would be paid.

The Air Force would pay me to leave and NTS would pay me to join them. This base closure stuff was pretty good, as far as I was concerned.

I didn't have to worry about a government pension because I didn't have one. I was hired under the government's newer system which relied on Social Security and a 401(k) program. I took both of those benefits with me to my new job in the private sector.

I also scored pretty high on the GMAT, which allowed me to get into the MBA program at Sacramento State University. I attended class in the evenings for the 18-month program, which I completed in the allotted time frame.

The Martins were doing well.

With the transition complete, the 24 NTS employees set about their daily duties performing the Air Force laboratory workload. You would think that, with 24 people, it would be very hard to complete a workload that had previously been done with 82 people. Actually, it was easy and no one was overworked; if anything, the lab folks were under worked. I was not surprised at all.

I was also bringing in outside testing and analysis workload from some of my Air Force contacts and Lockheed Martin.

I attended management reviews at NTS headquarters in Calabasas, California about every six months. During these sessions, I would usually push for a larger sales effort to bring more work into the Sacramento lab. The typical answer I would receive in return was that I was doing good work and our NTS division was making very good profits for the company, so don't worry so much and keep up the good work.

My new employers seemed focused on the Air Force contract, rather than looking to bring in private sector work to support the lab once the contract was over. It was a three-year contract after all, and we would have plenty of time to work through that issue. That turned out not to be true.

Any Air Force contract has escape clauses, and with political pressure from politicians regarding bases that were under worked, advancing workload transfer became the order of the day. We received word that the Air Force would cancel the NTS contract after less than two years. A very swift evaluation by NTS management came to the conclusion that a laboratory in Sacramento would not have enough work to sustain it, and should be closed.

I needed to explore my options. One of these was to start my own lab business.

Martin Testing Laboratories

The entire laboratory which NTS was operating was spread out in three buildings with more than 100,000 square feet of total space. That was way too big for the needs of our new business, Martin Testing Laboratories (MTL), which Denise and I founded together in 2000.

MTL was a 17,000 square-foot operation utilizing many of the capabilities of the USAF Materials & Processes Laboratories acquired after the closure of McClellan AFB. This was the best of the 80,000 square-foot NTS operation pared down to one building, instead of three.

At MTL, we would test anything that someone would pay us to test, but testing is seldom cheap. That means we were usually offered projects dealing with products that MUST work, or people die! Airplanes, auto air bags and medical devices are all good examples. Satellite payloads were another example of our work; they are very expensive to build and launch, so they must be tested to be sure they can survive the trip to space, as it would be very expensive to send a repairman.

MTL also offered Failure Analysis, which was the most "Perry-centric" activity. I performed all of that function myself, in addition to handling marketing, sales and all MTL quotes and managing all major test programs. I also had sign-off responsibility for the Mechanical Testing and Nondestructive Testing Labs.

Denise developed MTL's Quality Program and managed all equipment calibrations and personnel certifications. Her program achieved ISO 17025 certification for MTL. Denise also oversaw the chemistry testing, operated the fatigue testing systems and performed all thermal analysis testing (Thermal Mechanical Analysis TMA, Thermal Gravimetric Analysis TGA, Differential Scanning Calorimetry DSC).

Debbie (Hu) Wong was our operations manager. She scheduled the technicians to the various programs, processed the invoices, performed accounting and payroll duties, issued purchase orders and was the primary contact for MTL's customers.

I decided to use only Building 344 on the former McClellan campus. Its 17,000-square-foot configuration hosted the environmental test lab, mechanical testing lab and part of the non-destructive testing lab. We moved select pieces of equipment to the building to enhance that lab capability before we lost access to all the McClellan buildings.

I negotiated a 10-year lease with the new owner of the former Air Force base property, McClellan Park LLC, for the single building and all of the equipment associated with it. The portion of the lease that dealt with equipment was lease-to-own.

During the two years that NTS operated the lab, I was able to develop a small amount of local lab work, and that would serve as our main workload at the launch of our new company.

On day one, we started with a total of five employees and negative cash flow. I would need to fund expenses out of my pocket until we could develop enough workload to become self-sufficient.

Building workload in this niche field was a slow process, so negative cash flow meant I was making up the difference for MTL's first three years of operation.

I cashed in my 401(k) savings to acquire $400,000 for operations; this amount was reduced to $360,000 after paying a 10% tax penalty to the federal government for early withdrawal. Denise and I also cashed out our kids' college funds, took out a second mortgage on our home and maxed out our credit cards over this time period. We tried taking on a partner, which didn't work out. Things had gone from wonderful to dire in three years, and the stress was killing me.

Although Denise was very supportive of our new endeavor, we decided together to not tell our kids about the thin line we were dancing on financially. We didn't want to worry them about our family's money situation as we struggled at first to stay afloat, especially when our money outflow became extensive.

First, I was spending a lot of my time visiting customers and promoting our new business. During one customer visit, I connected with one of my customer's suppliers and sold some testing services to him. This opened my eyes to a new opportunity. Going forward, I would endeavor to identify all of my customer's suppliers and sell them services.

Second, McClellan Park LLC was starting to get more companies to locate at the business park and MTL was able to capture work from many of them. As we also slowly added their suppliers to our customer list, the cash flow began to stabilize.

After a nerve-racking start to our new endeavor, we were able to go a couple years keeping our heads above water. As we gained customers, we slowly moved into profitability. Once we started selling to our customers' suppliers' suppliers, we were actually comfortable again.

By 2007, which was just before the U.S. housing bubble burst, Denise and I had refinanced our home mortgage, consolidating our second mortgage and credit card debt into one 15-year mortgage. We implemented a Simplified Employee Pension (SEP) IRA plan for the lab and fully funded our individual accounts going forward. We started investing extra cash and, in 2003, we even co-founded a second company, TRUOX, a chemical business that specializes in advanced oxidizer technology.

We had been to the brink of disaster, barely kept our heads above water for a few years and then slowly built back all of the money we had invested in our original company. You would think we would play it safe.

One day in 2007, I came home from work and announced to Denise, "I want to buy a horse."

After all we had been through together, I could tell she didn't know whether she should laugh or cry.

4

OUR FIRST HORSE

When Denise and I decided to get into the horse racing business as Thoroughbred owners, we used the same approach you would take to entering a cold, deep swimming pool. First, we stuck in our big toes to check the temperature—and keep from drowning.

In 2007, we purchased 5% of a Kentucky-bred horse named Searchforthetruth from Blinkers On Racing Stable, a California-based racing syndicate which offers partnership opportunities for minimal buy-ins. We picked Blinkers On because Greg Gilchrist was the group's trainer. We wanted to learn the racing business, and the best way to do that was to watch a top trainer.

A mainstay on the Northern California racing circuit since the 1970s, Greg had risen to national prominence with his expert management of Lost in the Fog, a brilliant colt who had given him the first Grade 1 training victory of his career and who had been voted 2005 Champion Sprinter after winning 10 of his first 11 races.

Learning The Ropes

Blinkers On offered the complete owner experience, at a fraction of the regular costs. We got access to the backside at Golden Gate Fields on the shoreline of San Francisco Bay, and we took advantage of it. We showed up for workouts, picked up observations from Greg on what to look for, watched the care and feeding of the horses and asked a lot of questions as newcomers to the sport.

Searchforthetruth did pretty well, which was exciting; however, the experience of owning him in partnership was invaluable. The most important lesson Greg taught us was amazingly simple: Take care of your horses, keep them happy and healthy and they will take care of you.

Searchforthetruth raced during a period in the late 2000s when the California Horse Racing Board (CHRB) mandated the implementation of synthetic racetrack surfaces for the state's major racing venues. The smaller tracks on the Northern California fair circuit have short racing seasons of two to three weeks each year per fair, so these organizations were not forced to undergo the massive expense of overhauling their facilities, and were instead allowed to keep their natural dirt racing surfaces despite the mandate.

This titanic move away from traditional dirt was supposed to be for safety purposes; however, the data needed to be interpreted in a certain way to support that finding. Adding to the complexity of the situation, each of California's anchor racetracks selected and experimented with a different synthetic racing surface, including Cushion Track at Hollywood Park, Polytrack at Del Mar, Cushion Track, then Pro-Ride at Santa Anita Park and Tapeta Footings at Golden Gate.

Our horse, like many others in the California racehorse colony, would run okay at some tracks and not very well at other tracks when he did not take to those particular surfaces. The best analogy I can offer is this: If a world-class human sprinter outruns his competition on a man-made Olympic track, the outcome may be different if the race is contested on a sandy beach. That may be an extreme example, but it illustrates my point.

In my conversations with Scott Sherwood, the owner and manager of Blinkers On, I mentioned that I thought Searchforthetruth could be a stakes-quality horse if the racing surface was good for him. Scott was not convinced, but said he would run Searchforthetruth in a stakes race when the time was right.

I was excited when the 2008 summer fair season came around and Searchforthetruth was entered in an allowance optional claiming race at the Solano County Fair. I mentioned to Scott that I was glad the fair season was upon us, and that I thought Searchforthetruth would run well on Solano's dirt strip. That turned out to be an understatement.

Our 3-year-old Yes It's True colt won for fun that day, clearing the field in the stretch and completing the six-furlong race in 1:09.03, a very respectable time. Scott nominated him for the $50,000-added Bulldog Stakes at The Big Fresno Fair a few races later.

At the time, our family lived in Yuba City in Northern California. On the day of the stakes race, Denise and I woke up early and excitedly jumped in the car for the four-hour drive to Fresno. We were about three hours into our drive when the cell phone rang.

It was Scott. He told us they had to scratch Searchforthetruth from the race. He explained that there was a garbage dumpster outside the barn wall at the back of our colt's stall and when a truck pulled up to dump it, the dumpster was slammed into the stall wall. This spooked the horse, which caused him to rear up and hit his head on a low beam. A veterinarian had made the decision to scratch him.

This was our first major disappointment as racehorse owners. In the years to come, we would experience dozens of similar stupid anecdotes explaining why our horses did not or could not perform. So, if you are considering owning a racehorse, be forewarned.

By the way, Searchforthetruth never did run in a stakes race while under our ownership.

Love The Chase

Having done well the first year with Searchforthetruth, we decided to purchase a 5% interest in each of the five horses offered by Blinkers On the following year. One of these was a filly named Love the Chase, a lightly framed chestnut who had been purchased by Greg for $30,000 at an East Coast 2-year-old sale in 2008. She did not turn out to be a particularly good racehorse; however, I have found that there are usually reasons why horses with good pedigrees do not perform.

During our second season of ownership, even with all of the ups and downs, we began thinking about expanding our involvement in racing. The California Thoroughbred Breeders Association (CTBA) had recently announced several initiatives to draw in new owners and breeders of California-breds. We considered breeding horses, but, again, we did not like to jump into something without knowing what we were doing.

I began reading up and studying what the eminent Thoroughbred breeders throughout history had done. I pored over the pedigrees of the great champions, until several simple and successful breeding patterns were revealed to me.

Lord Edward Stanley, the 17th Earl of Derby, used inbreeding to reinforce desirable traits and outcrossing to correct deficiencies. Inbreeding along great sire lines was evident; however, the inbreeding of superior female families seemed very prevalent in the pedigrees of champions. I decided that, someday, when we would purchase a mare for breeding, female family inbreeding was what I would look for as the most desirable trait.

When I examined the pedigrees of the fillies we already owned in the partnership, my eyes went wide. Love the Chase had 3x3 female family inbreeding to the great mare Numbered Account! I thought to myself that I had found our first broodmare, but she belonged to the partnership, so we would need to wait until Blinkers On was ready to sell.

It did not take long for that to happen.

After a couple of poor races at the end of her 2-year-old season and the beginning of her 3-year-old season, the partners were asked if we were willing to sell. We were told that she had not grown, as hoped, and she was not showing much talent.

I called to inquire about purchasing her, and was told that $2,500 would be the price if the partnership decided to sell. Each partner had a vote, and I would be contacted soon. I was also informed that another partner in Blinkers On, a gentleman I had not yet met named Steve Coburn, was interested in buying her as well. I was given Steve's phone number, and I called him.

Steve and I both ultimately wanted the filly for breeding, but we wanted to wait until she was 4 years old before we bred her. Since she was already at the races and not doing well at 3, we felt we could campaign her in partnership together for the balance of 2009 without much risk of losing her in a claiming race.

We agreed to meet at Greg's barn at Golden Gate to discuss the idea a bit more before purchasing her. We decided to go 50/50 on her, at $1,250 each for the initial purchase. We assumed the sale was a relatively done deal. Blinkers On management was recommending a sale and we were both going to vote to sell. What could go wrong?

A majority of the partnership voted to race the filly one more time. Of course, she won, taking an $8,000 maiden claiming race by 3 1/2 lengths under jockey William Antongeorgi III. Denise and I were there for the race, and enjoyed a great celebration in the Golden Gate winner's circle with all the partners who were present.

The next day, I got a call from Scott. He had again called the partners and tallied a new vote for the potential sale of the filly. This time, the partners agreed to sell Love the Chase, but since she had won an $8,000 claiming race, her price would now be $8,000.

I immediately said I was in. I understood that this is how the game is played. She was now a winner, and a winning mare is more valuable than a non-winner. Because of that pedigree, I still believed she was a steal at the price.

A half-hour later, I got a call from Steve. He had just been given the same information by Scott.

"Perry, I'm sorry, but I'm out," he said.

I asked what was wrong.

"I don't do business like that," he replied. "We had a deal for $2,500 and now the price is $8,000. I'm out!"

He sounded upset, so I tried to explain why the filly was more valuable after winning a race. He was having none of it, so I went in another direction.

"Before we met, you were willing to purchase the filly by yourself for $2,500," I said. "Why don't you put in $2,400 and just take 30%?"

There was a quiet pause, so I continued.

"You would put in less than you had originally planned, still get to participate and have less expenses," I explained.

He thought about it, and said, "Okay."

So that is what we did.

5

DUMB ASS PARTNERS

Before the purchase, Steve and I agreed to meet on the backside at Golden Gate Fields in Love the Chase's barn. We stood in front of her stall and watched her eat hay. It was February 2009, the start of breeding season, and we were acquiring her in partnership for the purpose of breeding. Still, she had just turned 3, and we both thought it would be better to let her mature a bit more before she became a mother.

We discussed racing her for the remainder of the year, since she was conditioned and ready to run. Given her poor record to date—a win, a fourth and a pair of sixth-place efforts, all in maiden claiming company, we did not think anyone would claim her from us if we carried on with her, so all we would need was a trainer and we would be ready to roll. Greg Gilchrist had already told us he was not interested in training her, and had recommended another Northern California-based horseman named Monty Meier for the job. We decided to go with Greg's advice.

As we were about to finish our discussion, a groom who had been cleaning the stall next to us pushed a wheelbarrow full of soiled straw and horse manure past us. He stopped and turned in our direction.

"You guys looking to buy that horse?" the groom asked.

Steve and I simultaneously answered with a simple, "Yeah."

The groom looked down, began shaking his head disapprovingly, and said, "Anyone who buys that horse is a dumb-ass!"

Then he turned back and walked off with his wheelbarrow.

Steve and I looked at each other, both a little dumbfounded. I smiled and reached out my hand to him, exclaiming, "Dumb-ass partners!"

He shook my hand, and we walked over to the grandstand to watch the day's races.

Rocky Start

After we purchased Love the Chase, Denise and I met with Steve and his wife, Carolyn, to discuss some racing details over coffee.

What about the jockey silks? The concept for the silks design for our new partnership was accomplished in about two minutes.

Carolyn's favorite color was purple, and Denise's was green, so the silks would be purple and green. We did not think we could get away with spelling out "Dumb Ass Partners" on our silks, so we decided to have the letters "DAP" emblazoned on the front left area of the silks and the caricature of a donkey, or ass, on the back. All the design details, including the caricature that would later become quite famous, were done by Stephanie Searle of Classic Silks USA.

Our partnership silks were only carried twice by Love The Chase. And, for awhile, it looked like that brash-speaking groom in Greg's barn might have been right after all.

Over the next two months, Love the Chase performed very poorly.

In March, she never lifted a foot in a $12,500 claiming race, finishing seventh and last despite being reunited with Antongeorgi, the jockey who had guided her to her maiden victory.

We thought a return to the $8,000 claiming level for her next outing—ironically, on April Fool's Day—would shake her out of the doldrums. She was competitive for the first half-mile under a different rider, but quickly faded and struggled home eighth and last as a 28-1 longshot, finally reaching the wire more than 13 lengths behind the winner.

After each race, Love the Chase was given an endoscopic examination by a different veterinarian. I called and talked to each vet after the scopes were done: one had the opinion that she was just a nervous filly, while the other had an idea that extreme stress could have been causing breathing issues involving her epiglottis.

It was now early April, and recovery from epiglottis surgery would consume most of the remainder of the year. We were going to breed her for certain the following year, so there would be no point to have her undergo the surgery strictly for racing performance purposes. On the other hand, if the alternative possibility was true and she was just too nervous to be competitive, then why race at all?

We decided to take her off the track and try to breed her that spring.

A "Lucky" Twist Of Fate

After her second disappointing race for our new partnership, we pulled Love the Chase from training in early April and shipped her to Harris Farms in Coalinga, one of California's leading Thoroughbred nurseries.

All four of us were really impressed with the foals we saw at the farm who were sired by the Harris shuttle stallion Redattore, a Brazilian-bred son of Roi Normand who had won 15 races, including several Grade/Group 1 events in California and his native country, and who had earned just shy of $1.8 million. As a stallion, Redattore covered mares year-round: in California during the Northern Hemisphere breeding season in the spring and at a farm in Brazil during the Southern Hemisphere breeding season in the fall.

We decided to breed Love the Chase to Redattore for her first mating, so I negotiated a contract with Dave McGlothlin, the longtime manager of the farm's Horse Division. Dave noted that we were getting a late start to the breeding season, and explained that Love the Chase would need some time to let down after coming off the racetrack. But, he was sure that, with a little luck, we could get it done that season.

About two weeks later, Dave called to inform me that Redattore had been sold to Brazilian interests; therefore, he would not be available for breeding as he had to go through quarantine before being shipped permanently to South America. Dave asked if there was another stallion on the Harris roster to whom I would be interested in sending our filly.

I thought about it a bit, then said, "No, we will wait to breed her next year."

I actually felt a little relieved, as I thought she needed to mature a bit before becoming a mother.

When we hung up, I had the impression that Love the Chase had not been bred during the brief time frame when she arrived at the farm and that phone call. Years later, I found out that she had indeed been covered once before Redattore entered quarantine, but the pregnancy did not take. Although we had not been informed of this development, it actually worked out just fine, since it meant we could breed her early the following year.

As they say, everything happens for a reason.

Pedigree Perspectives

Most readers will find this section of our California Chrome story a bit boring, but to my fellow "pedigree geeks," I say, "Welcome."

My purpose is not to bore you, but to give an idea of what was happening regarding the thought process that was taking place behind the scenes. That painstaking effort has been highly condensed here to make it a little more palatable, but still provide the necessary background.

After Redattore became unavailable for breeding duties, our partnership considered other stallions for our filly. Taking the lead on this project, I evaluated many stallions who were standing in California, as well as some who were far away in Kentucky.

One of the prospective suitors was Lucky Pulpit, a young son of Pulpit who had been competitive in graded stakes company in Southern California, and whose oldest foals were yearlings at the time—an unproven gamble. As fate would have it, he also was on the Harris Farms roster.

I believe I used both available computer-based nicking programs, eNicks and TrueNicks, to evaluate the potential Lucky Pulpit/Love the Chase match. At that time, one gave me a "C" rating, while the other gave me a "C+." Anyone out there interested in breeding an average horse? Me either.

Why then would I ultimately select that match? Easy; I did not believe the computers.

By the way, I ran the same match on one of the programs after California Chrome was well established and got an "A." The ratings keep getting better over time as the programs learn and adjust to available data.

To anyone not familiar with nicking, the central idea is that all bloodlines are not the same and that some specific combinations do better in producing desirable offspring than other combinations.

What is better? Although the software algorithms are proprietary, they all look at some combination of percentage of starters, percentage of winners, money won and number of stakes winners. That is easy enough, but then the programs use proprietary biasing protocols, giving more or less weight based on generation (a closer generation carries more weight), sub-group populations (smaller groups carry less weight), and so on.

When evaluating the results, one must consider other biases that are not addressed in the software. One example that applied to Lucky Pulpit at the time was that new stallions usually do not receive the best mares.

Before concentrating on what stallion I would select for Love the Chase, it is probably best to take a step back and look at the process I used to find him.

Again, you must look at the mare's bloodline first. I made a decision that I would only look at "clusters." A cluster is the result of the inherent human nature of breeders. It occurs when one breeder produces a particularly good horse. Other breeders take notice of this and duplicate the pedigree cross, hoping to also get a good horse. The result is a fairly large population of a specific bloodline cross that is statistically significant. Being statistically significant simply means the results are more believable, and not a fluke.

As it takes multiple breeding seasons and years of racing results to develop a cluster, it is necessary to skip a generation in the pedigree for the analysis. For this reason, I looked at the performance of Mr.

Prospector mares against the major sire lines. Love the Chase was sired by Not For Love, a direct son of Mr. Prospector and a perennial leading sire in Maryland, where our filly had been foaled.

To make a long story short, one of the most intriguing crosses I found for Mr. Prospector mares was A.P. Indy.

Yet the sire line has its detractors. Many breeders in America point to a fragility of the line because there is too much inbreeding. Too many of the star racehorses who emerge from this bloodline are retired quickly due to injury. The poor showing of A.P. Indy offspring in Europe has breeders there saying the line has no talent on turf.

Wanting the high-talent benefit of the A.P. Indy/Mr. Prospector mare cross without the deficiencies meant I needed to look for a son of Pulpit who carried a beneficial outcross through his dam.

Being out of a Cozzene daughter, Lucky Pulpit was one such candidate. The fact that he stood in California, which would allow us to take advantage of California-bred benefits and race conditions with our foal, made it a no-brainer. Cozzene was sturdy and provided yet another line with turf influence.

Modern breeding theory in America has been highly influenced by the late Joe Estes, a longtime editor of "The Blood-Horse" trade magazine. Estes understood statistics and applied them successfully to breeding.

Before Estes, analysis shows that major successful breeders were obtaining one stakes winner from every 48 foals. Breeders using Estes' methods were able to obtain one stakes winner from every eight foals. That is rather good.

But not everyone really understands statistics. Over time, Estes' methods became oversimplified and sometimes misapplied. I have studied these methods; however, it is difficult for me to boil them down to reasonable length for this book.

Most proponents pare it down to just one sentence: "Breed the best to the best and hope for the best," which is not extremely helpful. What is "the best"?

Racing performance is an indicator of the presence (or lack thereof) of beneficial genetic factors. Would A.P. Indy be an inferior stallion had he never raced? I think not. How those factors combine across bloodlines is a different problem altogether.

There is entirely too much emphasis in media and public discourse on the fact that California Chrome's parents do not have a lot of black type (stakes success) and, thus, it is said he has a poor pedigree. This is wrong, and should only be used as an indicator for guidance, not an absolute. I believe that genetics is a better indicator; however, genetics is a science and many people do not do well at understanding science. So, statistical shortcuts using performance are used.

Think of it this way: grade point average in college can be used as an indicator for future success in business. So, should a company only hire those with extremely high grade point averages? I think that would be shortsighted.

For example, let us say there is a job candidate with only a "C" average in their schoolwork. Now let us say this candidate paid for college by working three jobs. I would think that this candidate would be very enterprising, and an excellent addition to my company.

There are many reasons racehorses do not perform. Here we see that our very first horse, Searchforthetruth, was aptly named! Just as with our hypothetical human job candidate above, you need to go beyond statistics to see truth. Searchforthetruth never got a chance as a stakes horse while we were involved with him because of circumstances, not lack of talent.

The highest stud fee does not make a stallion the best for your mare. The people who own that stallion will say differently, because that is how they make their money. A high stud fee implies the best. A low stud fee implies poor breeding to those ignorant of what is behind good breeding.

Again, you can be a successful Thoroughbred breeder through luck, but I believe it is much better to be successful through understanding chance. It means study, comprehension and extra work, but it is worth it.

Back to our story of how California Chrome came into existence.

With Love the Chase getting the remainder of 2009 to let down from the track, that gave me plenty of time to plan her breeding. It took about eight months of planning, looking at stallions, reading and studying, but I finally landed on Lucky Pulpit with some confidence.

I called Dave McGlothlin and told him that I wished to negotiate a 2010 breeding contract for Love the Chase. Dave actually recommended Lucky Pulpit as a good stallion choice for our filly based on the physical match-up. That made me feel better. I told him that Lucky Pulpit was the sire I had selected as well.

With the times being tough in the breeding industry, Dave was able to offer us a discount on Lucky Pulpit's advertised $2,500 stud fee. When you're a small breeder, every little bit counts!

6

IT'S A BOY!

At about 4 a.m. on Friday, February 18, 2011, Denise and I awoke to a phone call from someone who had been assigned to the night shift in the Harris Farms foaling barn. I was half-asleep when I answered the phone, but I distinctly heard the exciting news that Love the Chase was in labor. We were dressed and on our way to the farm in about five minutes.

It is usually a 3 1/2-hour drive from Yuba City to Coalinga, but we made it in three. Not a lot of traffic at 4 a.m.!

When we arrived, our new foal was already up and running circles around his mom. He was as shiny as a copper penny, with a huge white blaze on his expressive face and four white stockings. This splashy white coloration in a horse's coat is called "chrome" by horse aficionados.

Although the mating to Lucky Pulpit and subsequent pregnancy had been uneventful, and the colt was obviously doing well after making his grand entrance into the world, we were concerned about Love the Chase, who looked rather ragged and had an IV tube running into her neck. We were told that the birth had been difficult, and the foal had dragged a hoof, tearing her uterus. The IV bag was feeding a clotting agent to mitigate the bleeding.

Our mare was weak but, thankfully, on the improve. She stood very still while her newborn colt got the hang of his long legs by running laps around her in their stall. She would not be able to be bred back that year, but there was absolutely no disappointment.

We stood in joy and awe as our first foal continued to explore his new world.

"There is our Kentucky Derby horse!" I said to Denise.

We both smiled.

Two hours and several feedings had passed before the colt finally folded his white legs and nestled into the cedar shavings that covered the stall floor. We watched him sleep for a while before we dragged ourselves away.

We were so excited by that morning's events that we did not notice that we had not yet had breakfast, or even any coffee. It was a short drive from the foaling barn to the Harris Ranch Restaurant on Interstate Highway 5, where we shared breakfast and a lively discussion about what we had just witnessed.

"Isn't it amazing how much the foal looks like Lucky Pulpit?" Denise marveled.

"He sure does," I replied in agreement. "We should call him 'Junior.'"

That handle stuck.

Farm Visits

Over the next few years, Denise and I made many visits to both the Harris Farms main facility and the Harris River Ranch as Junior was growing up.

One of my favorite memories is visiting him out in the yearling pasture.

We pulled up in the Jeep and got out, then walked to the back of the vehicle to grab a bag of Mrs. Pastures horse cookies. As usual, it was a warm California Central Valley day, and the horses were enjoying some shade under trees at the far side of the pasture.

Rather than walk all the way around the perimeter of the pasture, we decided to open the gate and walk straight across. The horses just watched as we walked across the pasture. It wasn't time for feeding or anything like that, so they didn't feel a need to come greet us. That is until Junior, the "alpha" member of his herd, noticed that it was HIS people coming. That ALWAYS meant cookies!

Junior took off like a rocket, galloping toward us at full speed with the entire herd of about 20 yearlings following close behind him. Denise and I stopped in our tracks and looked at each other right there in the middle of the pasture.

I said, "Maybe this wasn't such a good idea!"

Before we could think about how to suddenly protect ourselves out in the open, Junior applied the brakes, kicking up a lot of dirt into the air; the other horses also slowed, fanning into a circle surrounding us. They all began to push in on us with their noses, sniffing and exploring this new experience.

Junior pushed his head into my chest, and I scratched him behind his ears. He started to sniff my pockets, looking for where I hid the cookies. After he got his treats first, we were allowed to feed some to his friends.

We played "hide the cookie." I hid a treat in one of my closed fists and let Junior guess which hand it was in. He always got it right; he has a good sense of smell.

After a while, Junior would get bored with our human games and just take off running in a circle around us. The other horses would try to follow, but they could not keep up. Eventually, Junior would steer himself to the center of the circle, where he could find more cookies. This pattern of behavior repeated itself until the cookies ran out, and we suddenly became a lot less interesting to our horse friends. But by the time Junior lost interest in us, we were fulfilled by our experience of communing with him on his turf.

A few years later, during another visit to a different group of yearlings at the Harris River Ranch, Denise and I were standing at the fence and watching one of Love the Chase's later foals when another group of about six people walked up.

It was a warm day, and the "babysitter" had the yearlings gathered under a large shade tree in the pasture to keep cool. The babysitter in this case was a retired mare who had been placed with the young fillies to provide guidance. Horses are very social animals and tend to stay in a group and take guidance from the alpha member; in this group, that leader was the babysitter.

If the mare walked to a water trough to drink, all the fillies would follow her, one by one, and take a drink as well. Whenever the feed truck would come for workers to load hay and grain into the feeders, the mare would have already anticipated their arrival at the usual time and would be waiting with the herd, keeping close.

On this day, it was hot, and under the tree in the shade was the place to be. Unfortunately, the chosen tree was out in the middle of the pasture, so the newly arrived ownership group could not get a good look at their pride and joy.

The man who was doing all the talking said, "We can't see them well from here; I'll go bring our filly up to the fence."

He proceeded to climb through the three-rail fence and walk out to the herd. He found his filly and tried to lead her back to the fence, but she was not having it. She stood her ground. These yearling fillies were about 400 pounds each at this point, so if they did not want to move, it would be no easy matter to move them.

The man stepped back and thought a bit. Then, to our surprise, he stepped forward and put his filly in a headlock! He planted his feet and tried to drag the horse to the fence where we were watching in amazement. This only went on for about three good tugs before the filly stomped her left front hoof down hard on the man's foot.

In great pain, he quickly released the horse and let out a loud scream. Muttering under his breath, he limped back to our group and climbed back through the fence.

"We have to go to the emergency room," he stammered. "Can somebody walk back and drive the car up?"

The wounded Thoroughbred owner handed the keys to a volunteer.

A short time later, Denise and I were alone at the fence again. We looked at each other and laughed.

"All he had to do was lead that babysitter mare to the fence, and the herd would have followed," she said.

I replied, "It may take two or three more broken feet before he learns that!"

The Name Game

As Junior progressed as a yearling, he got closer to transitioning back to the Harris Farms Coalinga facility where he was born in order to begin his training as a racehorse. This meant that our colt would soon need an official name, so the Coburns and the Martins needed to get together to choose one. Denise and I had been thinking of names for some time, so we were ready to discuss it with our partners; we just needed a time and place to meet.

One weekend in late 2012, I got a call that the Coburns, who lived just across the California state line in Nevada, were heading straight west to hook up with I-5 on their way to Harris Farms. Denise and I happened to be visiting Daehling Ranch in Elk Grove, south of Sacramento, at the time.

I suggested we should all meet for lunch about an hour later at Brewsters Bar & Grill in Galt. It was a restaurant I had happened across during my travels. Although it had been awhile since I had been there, our handy GPS system worked its magic correctly.

After we all arrived, we sat at a table and ordered lunch. Then we asked our waitress for a pen and paper so we could approach our task in a democratic manner.

When she returned with the supplies, we tore the paper into four squares and each of us wrote down the name we had selected for the horse. The paper squares were folded in half and placed inside Steve's cowboy hat. We asked the waitress to pull out the names, without looking, one at a time.

As the names came out, I wrote the numbers "1" through "4" on the papers. We opened #1 and the name written there was "California Chrome," which had been Steve's suggestion. I felt it was a fitting description of our colt. We finished our lunch, said our goodbyes and went our separate ways.

Denise submitted the potential names for our colt to The Jockey Club in the order in which they were selected. We sent in all four selections, but as our group's first choice was available and approved, the back-up names—Luckynlove, Big Mountain Breez and Seabisquik—were not needed.

This is perhaps not as interesting as some of the media reports I have read about how our horse got his name, but this is what actually happened.

After The Jockey Club made the name California Chrome official, I ordered two leather yearling halters with his name featured on brass plates. The next time we saw our boy, I placed one of the new halters on him. After a month, I traded that one out for the other halter. Then, I took the second halter off of him a couple weeks before he went into the training barn.

Our family still has those small yearling halters along with about 10 big, thick stallion halters from various points of time in his racing and breeding careers. My favorites, though, are from when he was young and playful. They often elicit comments such as, "You would think a big, strong horse like Chrome would need a more substantial halter!" That's when I remind folks that he was once a baby, too.

Denise, always generous to a fault and figuring we had two of these yearling halters as keepsakes, donated one of them to the Kiwanis Club of Yuba City for a fundraiser auction after Chrome hit the big time. I had to spend $1,600 at the auction to get it back! After all, we needed one for display at each of our homes, in Michigan and in Wyoming. In the end, I am extremely glad we have these as they are unique souvenirs of our great horse.

Throughout California Chrome's racing years, we always tried to collect his horseshoes and saddlecloths as memorabilia items. We even had three sets of special jockey silks made that were embroidered with the name of each race he would run in on the collar; his jockey wore a pair of these silks for each leg of the 2014 Triple Crown, but they subsequently went missing before we could collect them.

Early Education

As Junior, formally dubbed California Chrome, entered the fall months of 2012 as a yearling, he moved into the Harris Farms training barn. The beginning period of this educational process is like kindergarten for horses, as they learn the basic skills they will need for their racing careers.

Our colt was in expert hands. Overseeing his daily activities was the respected horseman Per Antonsen, trainer for the Harris Farms Horse Division since 1981. Many successful Thoroughbreds have excelled under Per's guidance, including the California-bred Hall of Famer Tiznow, the 2000 Horse of the Year and the only horse in history to win the Breeders' Cup Classic (G1) twice. It was the responsibility of Per and his team to develop Chrome during this crucial point in his young life.

There are four basic goals to this early training, often called "breaking."

The first goal is to get the horse used to racing tack (bridle and saddle) and the extra handling that comes with putting it on and taking it off. The second goal is to teach basic commands (stop, turn, back up, etc.) using long reins or a lunge line in a round pen. The third goal is conditioning, which comes as a consequence of galloping and exercising in the round pen. The final goal of this process is to get the horse used to someone climbing on its back. This step can be difficult because, in nature, only predators like mountain lions would climb on a horse's back. Breaking is a deliberate process of applying a little more weight on the horse's back every day, and slowly gaining the horse's trust.

At this point, even when the trust is developed so that a person could mount the saddle, the young horse is never ridden. Instead, the horse transitions to a mild conditioning and evaluation period to let down from the stress of the breaking process and to periodically have its knees X-rayed to determine if the growth plates have closed.

After the growth plates in the knees have closed, the horse will again go back to the familiar round-pen environment to finally be ridden. Following a week or two of riding within the secure boundaries of the round pen, the horse and rider will then transition to the training track.

Once on the training track, a morning routine is developed that will be repeated practically every day of the horse's racing career.

Repetition is very necessary to achieve a horse's forward development. Two weeks of jogging on a training track two to three miles each day with a rider aboard will help a horse build muscle and bone density and start developing its breathing techniques. When the horse is ready, he or she advances to galloping under the rider, and might be tasked with adding another mile to the exercise regime after that.

After the proper foundation has been laid, the horse progresses to a "two-minute lick," which is characterized by a horse covering one mile, or eight furlongs, in two minutes—15 seconds per furlong. After a few weeks, these licks transition to breezes, in which the last furlong or quarter-mile of the activity, at the discretion of the trainer, is run faster.

Once the young racehorse is breezing, he or she will be asked to slowly increase the breeze distance until it reaches three-eighths of a mile. At this point, the horse is usually ready for transition to the racetrack.

California Chrome was a fast learner and a well-behaved pupil. Per often referred positively to Chrome's intelligence, attitude and behavior.

Before we shipped California Chrome to the track, the critical decision of what trainer to use would need to be made.

Deciding On A Trainer

I believe the discussion about trainers occurred over the phone sometime in late 2012.

We knew we wanted to keep California Chrome based in his home state for our convenience and enjoyment, as well as to take full advantage of the restricted racing program and rich incentives available for registered California-bred runners.

Steve Coburn was in favor of Doug O'Neill because he had just won the 2012 Kentucky Derby with I'll Have Another. I agreed that the Derby experience was important, but I was leaning another way. I pointed out that O'Neill had a large stable, and explained that I wasn't sure that Chrome would get the level of attention he would require.

Also, Chrome has four white feet with yellowish-colored hooves. Yellow hooves are softer than dark or black hooves since the pigment hardens the hoof. Softer hooves are more easily damaged and need a lot of special attention. So, we would need a trainer who paid special attention to the horse's feet.

I told Steve that Denise and I had some horses in training at the Pleasanton fairgrounds and, as was our custom, we would poke around the backside to observe the operations of the different barns.

That year, the veteran trainer Art Sherman kept a string of 2-year-olds in training at Pleasanton, and we watched as Art's horses came off the track after training. Their first stop was usually the large rubber mats that formed the barn's wash rack. Here, the first order of business was the cleaning and inspection of the horse's feet. A bottom-up approach. Denise and I believed this outfit had their priorities right.

I was able to convince Steve of this too, so we agreed Art would be our guy.

Work Of Art

At that time, Denise and I had some horses in training at Golden Gate Fields with Steve Sherman, Art's son, so I gave him a call.

The Sherman family maintains training operations in both Northern California and Southern California. Although we lived in the northern part of the state, we expected Chrome to be a higher-quality, Southern California type of horse, as the races conducted at the tracks in the southern region typically offer larger purses. Art and his son Alan Sherman ran the family's Southern California barn, while Steve managed their Northern California counterpart.

When I called Steve, rather than ask for his dad's phone number right off the bat, I decided to be a little playful.

I said, "Hey Steve, I've got a horse that belongs racing in Southern California. Can you recommend a trainer down there?"

Without missing a beat, Steve immediately replied, "My dad trains down there. He'll do a good job for you!"

I said, "Why didn't I think of that?"

Then I proceeded to get Art's phone number.

Art and I had a productive conversation that involved training philosophies, expectations and rates. After he agreed to train Chrome, I told him I would give his number to Harris Farms so he could be notified when Chrome was on his way aboard the shipping truck. Art stabled his horses at Hollywood Park, just southwest of Los Angeles in the city of Inglewood, so the van trip from the farm would only take about four hours.

Chrome joined Art's Hollywood Park string as an early 2-year-old in 2013.

Whenever we could, Denise and I would either drive or fly down to Los Angeles on the weekends to watch Chrome's morning training sessions and timed works at Hollywood Park. After each work, we would follow him back to Art's barn and watch him get his bath, then follow him back to his stall, where we would watch him eat his breakfast.

Unlike the other horses in the barn who would consume their grain in one long, uninterrupted feeding session lasting from five to 10 minutes, Chrome would only eat a few mouthfuls of grain from his feed tub at a time, then go to his stall door where the hay net was hung at head-height level. He would grab bites of hay while contentedly observing the morning activities going on in the yard next to his barn. After several minutes of casually watching and munching hay, he would walk back to the feed tub and eat two or three more mouthfuls of grain. This cycle would repeat over the course of an hour until his feed tub was finally empty.

By this time, Denise and I had several years of backside experience, but we had never before seen this type of horse behavior. Art would tell us that Chrome was a fussy eater, but there was more going on here.

Being a scientist, I was curious to find out the root cause of this unusual behavior.

WHOA!

The Thoroughbred industry's Water Hay Oats Alliance (WHOA) is a grassroots movement of like-minded individuals who support the passage of federal legislation to prohibit the use of performance-enhancing drugs in the sport of horse racing. That is a noble cause and I support the stated effort. Yet the organization promotes water, hay and oats as the only "natural" substances a horse needs. Well, I guess two out of three isn't bad! Here is my argument for changing the organization's clever name.

In nature, a horse would only get grain in the fall when the grass the horse feeds on goes to seed. The horse would not eat just the grain, but would consume the entire plant that is above the ground. The grain would be mixed with a large amount of the horse's usual forage, which would pass through the horse's digestive tract at about the same rate as the grass without the seed. This natural procedure does not stress the horse's digestive system; instead, it provides extra concentrated nutrition at a time when the horse needs to fatten up for the winter months that lay ahead.

The first problem with feeding large amounts of grain to a companion horse or a performance horse is that it stresses the horse's digestive tract. The grain moves much quicker through the horse's system than forage, so the horse compensates by producing more acid to try and capture much-needed nutrition before the grain leaves its system. That acid is what causes digestive problems.

So, rather than feed the horse correctly, we treat, not solve, the problem by giving the horse drugs— in this case GastroGard, a treatment to prevent gastric ulcers. All horse owners know what GastroGard does to your monthly vet bill!

When watching morning works, you can get confirmation of this issue. Have you seen your horse jog by and poop in warm-ups? Do birds then swoop in and pick undigested grain out of the poop? If yes, you may have problems.

The second issue with oats is that this grain has an inverse calcium/phosphorus ratio (it's less than 1).

Like people, horses need phosphorus in order to absorb calcium, but too much phosphorus will cause one to lose calcium from one's body. In the 1970s, there was an issue with kids that drink too much soda (which contains phosphoric acid) breaking bones. Moms were encouraged to supply more milk to their kids and less soda.

Horses who are fed oats should always be given a calcium supplement in order to mitigate this issue, especially in the current environment of increased concern about horse safety and welfare. There are companies that produce horse feed pellets in which the grain is ground to flour and used as a binder with hay. Once eaten, the pellets expand and act like normal hay when moving through the horse's digestive system. Various supplements, including calcium, are available in these pellets. Feeding pellets is a little more expensive than oats, but nowhere near as expensive as GastroGard treatment.

California Chrome is a very intelligent horse. I gained more and more respect for him through observation of his behavior, and researching and learning what that behavior could teach me. He was not a fussy eater; he ate in a manner that he found to prevent digestive system discomfort. This is just one example of how Chrome is smarter than many humans!

The Grand Plan

There is a huge debate in the United States about the writing of, and need for, business plans. Some say that the time is better spent just running the business; others say that if you fail to plan, you are planning to fail. However, there is one thing that is certain: the intricacies of this discussion are simply not well understood in the equine racing culture.

Yes, as reported widely in the media, I did map out the races we wanted to hit with California Chrome on the road to the Kentucky Derby, and I provided that list to our trainer. I later learned by reading media stories about Chrome that my action was considered naive and laughable. Yet the races on that original list are the same races you will find on a list of California Chrome's past performances prior to the 2014 Kentucky Derby. Each race contributed valuable racing experience to Chrome or a valuable learning experience to his connections that would help to develop Chrome into the champion he was on that first Saturday in May of his 3-year-old season.

I feel absolutely privileged to compete in an industry where my competitors believe the opposite of what I believe. It is laughable, but not as they suggest!

According to the media, I mismanaged an ill-bred horse to $14,752,650 in earnings—the highest amount ever attained by any Thoroughbred in North America at the time of his retirement in 2017. I have stopped laughing, but I am still smiling.

7

AN AUSPICIOUS START

About five weeks before California Chrome's career debut, Art called me to discuss potential jockey options for the race.

He told me about Alberto Delgado, the brother of Art's morning exercise rider at the time, Willie Delgado. Alberto had just moved his tack to Southern California from the Mid-Atlantic region and was exercising horses in the mornings to help drum up business. I asked Art how he fit our horse and his overall impression was to give him a chance.

I told Art my first choice would be Mike Smith. A seasoned Hall of Famer, Mike had ridden Searchforthetruth to victory for our Blinkers On partnership group a couple times in Southern California back in 2008, and I was very impressed with him. Art replied that Mike was in great demand to ride horses and already had commitments to ride several 2-year-olds we would be running against. I relented; we went with Alberto.

Hollywood Premiere

Being precocious, and fortunately having avoided any setbacks in his training, Chrome made it to the races for the first time in late April 2013. As is customary with 2-year-olds who are just starting out, it was a short race, only 4 1/2 furlongs in distance, and restricted to non-winners who had been bred or sired in California.

The California-bred program was what originally drew Denise and I into breeding; now we were using that program to our advantage, supposedly running against weaker competition in a maiden special weight race at Hollywood Park for a purse of $53,000, which was greater than the standard purse for open-company races due to the Cal-bred purse supplement.

Everything was going to plan, until the race was drawn. We ended up with post nine on the far outside. That was a problem!

My road map to the Kentucky Derby did have Chrome starting his career at Hollywood Park. This track offered the benefit of being Chrome's home base, so he would not have to ship anywhere and he was already accustomed to the track's synthetic racing surface which was in mandated use at the time. However, the 4 1/2-furlong distance at Hollywood meant that it would be a short run to the turn and Chrome would be forced to run wide after breaking from his outside stall in the starting gate, causing him to run farther than the other horses.

I had a brief talk with Art, who offered the opportunity to scratch Chrome from the race. I declined, as the goal was to get some experience, not go undefeated.

On race day, April 26, we watched the race alongside the Coburns from a prime viewing spot in the middle of the grandstand's first balcony. We were far too nervous to sit, so we all stood up against the back aisle partition.

Chrome broke well and settled into a mid-pack position among the field of nine first-time starters. However, as expected, he was kept wide on the turn into the stretch. He also ran a bit "green," looking around at the screaming people in the stands. Fifty yards past the quarter pole, he regained his focus and surged up into second before he reached the wire just a length behind the speedy winner, Time for a Hug. Our horse didn't get the win in his first try, but he did gain a lot of valuable experience.

At 6-1, my $100 across-the-board bet paid alright. Alan, however, was upset; he had wagered $500 on Chrome to win.

We all walked to the backside after the race and watched as Chrome got his bath. He seemed very happy and proud of himself. There was no sense that he had just run in a race; his breathing was slow and even as he playfully nipped at his handlers.

Our First Winner's Circle

Three weeks later, Hollywood Park offered another race at the same conditions. This time, we drew post six in the original field of 10 entrants; however, the #1 horse was scratched from the race, so Chrome was able to move into the five-hole with Alberto aboard again as his pilot. The railbirds must have seen our colt's debut; he was installed as the 6-5 betting favorite.

Our group watched from the same location in the grandstand as the first race, but this time it was a little different. Carolyn was not able to be there, because her employer would not give her the time off.

With prior racing experience under his belt, Chrome broke alertly, but quickly found himself behind a speedier rival. Undeterred, our colt was relentless in applying pressure to the leader and the two horses pulled clear of the others. As Chrome was only two-wide around the turn, and not forced to give up as much ground in this sophomore effort, he was able to pull ahead after a quarter-mile of the private battle. He remained focused to the finish, and won by a commanding 2 3/4 lengths.

Our homebred was visibly proud of himself as he pranced back to the winner's circle. His owners, however, were not quite as graceful. Instead of prancing demurely, we all flat-out ran with excitement to greet our horse and get our picture taken with him. It was only luck that kept us from knocking down other Hollywood Park patrons.

This gathering ended up being the winner's circle with the fewest number of people in it throughout all of Chrome's career—only a handful of us, but I actually knew everybody in the group. I can't say the same about many of the later post-race celebrations. With the number of folks in the official photo being so manageable, we quickly shook hands with everyone and walked back to Art's barn with Chrome and his groom, Raul Rodriguez.

It was May 17, 2013: exactly one year until the 139th running of the Preakness Stakes (G1).

Weekend Workouts

Occasionally, Denise and I would make it down to Southern California for Saturday workouts. Arriving at the barn before sunrise, we would usually bring donuts and leave them in Art's tack room/office near a large coffee pot, where everybody in his crew could get one. With a cup of coffee in one hand and a donut in the other, we would each watch the morning goings-on with great interest.

One morning work in particular stands out in my memory. It took place between Chrome's maiden win and his first start in stakes company.

After securing our coffee and donuts, we overheard Art giving instructions to the exercise rider while Raul finished tacking up our horse.

"Not too fast today; we just want a maintenance drill," Art directed. "We'll go five furlongs; keep him around a minute two."

That was our cue to head to the grandstand. Walking briskly with anticipation, Chrome quickly passed us by on his way to the track, but we weren't worried about missing him; he usually did a warm-up lap before the real action started.

We made it to our viewing platform before the workout. Once we were situated, it was easy to find Chrome out on the track. Under the track lights in the early morning darkness, his distinctive white blaze and four white stockings made him a real standout.

We watched as Chrome increased his gallop speed approaching the five-eighths pole. He was off.

I started my stopwatch just as he reached the five-eighths pole. Chrome tugged against his rider, who was trying to moderate his speed. The rider became more aggressive, pulling the reins back tight, to no avail. Chrome was in his glory now, running like the wind, ears pinned back with all concentration forward. I stopped the watch as he crossed the wire in :59.2.

Chrome continued past the finish, even with the rider standing up and pulling back hard on the reins. He galloped a full quarter-mile past the wire before he finally slowed.

Art looked at me as I looked at my watch.

"A little faster than I had wanted, but it will do," the veteran trainer said.

We made our way back to the barn while Chrome cooled out.

As Denise and I watched our horse get his bath, we felt warm and content. A seven-hour drive to Los Angeles, an overnight stay, then a seven-hour drive home—all for a one-minute workout. Some folks might think it wasn't worth it. Glad we weren't those folks!

Again, Chrome was teaching me. He knew what he needed to do was what he loved to do. The horse had no bad habits.

Jumping Into Open Company Stakes

Most Thoroughbreds in the U.S., after winning their first race, will next try an allowance race in which the competition is again limited to horses who have the approximate same racing experience; in this case, non-winners of one race other than maiden. This methodical way of moving up the ladder allows each horse to go through his or her conditions, or race requirements, in a steady, unrushed pattern.

But California Chrome was not like most horses. After he broke his maiden in his second start at 2, he never ran in an allowance race; it was stakes races only for him from that point on.

This is perhaps another fact the racing industry would point at to reinforce their assertion that Chrome was mismanaged. They would say we left easy money on the table. I would say that easy money does not always sharpen your horse on the road to the Kentucky Derby. I have no aversion to easy money, which is why we availed ourselves to a set series of California-bred stakes races along the way.

Let me point out that when I say "easy money," I am not trying to disparage the other California-bred horses against whom Chrome competed. In fact, I will point out that Chrome sometimes had a more difficult time in some of these restricted state-bred races, but we always gained valuable experience and learned from the mistakes we made. I will say that when we lost in a Cal-bred race, it was not because of the quality of the other horses; it was because of human miscalculations. The number of human miscalculations interspersed throughout Chrome's racing career was reduced along the way, but never completely eliminated.

Hollywood Park's Willard L. Proctor Memorial Stakes was an open company race—a race in which a horse who has been bred in any state or country can compete. The purpose of selecting this $100,000-guaranteed race for Chrome's third lifetime start in June of his juvenile campaign was simple: to get an early measure of Chrome's ability against open company horses, while taking advantage of the race being offered at his home track.

Unfortunately, our regular rider, Alberto Delgado, was injured and could not ride Chrome this day. We turned to Corey Nakatani as the replacement rider. Mr. Nakatani had an excellent reputation and a long, distinguished record as a jockey, so we had high expectations for this race. We drew a post on the outside, which meant Chrome would break from the seven-hole among nine starters, but this race was 5 1/2 furlongs, so he and his new rider would have some extra distance to maneuver for position before entering the turn.

With Carolyn back in attendance, our group of four Dumb Ass Partners once again watched the race from our usual perch in the Hollywood Park grandstand.

Chrome broke sharply from the gate and was well-placed in the early going. However, I became concerned when I noticed that he was running with his head held much higher than usual, and his ears were twitching back and forth while he would toss his head from time to time. I felt this indicated that he was in some sort of distress. My concern was justified as he showed no kick in the stretch, but instead finished evenly to capture fifth, more than seven lengths behind the race winner, Kobe's Back.

As our group walked to the backside to see our horse and review the race with his trainer, Carolyn made an observation.

"Maybe I should stay home," she suggested. "When I'm here, Chrome loses and when I'm at work, he wins!"

I smiled and said, "Carolyn, you're not superstitious, are you?"

The group laughed.

When we arrived at the barn, the vet was just pulling the video scope from Chrome's nostril.

"There is no bleeding," he told us. "The only issue is that his sinus cavity is red and irritated and there is a lot of mucus which hinders his breathing. I'm thinking that the smoke from the nearby wildfires, along with L.A.'s normal smog, is irritating his sinuses."

"If we give him a pre-race shot of Lasix, that will help prevent excess mucus and he should be able to breathe normally," he said.

So, after two good race performances without Lasix, one poor effort had California Chrome added to the Lasix list. Chrome never had bleeding issues and was only given half the normal amount of Lasix to address the irritation caused by Los Angeles' poor air quality. All the speculation and manufactured controversy which would later occur about Chrome running in jurisdictions where Lasix was not allowed was never a concern for us, as we knew it would not be a problem for him. We also knew that we had found and solved an issue which hindered Chrome's performance. This issue would never hurt us again!

Besides learning a little more about how to optimize our horse's performance, there was another positive benefit to Chrome's loss. The oddsmakers would see this middling effort as Chrome not being able to compete in open company. As he progressed in his career and performed well in California-bred races, the oddsmakers would view him as just a good Cal-bred and nothing more. This would help boost his odds tremendously.

Chrome Graduates In Style

After attending three consecutive races at California Chrome's home track, Hollywood Park, Denise and I traveled even further south to watch him run next "where the surf meets the turf" at Del Mar racetrack, a couple dozen miles north of San Diego. We made a mini-vacation out of this trip, staying at the Hilton hotel located across the street from the track's stable gate.

It was the last day of July in 2013, and the weather at Del Mar was simply perfect for Chrome's next outing.

Denise and I strolled across the street from our hotel and entered the track's stable area to find Chrome's stall. After we said our hellos to Art, Alan, Raul and Chrome, we made our way across to the racetrack and wandered into the grandstand area. We had been to Del Mar once before, when our kids were 4 and 6 years old and we had taken a family vacation to Southern California to enjoy Disneyland and the San Diego Zoo.

On this visit, we spent most of our time going back and forth between the track apron and the paddock's walking ring. We would occasionally divert our path over to a refreshment stand to purchase another round of delicious Del Margaritas. All indications pointed to a good day ahead.

The $100,000-guaranteed Graduation Stakes for California-bred 2-year-olds was scheduled as the seventh race on the card, with a post time just after 5 p.m. We had our regular jockey back for the 5 1/2-furlong event, so hopes were high. I had brought a little extra money for this trip, since we were on vacation and I thought we would need extra funds for some of the side excursions we were planning to take.

When the seventh race arrived, we walked into the paddock area to watch our horse get saddled. I had already bet the race, but when I looked up at the tote board and saw the live odds of 8-1 on Chrome, I knew those extra funds I had brought with us would be put to work. As the horses left the paddock, we followed; but instead of walking straight to our race viewing spot, I made a pit stop at the betting windows. Chrome ended up going off at 6-1, in no small measure due to the wagering of our vacation fund!

Meeting up with Denise again at our viewing spot on the track apron, I settled in for the start of the race.

Chrome broke well under Alberto's handling and settled into fourth running position among the seven starters. As he entered the turn, he moved up slowly into third. He improved his position as they progressed in the turn and, by the top of the stretch, he had taken the lead. Chrome continued his drive and increased the winning margin to a dominant 2 3/4 lengths at the finish, stopping the clock in an official 1:03.48.

Boy, was I excited! We ran to the winner's circle and positioned ourselves in a good spot while we waited for Chrome to make it back for the commemorative picture. Our friend John Harris, the owner of Harris Farms, met us at the winner's circle and joined us for the photo.

After the track photographer finished, the TVG personality in the winner's circle approached me with his microphone. We talked about the race a bit, then he asked, "Isn't it great winning here at Del Mar?"

I looked at him a bit, puzzled, and replied, "It's good to win anywhere!"

I guess I didn't get the memo.

Our horse earned $57,000 and I made some good money at the betting windows that day; unfortunately, I would give much of it back in the next race that Chrome would run. The Coburns didn't make it to the Graduation Stakes, and Chrome had won again. Hmm, maybe there was something to that superstition...nah!

After we returned home, I was thinking about our horse now being a stakes winner, and the team effort it had required to make that happen.

At that time, our deal with Art was that, as California Chrome's trainer, in addition to his day rate, he would receive 10% of any purse money won plus a 1% stable stake which was distributed to the folks working in his barn: Chrome's groom, exercise rider, hot walkers and others. I talked it over with Denise, and we both felt we should double the stable stake. I called Steve and he agreed as well.

So I asked Art to make the stable stakes 2% on our monthly training bill. The track bookkeepers automatically took out 10% for the trainer and 10% for the jockey on any purse money Chrome earned.

8

THE BIG LEAGUES

When you are fortunate enough to find out that you've got a good racehorse on your hands, the stakes are quickly raised—both figuratively, and literally. Now a restricted black-type winner at 2, California Chrome was on the right road to a promising career. We buckled our seatbelts, double-checked our roadmap and set off for the ride of our lives.

Going For A Grade 1

The next race on our young colt's agenda was the $301,500 Del Mar Futurity, a Grade 1 test for juveniles that was scheduled at Del Mar five weeks after Chrome's breakthrough performance in the Graduation Stakes.

A Grade 1 classification is the very top level in racing. An early test of Chrome's ability against the top level of horses in his age group was the best way to find out exactly where we were in his development. This also would be another step up in distance for Chrome, with the race going seven furlongs; however, Del Mar uses the chute, a straightaway lead-in to the backstretch, for this race, so it is still contested at just one turn.

This race is also a good example of why you need to plan ahead as a Thoroughbred owner. Nominations for the 2013 Del Mar Futurity were due in early June; the race was not contested until September.

There would not be a short Southern California vacation for Denise and me this time; we decided to fly in and fly out the day of the race, as we had a testing program running at our lab a few days later. Working folks gotta work; I don't know what it is the others do.

Once we made it to the track, it took 20 minutes to navigate the heavy traffic and find the owner's parking lot. No time to tour the backside on this visit, so we made our way to the track's paddock and walking ring and waited for our race. It seemed a very long time, but it was probably less than two hours. I had a beer to help calm my nerves while Denise chose a cup of wine.

After we watched our colt get saddled and walked by hand in the paddock's oval ring, we made our way to the track apron on the front side of the grandstand at the official call of "riders up." Even though he was a California-bred competing in an open race at the elite Grade 1 level, Chrome was sent postward at respectable odds of 5-1 by the betting public in recognition of his stakes win on the same all-weather strip in his previous race. He looked good in the warm-ups and was reunited with his regular rider, so we had high expectations despite the huge class jump.

When the starting gate opened, Chrome broke a step late and was forced to run mid-pack in between rivals on the long backstretch. As the horses approached the turn, Alberto moved Chrome up along the rail into a pocket where he was trapped. He seemed to realize his mistake and slowed Chrome to back out of the pocket, then steered him to the outside where he progressed to the top of the stretch.

At the top of the stretch, Chrome was in the middle of the track behind a wall of four horses. As they raced for the finish line, Chrome simply followed the four horses in front of him, waiting for a hole to open. This was another riding mistake, as the finish line was fast approaching and there was no time for indecision. While Alberto waited for a hole to materialize, Tamarando and Dance With Fate had found clear paths on the far outside and were closing fast. Alberto thought he saw a hole inside of Guns Loaded and pointed Chrome there while encouraging more run. Chrome responded and surged toward the hole.

With the speed he was moving now, a rush of adrenaline coursed in my veins.

"He's got it!" I yelled. Too soon, it turned out.

Just then, at the sixteenth pole and in close quarters, Joe Talamo whipped Chrome across the nose, causing him to duck back as he shied away from the whip. Chrome ended up finishing sixth, but at that instant, I knew we had a Grade 1 quality horse.

We had to catch our plane, so we did not visit the backside postrace. It was a sad and quiet trip home, but that was good as I had a lot to think about.

The next day, I called Art to get an update on how Chrome came out of the race and talk to him about my expectations going forward. I explained that, up until this race, we had been in short sprint races where it is more about the horse's mindset and ability. At these short distances, all Thoroughbreds run pretty much flat out and separate themselves through the horse's ability. The two races we lost I attributed to luck of the draw (being on the outside) and a breathing issue we had solved. This was the first race at a longer distance in which the jockey's skills came into play, and I was not happy that I had, in my opinion, witnessed two riding errors in one race!

I told Art that we didn't need to make a change immediately; anyone could have one bad race, but we could not afford to wait too long to make a change, if needed. Art agreed with my assessment and assured me he would do whatever was needed when the time came.

As our team continued to learn about Chrome and address his needs to help optimize his performance, all the oddsmakers would see is a Cal-bred who failed in his two attempts in open company.

Back To Cal-Bred Company

It was a tough decision. I knew we had a Grade 1 quality horse and the 2013 Breeders' Cup Juvenile (G1) would provide valuable Kentucky Derby points for 2014, but I chose to go with the $200,000-guaranteed Golden State Juvenile Stakes that was run on the Breeders' Cup undercard at Santa Anita that year.

I felt it was important to give Chrome an easier race to help build back his confidence. He had run well against most of these horses before, which explains why he was only 3-1. This race would be one mile in distance, Chrome's longest race ever and his first around two turns. Just another notch up as he got ready for the 10 furlongs that would be required on the first Saturday in May the following year.

Denise and I stayed at the Embassy Suites near Santa Anita. Not only was this a nice hotel, but we could also walk to The Derby, the famous restaurant founded in 1922 by Hall of Fame jockey George Woolf, for dinner, as it was just next door to the hotel. Denise and I also enjoyed walking the sidewalks of the Arcadia business district where famous horses, jockeys and trainers had brass plaques embedded in the sidewalk concrete. We walked slowly and stopped to read the plaques just before sunset.

Chrome shuttled across town from Hollywood Park to Santa Anita the day before the race. Everything was a go, as far as we knew. We watched the race from the track apron, as was our custom, since we enjoyed being close to the action.

Chrome was starting from the one-hole on the rail. He would be the first horse loaded and spend the longest time in the gate. This can be hard on a nervous Thoroughbred who is anxious and raring to go! It would be Alberto's job to reassure him, but still keep him focused.

The gate opened and Chrome jumped straight up into the air. By the time he landed and started moving forward, he was last of nine. Alberto put Chrome into high gear early and ran up the inside past several horses to position in mid-pack. That was about all our duo could muster that day, finishing sixth again! It was very disappointing for us, as we had forgone the Breeders' Cup to run him in a perceived "easy" race. Denise and I headed back to the barn after the race.

The vet was scoping Chrome as we approached.

"No bleeding" the vet said.

I approached Art and asked his opinion of the race.

"I think we need to make a change," he offered.

Art was right.

Denise and I were tied up with work the next couple weeks, but I stayed in touch with Art and Steve via phone. I had again emphasized my preference for having Mike Smith ride Chrome and Art set up a morning meeting at his barn with Mike on a weekend Steve was there to view the work.

I was told that Mike showed up with fellow Hall of Famer Gary Stevens and was interested in riding Chrome. In fact, one of the two stated that, with Mike, you get two for one, because if Mike had to ride another horse, Gary would fill in. Perfect; I couldn't ask for more.

Mike was scheduled to ride Chrome in his next race, the King Glorious Stakes for Cal-breds. That arrangement lasted about a week until we got the word Mike would not be available to ride as he had a commitment to go to New Mexico for his indoctrination into the New Mexico Sports Hall of Fame. Of course, his best friend Gary Stevens was going with him and would also be unavailable to ride.

In a few days, Art called me with a question. Victor Espinoza was interested in riding Chrome, and would I be okay with letting him ride? I had to think hard, as that was not a name that I'd heard a lot about lately. I did know Victor had won the Kentucky Derby in 2002 with War Emblem, but that was more than a decade earlier. While I was thinking, Art was making a good case that Victor was a top jockey and had a very intense desire to ride the horse. In the end, that desire is what convinced me.

I said, "Art, I'm on board with this. Let's do it!"

Leaving His Mark At Hollywood Park

Sometimes when we had time to do so, we would drive to Los Angeles from Yuba City, stopping to stay at Harris Farms, about halfway down Interstate 5, so we could visit with Love the Chase and our other horses there. But not today! This would be another fly in, fly out day at the races for the Martins.

As Hollywood Park was near LAX airport, we jumped in a cab for the short ride to the track. This was a new lifestyle for us, jetting up and down the state to catch races. With having to show up at least an hour early, security delays, airline maintenance delays and other issues, we would have to find a better way.

Victor was named to ride Chrome for the seven-furlong, one-turn King Glorious Stakes for Cal-breds, the last stakes race to ever be run at Hollywood Park, on the last day of racing before the track closed forever after 75 years of racing. This was a racetrack with a deep history: the first Breeders' Cup was run here in 1984. It would be missed by racing fans, who showed up 13,000-plus strong to say goodbye to Southern California's grande dame.

In the future, many Chromies would point to December 22, 2013 as their introduction to California Chrome. In the future, I would cherish my memories of Chrome running at this great track that featured such Thoroughbred stars as Seabiscuit and Zenyatta and Triple Crown winners Citation, Seattle Slew and Affirmed.

Denise and I watched from our usual Hollywood Park perch, on the first balcony, one last time.

Chrome broke well under his new rider and charged into fourth place about four-wide on the backstretch. He stayed there stalking the leaders until the turn, where he slowly floated up to be even with the leaders, then at the top of the stretch exploded to clear the field. The announcer screamed, "California Chrome is gone!" to the cheers of the crowd.

About 50 people joined us in the winner's circle for the victory photo. I think I knew maybe eight of those people. This would be a scenario that would repeat itself over time, with ever increasing numbers of people cramming into the winner's circle as Chrome's reputation and fan base grew.

At the end of the evening, Denise and I walked out of the racetrack and waited at the cab stand. A "cab" pulled up and we got in. We told the driver we wanted to go to LAX and he took off, occasionally peppering us with small talk. It was to be a short ride, but it was much shorter than we imagined.

The driver pulled into a rental car lot near the airport and told us this was the end of the line, demanding payment.

I said, "But we want to go to LAX!"

He said, "I don't have a cab license for the airport, so you need to take a shuttle here."

I was disgusted. We got out and I threw him a couple bucks. We took the rental car shuttle to the airport. I just wished he would have dropped us off at a rental car company we regularly used; then I wouldn't have felt so cheap. Again, we need to find a better way to travel. The entire travel industry is a service industry where the only thing missing is service!

On a brighter note, we actually received two commemorative trophies for this race: one from Hollywood Park and one from the CTBA, the latter since it was a Golden State Series race. The Hollywood Park trophy is the only trophy we display in our bedroom.

Wedding Present

Our daughter, Kelly, was planning an early January 2014 trip to Las Vegas to attend a bachelorette party for one of her friends. Before she left, we sat down together and had a good, old-fashioned "father-and-daughter" talk: I explained to her how to wager on Kentucky Derby Futures.

I had checked the internet for odds on California Chrome to win the 2014 Kentucky Derby, but I could not find any. He was not yet listed, as the organizers had not yet posted the horses nominated to the Derby. They were basically just listing the horses who had acquired points, or at least had run in Derby point races.

I gave Kelly $500 to bet for me and told her she would first need to ask one of the Vegas sports books or race books to add California Chrome to the official list of horses for the future bets. I told her the addition would take some time, so she would probably need to leave, then go back the next day. I then added that she would need to do this at every sports book/race book on the Vegas Strip.

I explained that, after they assigned Chrome a number and his opening odds, she could bet up to $100. After that, she would need to ask to bet another $100 and they would assign new odds for that bet. I told her that when the odds dropped below 200-1, she should go to another sports book and start again.

I gave her an extra $100 so she could bet for herself, as a thank you for performing my complicated errand. I thought she would bet it all on Chrome; however, she used the money management skills she had learned from Dad and only bet $20 for herself, explaining, "No matter the outcome, I was still $80 ahead!"

After one day, Chrome began to show up on the Futures Bet lists for the Derby, with opening odds of 300-1.

Kelly is blessed with a cute baby face and a quiet voice, so when she asked to bet California Chrome, the teller would usually need to look up his race record. After studying his past performances, the teller would say to her, "He is just a nice Cal-bred, are you sure you want to bet him for the Derby? He doesn't even have any of the points needed to get into the race!"

Kelly told me she would reply by smiling, shrugging her shoulders and then saying naively, "I just think he's such a beautiful horse!"

She was able to bet all of the $500 for me at odds of 300-1 down to 200-1, and her own $20 Futures bet at 300-1.

The bride of the bachelorette party also bet on California Chrome in the future wager. She was able to purchase both a living room set and a dining room set for her new home after her wedding.

9

DREAM SEASON

Each year on January 1, all Thoroughbreds who were foaled in North America mark their birthday, no matter their actual date of birth. January is also when the early nominations for each year's Triple Crown races are due. I sent in the nomination form and $600 check for Chrome during the last week of December in 2013 and received confirmation by the end of the year that we were registered.

Our Kentucky Derby Futures bets were in our pockets as we headed to Santa Anita on January 25, 2014 to watch California Chrome make his sophomore debut. The $250,000-guaranteed California Cup Derby was written for state-bred 3-year-olds at a distance of 1 1/16 miles. This would be Chrome's second two-turn race with a small bump up in distance to get us ever closer to that classic distance of 1 1/4 miles that he would need to master in May.

An interesting aside is that all races listed as a "derby" in North America are limited to 3-year-old horses only. This fact was always well-known to me, but just to push some people's buttons, I would sometimes pretend to be the clueless neophyte the press would portray me as.

I remember the social media outcry after I once told a reporter, "One main goal for Chrome is to be the first two-time winner of the Kentucky Derby!"

I was sure everyone would know I was joking; I was wrong.

I found the names some people would call me very entertaining, which always encouraged me to push even more buttons. Unfortunately, my wife seemed to take these insults to heart and was very hurt. I would try to tell her that it was a compliment these people found me so important that they would take time out of their busy day of reading the captions in "Sports Illustrated" to write these long dissertations on how smart they were and how dumb I am. She would smile and agree with me, but I could see she was still hurt.

Sprouting Wings

Our second race at Santa Anita would not go the same way as the first. Instead, this race was similar to Chrome's first race under Victor Espinoza, in the King Glorious Stakes.

Chrome broke a bit slow but hustled up into third where he stalked the pace. Things remained unchanged until the last turn where, again, Chrome picked it up and pulled even with the leader. At the top of the stretch Chrome again displayed his now familiar surge to pull away by five or six lengths, holding that margin while cruising to the finish as a 5 1/2-length winner. As track announcer Trevor Denman said, "They would need to sprout wings to catch California Chrome!"

Chrome's old nemesis Tamarando, who was voted 2013 California Champion 2-Year-Old Male instead of Chrome, closed late for second as the 9-5 favorite. But Chrome was clearly superior this time, as Tamarando never did sprout wings.

I wrote several letters to the Red Bull energy drink company, trying to get a sponsorship for Chrome. I always felt their "Red Bull gives you wings" advertising slogan would fit perfectly using video footage of this race and Trevor's call in the stretch. They never answered any of my letters.

Interesting sidenote: My cousin, Jack Dadam, actually discovered Red Bull in Europe under another product name. He purchased U.S. distribution rights and introduced it to America as Red Bull in the 1990s. He eventually sold his distribution company, so he would not have been any help to me for this potential cross-promotional effort.

The San Felipe Stakes

Santa Anita's historic San Felipe Stakes is a Grade 2 event for 3-year-olds that is typically held in early March and carded at a distance of 1 1/16 miles. Most importantly, this race offers 50 points to the winner on the road to the Kentucky Derby.

This was the first Kentucky Derby points race in which Chrome competed. I was not worried about gaining points in the earlier points races for 2-year-olds, as the points series is structured so that more points are awarded as the series moves closer to the Derby; this way, the horses who are coming into form closest to the Derby are the most likely to get in and compete. Winning this race for 50 points would likely punch our ticket to the Derby.

Being back at Santa Anita, and being creatures of habit, we again stayed at the Embassy Suites. Anticipation and anxiety were running high, as we needed to get over the hump and win, not only an open stakes race but a graded stakes race to boot!

Race days are hard, since the premier race of the day usually happens near the end of the program. That means waiting and more waiting as the butterflies seem to build a nest in my stomach.

Chrome was looking brilliant the morning of the $300,000-guaranteed San Felipe. Still, as was my custom, I asked his groom, Raul, how Chrome was doing. Raul was very close to Chrome and knew him better than anyone. He would prove to be the very best provider of inside information concerning Chrome.

On this morning, we got a very positive affirmation.

"Chrome is strong; very strong today!" Raul beamed.

That was all it took for me to empty my wallet at the betting windows. You would think that never having won a stakes race of this caliber would keep the betting odds fair. Chrome went off a little better than even money, as the 7-5 favorite.

Raul was right.

After emerging like a rocket out of the four-hole, Chrome shot straight to the lead. This was a first for him. After he ran a very quick opening quarter-mile in :23.09, Victor slowed the pace slightly the next quarter, while keeping the competition a half-length back. They were traveling at Chrome's high cruising speed and many of the horses were having difficulty keeping up.

This intense pace continued to the top of the stretch, where Victor dropped the reins and Chrome accelerated, quickly putting three lengths between himself and the closest horse behind him. The whip was never used as Chrome never needed urging. The margin of advantage continued to increase down the stretch until the final sixteenth of a mile, when Victor allowed Chrome to just canter home. The victory margin was 7 1/4 lengths, and the final time of 1:40.59 was only one second slower than the 21-year-old track record! This was one of many races in which Chrome could have broken records if not eased to save it for another day.

The First Offers

After traveling back to Yuba City, we settled into our "normal" routine, getting up at the crack of dawn and going to work. The next two weeks of work, however, were going to be a bit different.

I first got a phone call from a bloodstock agent who said he was representing a client from the Middle East. He said his client would like to offer $6 million to purchase California Chrome.

It actually did not register with me right away. After several seconds had passed, I said, "That is an interesting offer, I need to discuss this with my partner."

I quickly checked my cell phone to be sure I had the agent's number, then told him I would call him back. I was leaning "no" on his query, but I called Steve anyway to let him know of the offer.

We promptly agreed that $6 million would not be enough to sell our dream. I called the agent back and told him the bad news.

I got back to work.

Fifteen minutes later, my phone rang again. It was the same agent. This time, he offered $6 million for 51% ownership of Chrome. Again, it just didn't sink in right away. A few seconds later, it registered, so I asked for clarification. The clarification was simple: Chrome would be trained by the new majority owner's trainer and would wear the new owner's silks. I told him I would discuss it with my partner and get back to him.

I again called Steve and told him of the new offer. Steve told me again that he was out; his dream was not for sale at any price. I told him I would relay that to the agent.

It was about 45 minutes before I called the agent back. I was thinking that I could sell 51% from my 70% share, put $6 million in the bank and still participate in Chrome's career, owning 19%. I thought that a $12 million valuation was quite fair, and maybe even excessive as Chrome had only won one graded stakes race at this point.

I talked it over with Denise, and she agreed that $6 million was a lot of money. In the end, we couldn't in effect take Chrome away from Art, so we said no and went back to our day jobs.

Enter The Press

After the San Felipe romp, we had enough points that we were now officially on the media radar as a Kentucky Derby contender.

There were three levels of media involved.

The first media exposure would be from the on-track press corps. This consists of various newspaper, radio and equine print media (such as "Daily Racing Form" and "Blood-Horse"), as well as the on-track broadcast media groups, such as TVG. They would usually want a one- or two-minute statement explaining everything of importance—a sound bite. I do not speak well in soundbites.

The second media exposure would be from our regional Sacramento/Yuba City news organizations. This consisted of the local newspaper (the "Sacramento Bee") and local radio and TV programs such as "Good Day Sacramento." This program was my favorite, since it featured former TVG analyst Ken Rudolph as one of the hosts. It was fun discussing horse racing with someone who knew something about the sport.

The third media exposure was national. NBC called, wanting to arrange to shoot some background footage with me at Martin Testing Labs for their Kentucky Derby broadcast.

This was just the beginning of our media adventures.

Mom

There was a lot going on behind the scenes in my life that people do not know about. It is still difficult for me to talk about without getting too emotional, so maybe writing about it will be good therapy.

A year before our run to the Kentucky Derby, my mother had been diagnosed with lung cancer. She had a lung removed and the doctors were confident it had not spread, but it was a long, hard road of physical therapy to gain some sort of "normalcy" in her life.

We called often and visited when we could. She always asked about our horses, especially the young filly that was named after her, Catherine's Cause. She also had a special interest in Chrome, the horse I told her was going to win the Kentucky Derby.

"I'm working hard," she said. "I need to be healthy enough to travel and see my filly run and Chrome win the Kentucky Derby."

That strong will of hers drove her to better health. Within six months of having a lung removed, she was walking up to a mile and working in her garden.

Things were looking good as we worked our way closer to the Derby: Chrome was on a winning streak, while my mom kept getting stronger also. Moments after every Chrome win, we would call her to share the good news. She was always excited and looking forward to the first Saturday in May.

We called after the San Felipe win, and immediately I knew something was wrong. There was no excitement and no energy, she sounded tired and I was sure I heard a muffled cough. I asked her what was wrong, and she said that there had been an early snow melt in her hometown of Iron Mountain, Michigan, so she had gone outside to do a little clean-up in her garden and get ready for spring. She said she must have caught a little cold. I made her promise to see the doctor before I would let her hang up the phone.

A week later, we were on a plane to visit her. She was in the hospital with pneumonia. That is rough enough for any elderly person, but especially serious for one with only one lung!

When we got there, she put on a good show. She was going to be up and around in no time. We consulted with her doctor, and he had other ideas. In addition to the pneumonia, there was some filling around her heart. He assured us there was no immediate danger, but recovery would be slow and limited in nature.

He felt that, by the time of the Derby, she would still be on oxygen therapy with bed rest along with targeted physical therapy. He thought she should be able to watch the Derby on TV.

We visited for a few days and tried to let her down easy, repeating over and over the doctor's outlook. She kept saying, "I'm not going to miss the Derby!"

The Santa Anita Derby

With three consecutive wins in stakes company, Chrome was now on a roll, and seemingly doing better each race as we approached the Kentucky Derby. This is exactly what you would want as an owner of a Derby contender. We were now operating on cruise control, as we had made the difficult decisions to support our horse and the results were validating the choices we had made.

It was more tradition and convenience, rather than superstition, which kept us going back to the Embassy Suites in Arcadia. Just like the mantra of the horse industry, "If it works, don't change it!"

One thing we did change, however, was getting to the track early. Waiting out the long day is just too stressful.

On the day of the 2014 Santa Anita Derby (G1), the West Coast's major prep for the Triple Crown series of races, we decided to sleep in and go to a long brunch before arriving at Santa Anita. It's just so much easier to relax without everyone in your face.

Knowing we were again in a later, marquee race, we opted to arrive around Race 5, about 90 minutes prior to the Santa Anita Derby. I would not have a chance to ask Raul about Chrome on this day, but I would only make a token wager since Chrome was the 3-5 morning line favorite. It's not worth risking money for 3-5, especially when the winner of the race gets a $600,000 check.

Having the favorite in a Grade 1 race does offer some perks. We watched the races leading up to the Santa Anita Derby from a complimentary owner's box, rather than from our normal, unassuming spot. But for our race, we would go from the walking ring to our regular spot on the track apron.

Chrome did not get a flyer out of the gate this day, and was in very close quarters early. He was able to accelerate and moved up to second while the crowd's second favorite, Candy Boy, kept pressure on him to his outside. The pace slowed on the backstretch and Chrome and Victor, who were really starting to gel as a duo by now, bided their time.

There was no change in leadership until mid-turn, when Chrome applied his usual kick for home. By the top of the stretch, he was in front by three lengths and his lead was growing. He was more than seven lengths clear of the closest competitor when Victor let off the gas at the sixteenth pole, and cruised home to win by an easy 5 1/4 lengths. Our horse had run his furthest distance yet, at 1 1/8 miles, and was showing no signs of difficulty with longer distances.

Keeping with tradition, I called my mom's hospital room after the Santa Anita Derby win. She already knew we had won, as the nurses had thoughtfully set up a computer in her room so she could watch the race via streaming.

"He won by a mile!" she said. She was excited, but I could tell she was also tired and weak.

Before we hung up, she again told me she was going to the Kentucky Derby. What could I do? I did not want to upset her. Even though I knew she would be ignoring her doctor's advice, I said, "Okay, mom."

Despite the fact that he got a late start running in qualifying points races, with his Santa Anita Derby win, Chrome now had 150 Kentucky

Derby points and was ranked on top as the new points leader. With most of the major prep races in the books, no other horse would surpass his point total. Chrome might just be the Derby favorite!

Chasing Chase

This fact was not lost on the equine marketplace, as I got a call from an old acquaintance, Greg Gilchrist—the trainer of our first racehorse, Searchforthetruth. Greg was acting as an agent for one of his well-heeled clients who was interested in purchasing Love the Chase, California Chrome's dam whom Greg had originally picked out at auction as an unraced 2-year-old. The offer was $750,000.

As I was now experienced in these matters, I was quick to answer this time. I told Greg I would need to pass the offer by Steve before I could give him an answer.

I called Steve and we discussed it, agreeing that Love the Chase was worth much more as the young dam of the likely Kentucky Derby favorite. I relayed this information to Greg, who thanked me for my time.

A few minutes later, he called back. His client had upped the offer. His base offer was still $750,000, which he would pay immediately, plus a bonus of $250,000 for each of the Triple Crown races won by Chrome to be paid after each race. I needed to call Steve back.

We again agreed that Love the Chase was worth more, so we declined the offer. Greg would not call back again. That was fine with us.

I read in stories on the internet that we were offered $2 million for Love the Chase. I was never offered that amount of money, nor informed of any offer of that size. Greg's offer was the highest of which I'm aware, coming in at $1.25 million since Chrome went on to win two Triple Crown races. Others offered less and were turned down immediately.

10

OUR RUN FOR THE ROSES

For almost 11 years, I worked for the United States Air Force at McClellan Air Force Base in California, as I detailed earlier. When the base closed, I worked as a manager for NTS, a nationwide testing and laboratory company that received a federal contract to operate the Air Force labs as the base was shuttered. When NTS closed, my wife and I started Materials Technology Laboratories (MTL), dba Martin Testing Labs, using the exact same facilities.

I mention this because my experience for the United States Air Force included doing failure analysis and crash investigation. In actuality, I only did crash investigation for one year. The Air Force then adopted a new, better sounding terminology; there were no more "crashes," only various magnitudes of "mishaps." From that day forward, I did Mishap Investigation.

This work made for some interesting discussions around the dinner table when our children were growing up. It may not be surprising, then, that my son, Perry Jr., has an aversion to air travel.

For this reason, my immediate family decided to take an Amtrak train to the Kentucky Derby. That meant we would have to leave a few days early, but that was fine as it would keep us off the media radar for a few days, or so I thought.

The Fame Game

The media had gotten word that we were taking the train, porter met us on the train platform in Sacramento. We had a s⎽ ⎽⎽s- cussion about why we were taking the train and the reporter seemed to get bored. That was fine with us. When the train arrived, we loaded aboard.

The four of us settled into our two compartments. We sat and contently watched the trip unfold, enjoying glorious views of the Sierra Nevada Mountains as we slowly made our way out of California. We made reservations for dinner the first night in the dining car. We timed our reservations for just after our short stop in Reno, Nevada.

The whole train experience was new for me, and I quickly learned that the railroad personnel expected to be tipped for every little thing. This was not at all like flying in a commercial airplane. The food was fairly good, however very salty. After dinner, and a long discussion of our adventure to come, we made our way back to our compartments and reconfigured them for sleeping. When night fell, we hit the sack, as there was no point of trying to view scenery in the dark.

I cannot speak for everybody in our group, but sleeping was almost impossible for me. Every time I started to drift off, we either went over some cross-tracks or went through a tunnel or another train would go by in the opposite direction. By morning, I was exhausted.

Sightseeing became more boring the further east we traveled. The beautiful scenery had disappeared and there was nothing but empty space. The whole family began to look forward to our dining car visits as the most enjoyable experience on the train.

There was one interesting thing that happened. Denise had splurged on a new iPhone, and when we were in "good" areas, she could access her email and the internet on it. At one point, she received an email from our friend Debbie, who sent a link from the local Sacramento TV news, saying, "You've got to see this!"

Denise clicked the link, and we watched on her phone as a news crew in front of our Yuba City home interviewed our next door neighbor!

I turned to Denise and said, "I knew I should have mowed the lawn before we left!"

She shushed me and we continued to watch the tiny screen.

The reporter asked, "How does it feel to live next door to the family that owns the favorite in the Kentucky Derby?"

I should say right now that this neighbor had just moved in a few months earlier, after our longtime neighbor had died. We really did not know her very well; still, her answer was quite interesting.

"All I know is that the City of Yuba City saw fit to fine me for having chickens in my yard!" she stated sharply. "If I can't have chickens, how do those people get away with having a horse?"

The reporter, without missing a beat, said, "And there you have it from in front of the Martin home in Yuba City. We'll bring you more remote broadcasts later on as we query the folks of Yuba City on their thoughts about this historic event."

We all laughed.

I guess these remote broadcasts were shown at various points throughout the local news morning show on TV. As was the current custom, the video clips for the morning show were posted on the TV station's website.

Denise scrolled down to the next video clip and clicked on it. The news crew had found their way to a Yuba City hotspot called The Happy Viking Sports Pub & Eatery. Before the camera rolled, they probably gave the crowd a briefing on what they were doing, because everyone was aware of California Chrome and the Yuba City connection with his owners, the Martins.

They quickly walked through the bar getting soundbites from at least five different people. The main essence was always something like, "The Martins are great people; they are in here all the time."

I asked Kelly and Perry Jr. if they had ever been in The Happy Viking. They shook their heads and said, "No!"

I asked Denise the same question, and she said, "I have never even heard of The Happy Viking."

I said, "Me either. I would like to meet that other Martin family, though; they sound pretty nice!"

We all laughed.

Our Churchill Downs Experience

I have been told it went down something like this.

My mom called my brother Roy and told him to come pick her up "right now!" from the hospital. Once he agreed and she knew he was on his way, she asked the nurse to call her doctor. The doctor had a long talk with her about traveling to the Kentucky Derby and tried to convince her she needed rest and should not go. She would not listen. He finally told her they needed to wait until my brother arrived and they could all discuss it together.

After a six-hour drive from Chicago, my brother got there to find my mom sitting up in bed with her arms crossed, absolutely stoic. The doctor called my brother out of the room and talked to him first, then the two of them approached our mom. She just kept repeating that she was going to the Kentucky Derby!

They backed out of the room and sent in her favorite nurse to try and talk to her. The nurse said, "But Mrs. Martin, if you leave the hospital, you could die."

My mom replied, "Honey, I'm going to die, but not before I see my son's horse win the Kentucky Derby!"

The doctor knew he was beat. My mom was so tough, he never had a chance. He pulled my brother aside and started writing down a checklist of everything he would need: wheelchair, portable oxygen, etc.

The next day, after a visit to the medical supply store, everything required was packed into my brother's van and they were literally off to the races. My brother called me and told me the story while they were on the way. Mom was going to the Derby. It was no longer just about the horse, but something much more important: family.

We disembarked the train at a small Illinois town, rented a car and drove the rest of the way to Frankfort, Kentucky, our home base for the entire Derby trip. Churchill Downs had reserved blocks of rooms in Louisville for owners of the Kentucky Derby runners and offered us reservations at these more convenient in-town hotels, but we felt the $1,100 to $1,500 per night charges were a bit hefty. The Frankfort hotel we stayed at had raised its rates up to $165 per night for Derby week, and we felt an extra 45-minute ride each way was a small price to pay for better value.

Our whole group stayed at the same hotel: Denise, me and our kids, Denise's brother Andrew and his family, my brother Roy and his family and my mom and her guest, Mary, who was her neighbor and a friend of the family.

On Derby day, my entire family, including my mother, piled into three cars and we headed toward the track. The traffic that day was horrible, which should come as no surprise. It took us more than 20 minutes just to make it down the highway exit ramp. It took another 40 minutes to make it to the correct parking lot where I already had a parking pass. Unfortunately, that lot was the furthest from the Churchill Downs barn area.

After making such an effort to travel to the event, my mom really wanted to visit with California Chrome, so I pushed her wheelchair all the way to the barn area with my family following in attendance. I showed my credentials, and we were allowed access to the backside, but when we arrived at Chrome's barn, we were stopped by a sheriff who was guarding access to Chrome.

I showed the sheriff my credentials and told him I was Chrome's owner. The sheriff shook his head and said, I've seen the television reports and Chrome's owner is a guy with a cowboy hat, and you aren't him.

I asked the sheriff if my name was on the access list. He checked, and it was not!

I asked him if he knew Art Sherman, and if he would believe it if Art told him who I was. He said yes, Art Sherman is on the access list and if he said I could see the horse, we could see him. I tried calling Art, but got no answer. It was Derby day, and he was very busy. The sheriff was adamant, so we turned around and made our way to our box seats without seeing Chrome.

The only other noteworthy incident at the Derby concerned where we would watch the race from. At the time, Churchill Downs only had one hydraulic lift for wheelchairs, and it was at the far end of the grandstand. It took some time to get my mother situated in our box, but once there, we had an excellent view of the entire track positioned just past the finish line. This was a magnificent vantage point.

Our volunteer host had some concerns that it would take a considerably long time to navigate my mother to the winner's circle if we were to win the Derby. She suggested that we pre-position my mother near the rail by the finish line. I told her that it was my experience that the rail near the finish line gets awfully crowded, and I was afraid we would not get a good view of the race. I was assured that the area in front of us would be kept clear. I said I prefer to remain in the box.

Some time passed, and we were another race closer to the Derby. Our host's supervisor came by to talk to us. I was again assured that we would have a great view of the track if we moved now. I knew I shouldn't, but I relented, and we made our way down to the rail.

Staying with my mom down on the rail, I missed the ceremonial walkover of the horses from the barn. Mom and I were right there when they turned to come off the track and into the paddock tunnel; this area had several people in wheelchairs. My mom screamed, "There he is!" as Chrome walked by.

After that brief sighting, we waited a bit. Eventually, the horses were saddled in the paddock and headed back out through the tunnel and onto the track for the post parade. That was great, but an army of "owners" walked out with them, then positioned themselves out on the track right in front of us, backing up to lean back on the rail just outside the chain-link fencing. Being on lower ground, we could not see a thing!

I flagged down our host and complained. She walked over and talked to two security guards who then moved the people on the rail in front of us, telling them to keep the area clear as there were folks in the wheelchair area who wanted to see the race. They complied until just before the race started, when the guards walked over to move people that had wandered out too far onto the track. As soon as the guards moved away, the "owners" moved back in front of us.

I raised my voice, reminding them that there were people here in wheelchairs who wanted to see the race. They pretended they didn't hear me, so I yelled louder. One laughed. Just then, I had a wonderful thought. I bet if I crack that guy's head open and dump him in the trench along the rail, everybody else would move! Even after 15 years of living in genteel California, my Chicago upbringing kicks in when I need it.

I started to climb the fence and my mother grabbed my arm.

"Leave it be, I can see the race on the big board," she assured me.

The flush left my face and I smiled and returned to her side. Too bad; someone almost had one of those unforgettable Derby experiences!

Mom and I held hands when the starting gates opened to unleash the 19 Derby hopefuls. Neither of us said a word as we watched the race progress on the large, elevated video screen in the infield. We huddled in silence while engulfed in an excited roar of the crowd.

At the turn for home, I could see Chrome just off the leader on the outside. I saw Victor drop the reins. Chrome's ears pricked forward, and he dropped about a foot in height as he stretched out to accelerate.

"It's all over!" I shouted as Chrome quickly drove out to a five-length lead.

My mom was squeezing my hand with all the strength she could muster.

A few seconds later as the horses flashed by, I looked at Mom and beamed, "We won!"

We must have hugged for two minutes.

The Churchill Downs staff showed up. Four guys picked up my mother's wheelchair and carried it, with her in it, across the dirt track to the Kentucky Derby infield winner's circle. I followed behind, tears welling up. It meant so much that my mom could share this moment with me.

Steve Haskins from "BloodHorse" magazine stopped me as I crossed the track.

"Perry, what are you feeling?" he asked.

I could not utter a word. Steve probably thought I was overwrought by winning the Kentucky Derby. In actuality, that was just a small part of the emotions that were swirling inside me.

I slowly made my way to the stage in the winner's circle, stopping to acknowledge the offerings of well-wishers. I walked up the stairs and over to the trophy presentation area. Denise and I stood in the background, trying to blend in. Bob Costas of NBC signaled me over to ask a question. This was it; this is why we had to stand down at the rail with a bad view of the race. This is what I could not miss, the moment the world's TV audience couldn't miss.

I looked down at the crowd in the winner's circle. There was my mom, waving from her wheelchair and smiling.

When I got over to the microphone, Mr. Costas asked me, "Perry, this is a horse that was bred for barely $10,000. You turned down $6 million for half-interest in the horse. You must have had a real belief in the horse?"

I hesitated. Being me, the first thing I wanted to say was, "Duh?"

However, I thought better of it and simply repeated, "I had a real belief in the horse, yes!"

There, now the world can rest easy.

I skipped the press conference after the race. I felt I had already contributed more information than the world could handle. Besides, I had a lot of tickets to cash. First things first!

My mother, Katherine Martin, held on for five more months, but passed away in September of that incredible year. She never got to see her namesake filly run—and win!—but she did get to see her son's horse win the Kentucky Derby. I am so very thankful for that.

11

THE SECOND JEWEL

Much was made in the press about how I was treated badly at the Kentucky Derby and that was why Denise and I did not attend the 2014 Preakness Stakes at Pimlico Race Course in Maryland. That is complete and utter nonsense!

My wife and I had pre-arranged plans to celebrate our 28th wedding anniversary at the Wynn Las Vegas. As I mentioned in an earlier chapter, we had spent our honeymoon at the Desert Inn, and when that hotel was torn down and replaced by the Wynn, the Wynn became our go-to place to stay in Vegas.

During the Kentucky Derby after-party, we were discussing canceling our plans and going to the Preakness, but my mother overheard us and said, "You'll do no such thing; family first."

We immediately promised her we would follow through on our original plans.

Letting It Ride

Denise and I arrived in Vegas a few days before the May 17 race. Our first day of vacation was spent walking up and down the Vegas Strip, cashing the Kentucky Derby Futures bets that Kelly had placed for us back in January. In all, these bets totaled more than $100,000, which fit nicely into a small tote bag that we had taken with us just for that purpose.

The day of the Preakness, I decided it would be fine if we gave some of the casino's money back, so we left the tote bag with a little over $90,000 inside it in a large safety deposit box in the casino's safe and took the remainder to the Wynn's race book. What happened next was what I would describe as my most remarkable day at the betting windows ever!

I like gambling at a race book, since there is a large offering of races to choose from and there is no need to place a wager in races that are wide-open. I usually handicap the races, then bet $20 in a race in which I estimate a good likelihood of being successful and $100 in any race in which I feel the likelihood of success is high. These bets for a $20 race are typically in the form of $5 to win, place and show and then $5 in some form of exotic bet, such as an exacta or superfecta. In a $100 race, these same bets would be five times larger.

On this occasion, I was feeling lucky, so I indulged on $1,000 worth of bets on each race. For a four-hour period, from about 11 a.m. until 3 p.m. Vegas time, I made dozens of bets and cashed all but one ticket! It got so that when I walked up to the betting window, the tellers at the adjoining windows would ask their customers to please stand by while they leaned over to hear what horse I was betting.

There was one teller all the way at the end of the windows who would stand up, walk over and stand behind the teller I was using. I would bet a horse that was 8-1, and by the time I walked back to my seat and looked up at the tote board, the odds would drop to 4-1. Those tellers must have really jumped on my picks.

Before leaving the race book, I parlayed everything we had won that day on California Chrome in the Preakness. I was absolutely sure our colt was going to make it six stakes wins in a row that day.

Family First

I have to say, the Preakness was my favorite Triple Crown race.

Denise and I watched the race coverage in our suite on TV with the sound turned off. After Chrome won, we hugged, then turned off the TV.

We took a long, slow walk down the Strip to the restaurant where we had our dinner reservations. This was so much more relaxing and enjoyable than any of the races we had attended.

We waited until the next day to cash our tickets on Chrome. After all, we needed to do a little shopping before we collected our winnings. We needed a larger tote bag.

You would think that having such a pleasant experience away from the track, we would opt to miss the races more often. In all, though, we missed only two races in Chrome's entire career: the Preakness and the Hollywood Derby (G1)—although I can think of a couple races I would have liked to miss.

You already know why we missed the Preakness. We missed the Hollywood Derby six months later when we attended my mother's memorial service.

This service was held several months after her death in order to accommodate everyone's schedules. My father, per his bequest, had his ashes scattered at his favorite place to be: his neighbor's deer camp in Michigan's Upper Peninsula. My mother wished to have her ashes scattered at the same site, so we gathered with her friends and neighbors to do just that.

It was very moving to be in pristine forest, hearing only the sound of the rushing Sturgeon River, which was nearby. Everyone talked for a few minutes about their favorite memory of my mother. It was very poignant.

Banking On Success

As an everyday kind of guy who grew up in the Midwest, I am still confused why anyone would want my autograph. I never refuse to give it; I just grimace a little.

The coolest experience for me regarding my newfound fame (and fortune) was taking California Chrome's Kentucky Derby winner's check to my credit union in Sacramento.

I stood in line and waited my turn, then I approached the teller, showed her my ID and gave her my account number. She pulled up the account on her computer terminal while I signed the back of the check. She again looked at my ID and saw that it matched the information on the computer screen.

"Hello Mr. Martin, what can I do for you?" she asked.

I turned over the check and presented it to her. She flipped it back over and looked at the signature, comparing it to my signature on file that was presented on her computer screen. Satisfied, she again turned over the check and looked at the amount: around $800,000.

Her eyes opened wide, and she gasped, "What is this for?"

"It's for deposit," I replied, matter-of-factly.

"No, no," she said, "Why did they give this to you?"

"Because they owed me the money," I explained.

Now she was flustered.

"Why do they owe you the money?"

Not wanting to hold up the line too long with my Kentucky Derby tale and the inevitable question-and-answer period it would have generated at my community banking center, I replied, "An investment paid off." It was the simple truth, after all.

The bank teller proceeded to warn me about all the investment scams out there, and notified me that she was going to have to place a hold on the funds. Good thing I did not tell her about the Nigerian prince I have dealings with through email!

Adding A Little Flair

Before Chrome ever ran, I recommended to Art that our colt should use a Flair Equine Nasal Strip as part of his regular equipment. This drug-free, adhesive patch for horses is similar to Breathe Right nasal strips for humans; however, for horses, it is worn more for safety reasons.

A horse only breathes through his nose, not his mouth, and the nasal walls depend on blood pressure to keep the passageway rigid. If, at the end of a race, the horse is spent and his blood pressure drops, the nasal passage walls will become flaccid like a wet paper soda straw and collapse when the horse breathes in. This will cause exercise-induced pulmonary hemorrhage (EIPH), which can damage a horse's health when blood enters the lungs.

The Flair strip holds the passage open, helping to allow air flow through the nostrils and reduce the damage. Studies have shown that the nasal strip does not enhance performance.

Back in 2014, New York racing officials did not allow nasal strips to be used during races, which presented a problem for us after Chrome won the Preakness. When giving an interview prior to Chrome's Triple Crown attempt, Art mentioned that I might not let the horse run if he could not wear his nasal strip. My being a media "loose cannon" would now be useful.

A few weeks prior to the 2014 Belmont Stakes (G1), the three stewards at Belmont Park, prompted by a formal request from Art and encouraged by expert analysis from the New York State Gaming Commission equine medical director, announced they had unanimously agreed to allow the use of equine nasal strips for all horses running at New York Racing Association (NYRA) tracks, and that Chrome would be permitted to use a nasal strip when he competed in the third leg of the Triple Crown.

In response, Flair provided us with a one-year supply of nasal strips and told us to ask when we needed more.

Around this time, we also started working with Leverage Agency, a sponsorship agency based in New York City that secured our first official sponsorship: Breathe Right nasal strips. The company announced they would provide free nasal strips to the tens of thousands of racing fans who attended that year's Belmont Stakes, and we entered a new phase of marketing our California-bred colt to a wider audience.

Not bad for a couple of Dumb Ass Partners who started out with an $8,000 mare.

12

TRIPLE CROWN LETDOWN

The Belmont Stakes is a race that I probably would have liked to miss.

Denise and I decided to go to the race because we didn't want to miss the history that was hopefully in the making. We were joined in New York by Kelly and her boyfriend at the time, Jason, as well as her friends Robin and Leah. Perry Jr. stayed home to watch our Golden Retriever, Tizzy, for us.

In case you are wondering, yes; Tizzy was named for Cee's Tizzy, the Harris Farm stallion who sired another superlative Cal-bred Tiznow, who was foaled and raised at Harris Farms, and who also was lauded as Horse of the Year, in 2000. The pensioned Tiznow, who will turn 25 at his longtime Kentucky home of WinStar Farm in 2022, reigned as the highest-earning California-bred in history with his $6,427,830 bankroll until Chrome came along and smashed that record by more than double.

Denise and I took a young unnamed golden retriever pup with us to Harris Farms one day as Dave McGlothlin was touring us around the stallion complex. She wandered into Cee's Tizzy's paddock where he was lying down resting and lay down next to the stallion's nose. Dave got a bit excited as the stallion was known for his aggressive nature and Dave was worried for the pup's safety. The stallion rolled halfway up and sniffed the quiet puppy, then rolled back to continue resting. We called and the pup came running, unnamed no longer.

Media Frenzy

The Belmont Park folks set us up at a very nice hotel in New Jersey. We really enjoyed walking around the neighborhood and found several nice restaurants where we could have our evening meals. I must say that I had the best mussels that I'd ever eaten at an Italian place which was just around the corner from our hotel.

In the days leading up to the race, there were several public relations events that the Belmont representatives had set up for us to help promote the big race. It was a whirlwind.

Denise and I skipped everything, preferring instead to let our partners, Steve and Carolyn Coburn, enjoy the lion's share of the glaring spotlight that always shines whenever an elusive Triple Crown win is on the line. Our partners rang the bell to open the New York Stock Exchange and appeared on the "Good Morning America" television program, among other pre-race activities.

It seemed that every time we came downstairs to the hotel lobby, we were ambushed by the media wanting an interview or to discuss Chrome's prospects for securing the Triple Crown in the Belmont. We had accumulated six stakes wins in a row, and our nerves were starting to get frayed. After all, Denise and I were just a normal married couple who had no formal experience or training in dealing with the media, or how to handle our instant celebrity status. It was overwhelming.

The night before the Belmont Stakes, our small group went on a pub crawl to let off some steam. After a few drinks, Jason and I had a grand time communicating the rest of the evening with Scottish accents. Aye.

We happened to run into Art Sherman's group while we were moving between pubs. It seems that his group had the same idea we had, and Art was certainly a little bit worse for wear. The next day there was going to be a small price to pay, but I'm sure it was worth it.

The morning of the Belmont, we took the shuttle provided by Belmont Park to the track, where I ran into my old friend Ken Rudulph from the "Good Day Sacramento" TV series at Chrome's barn. We talked for a bit on camera to provide an update on Chrome's progress moving toward the Belmont for his morning show.

Then Ken acted as my chauffeur by driving me from the barn area over to the rapidly filling grandstand. We made some small talk during the drive, and I remember discussing my favorite type of music—Hard Rock—and my favorite band, Metallica. I joined my wife and our very small group to enjoy the races leading up to The Big One.

After the completion of the race prior to the Belmont, Denise and I got up and made our way toward the paddock and saddling area, which was now jammed with people. As we approached, a guard at the gate stopped us and would not let us enter the paddock. I had a collection of tickets and passes on a lanyard around my neck and I pointed out our paddock pass for this specific race to the guard. In fact, I held it up in front of his face so he could read it quite clearly.

The guard must have been able to read, since he said, "I don't know where you got that, but the owner of California Chrome is already in the paddock and I'm not letting any more people in there."

In the heat of the moment, I said some things to that person that I'm not proud of, but I'm sure with him being from New York, he has likely heard worse.

Disgusted, we walked back to our box seats after again being denied access to our horse. It seemed that we had only avoided the triple brush-off by not attending the Preakness. Staying home was looking better and better!

We actually watched the Belmont from our box, rather than from our favorite viewing area of any racetrack: the apron. Maybe that is what jinxed it for us.

Fate Steps In

When the starting gate opened, I saw Chrome bump against Matterhorn, a maiden winner and, at 40-1, the longest shot in the 11-horse field who had drawn the starting stall next to him. But, of course, from my faraway vantage point, I could not see that Chrome's right front hoof had been stepped on, and a portion of it had been torn off.

What I did notice was that Chrome was running with his head held much higher and he was tossing it from side to side, much like he had in the Willard Proctor Stakes at Hollywood Park the previous year. I knew Chrome was in distress, so I mentioned this to Denise. She concurred and said, simply, "I hope Victor takes care of him."

Chrome tried his best despite the early trouble and ultimately finished in a dead heat with Wicked Strong for fourth in the grueling, 1 1/2-mile test, reaching the wire together an admirable 1 3/4 lengths behind the 9-1 winner, Tonalist.

Like so many others before him, California Chrome had just missed winning the Triple Crown. It was certainly disappointing, but at that moment, Denise and I had other concerns, such as why was our horse distressed during the race?

We watched as Chrome completed his post-race gallop-out and returned in front of the grandstand to be unsaddled. Our focus was on the horse, so we were not paying attention to the raised voices six rows up behind us, as other members of our racing partnership were interviewed by NBC reporter Kenny Rice in the immediate aftermath of the race. We did see it on TV ourselves later and, of course, those heated moments live on in infamy on YouTube.

In front of us, we watched more important drama unfold, as Chrome was inspected by the track veterinarian and then led off back through the tunnel by Raul. Just as I had finished telling Denise we would need to walk back to the barn to see how Chrome was, a young man ran up to our box. He was a little winded, but managed to get out these dire words, "They sent me up here to tell you your horse is bleeding."

As he suddenly turned to walk off, I yelled, "Bleeding from where?"

The young man stopped and turned back for just a moment, shrugging that he did not know, then continued on his way.

Just one row behind us was Art, who was focused on the loud distraction a few rows up. I reached back and tapped him on the shoulder, "Art, they told us Chrome was bleeding."

Art snapped around, the concern evident.

"From the nose?" he asked.

I told him we didn't know; we were not given any additional information.

Denise and I left with Art, and walked together quietly back to Chrome's barn. The lack of noise that enveloped us as we approached Belmont's bucolic backside was a complete turnaround from just 15 minutes earlier, when excitement and adrenaline from a raucous crowd of 102,199 racing fans had lifted the rafters of the venerable old track.

By the time we reached the barn, the vet had already blocked Chrome's right leg, which means he was given an injection to stop the pain, much like a dentist does before working on your teeth. He had also disinfected and wrapped the wound.

Alan Sherman showed us a picture of the wound he had taken with his phone. It was ugly.

"Ouch," I cringed.

Fortunately, the vet said Chrome would need some time to heal, but would be fine. We instructed Art to send him home to Harris Farms in California for a little rest before we left to find our group.

After our stop at the barn to check on the horse, Denise and I met up with our friends and family, as well as a few folks from the Coburns' entourage, and looked for the shuttle that would take us back to the hotel. We had a pre-arranged place to meet it near the grandstand, but it was nowhere to be found. We tried calling the shuttle driver, who had given us his business card. But the crowd at the Belmont was so large that the cell towers had been overwhelmed and calls were not going through.

We looked at the streets around the track; they were filled with cars that were not moving. We watched as a stoplight changed from red to green and one car pulled into the intersection, with its driver anticipating that the line would move. It did not. The car stuck in the intersection was now blocking cross-traffic, so there was a chorus of car horns. We could hear car horns in the distance as well, as this scenario repeated itself everywhere with tens of thousands of people all trying to leave the track at one time.

Our small group huddled. We came up with a simple plan: just start walking back to the hotel in New Jersey. Our thinking was that the further we got away from Belmont Park, the less congested the streets would be. Also, eventually we would pick up a cell tower that was forwarding calls.

When we got about 10 blocks away from Belmont Park, our call to the shuttle driver finally got through. He had taken the Coburns back to the hotel and was awaiting our call. We told him the names of the streets at the intersection where we were standing, and he instructed us to wait there until he arrived.

It was another half-hour until we saw the shuttle pull up, but that was actually the best thing that happened to us on that dreadful day. I repeat, there has got to be a better way!

In 2015, Belmont Park officials implemented an attendance cap of 90,000 for future events, due to the madness and unpreparedness that permeated the facility on the day of Chrome's Triple Crown attempt.

13

THE EYE OF THE STORM

A week after the Belmont, we were invited back to Churchill Downs for the official presentation of the Kentucky Derby trophy.

For most of the big races, the trophy is engraved with the name of the winning horse and the names of the horse's connections: owner, trainer and jockey. For most races, the trophy is simply shipped to the designated owner. For the Kentucky Derby, however, there is an official presentation which is part of a daylong series of other events such as the unveiling of the Derby winner's exhibit in the Kentucky Derby Museum, which is adjacent to Churchill Downs.

As the owners of the newest Derby winner, we were the first of the public allowed to view the exhibit. It started with a life-sized replica of California Chrome being ridden by a Victor Espinoza replica outfitted with our Dumb Ass Partners silks. The Chrome replica was draped with the familiar garland of roses. Behind the horse was a replica tote board showing the final odds and final finishing time of the 2014 race. We marveled over the detail; Chrome's freckle on his white blaze was perfectly positioned.

We were then escorted to the Museum's video room, where there was an audiovisual presentation about the history of the Kentucky Derby with "My Old Kentucky Home" softly playing in the background. The stretch call of our race, the 140th Kentucky Derby, was played along with the race video. I needed to wipe a tear from my eye at this point, as the memories were overwhelming. I took a quick look around to make sure that nobody saw.

At the conclusion of the museum tour, we were escorted to seats in the Churchill Downs clubhouse to enjoy the evening's live racing program, which featured the Grade 1 Stephen Foster Handicap, a race which was named, appropriately enough, after the composer of "My Old Kentucky Home."

I believe our trophy presentation took place just before they ran the marquee race. I was able to get through the brief ceremony without saying anything controversial. I'm not sure how that happened.

Kentucky Derby Keepsakes

A lot of people have asked me about the logistics of winning such an important and historic race as the Kentucky Derby. For example: Do you get to keep the trophy? And: How do you get the trophy home? Here is our experience.

Churchill Downs paid for round-trip first-class airfare for Denise and I to attend the on-track trophy presentation in June, approximately six weeks after our horse won the Run for the Roses.

Through Dumb Ass Partners, we used race proceeds to purchase a replica trophy for every race up until the Triple Crown. As the Derby trophy costs more than $100,000 to produce, we did not replicate it.

Because we owned the winner of two legs of the Triple Crown in partnership at the time, Denise and I kept the Kentucky Derby owners' trophy and Steve and Carolyn kept the sterling silver owners' trophy from the Preakness Stakes. Art and Victor received their designated trophies from these two American classic races as well; these are replicas created for the winning trainer and jockey.

Our engraved Kentucky Derby trophy was shipped to us in two padded transport cases via private courier. One case was for the 18-karat gold trophy and lid and the other was for the jade base.

So, in answer to a question I receive often: No, we did not have to run our Kentucky Derby trophy through TSA as a carry-on item on our flight home!

Another memento from winning the biggest race in America is the Kentucky Derby ring, the brainchild of the late Churchill Downs executive Donnie Richardson.

Although similar to the idea of championship rings in other sports, I've been told that these rings have a special origin story. Excess gold from the making of the Kentucky Derby trophy, such as filing off the flash from mold seams, sprue hole material and so on, is added to additional gold to make the rings. One ring each is given to the jockey, trainer and owner of the winning horse.

As Denise was my partner in all things, we asked Churchill Downs' Kelly Danner, who implemented the Kentucky Derby ring concept, if we could purchase an additional ring in Denise's size. Both of these rings were inscribed on the inside with the same words, "Partners Forever." We never wore these rings in public, but simply kept them as keepsakes.

If I am so lucky as to win four Kentucky Derbies, like NFL great Terry Bradshaw has four Super Bowl rings, then I'll start wearing them in public. As I started breeding horses in my late 50s, it would be too much to ask to win seven rings, like Tom Brady.

Chrome Goes Home

Following his rigorous Triple Crown campaign which unfortunately concluded with a partially sheared-off hoof, California Chrome was shipped via a Tex Sutton flight back to his birthplace of Harris Farms in California for a rest, although "rest" might not be the right word for our colt's first extended break since he had begun serious race training as an early 2-year-old.

We were able to visit him twice while he was there over the summer of 2014. Farm manager Dave McGlothlin showed us the stallion paddock where Chrome was staying. Chrome seemed right at home about 50 yards away from his sire, Lucky Pulpit.

Dave showed us the secret stash of Mrs. Pasture's horse cookies that was hidden in the crook of a tree just outside the paddock fence. Dave said we were welcome to feed Chrome a cookie whenever we visited. Apparently, so were the dozens of reporters, camera crews and distinguished visitors that dropped by that summer, providing free publicity to the farm where California Chrome was born and raised.

After six weeks at the farm, Chrome's hoof was as good as new, so it was back to Art's barn to start training and burning off those cookies.

With the closure of Hollywood Park the previous December, Art had moved his training operation to Los Alamitos Race Course in Orange County, primarily a Quarter Horse track and located not too far from Disneyland. Los Alamitos owner Ed "Doc" Allred, who had expanded his facility to better accommodate Thoroughbreds after Hollywood Park was shuttered, was quick to capitalize on his famous new tenant, rebranding Los Alamitos as the "Home of Chrome."

The Pride Of California

The California Thoroughbred Breeders Association is by far the largest promoter of Thoroughbred racing in California, even to the extent of hiring a lobbyist to promote the sport to lawmakers and represent racing's interests in the California State Legislature. So, when the opportunity arose to highlight the California-bred program's success in having produced California Chrome, it was a no-brainer for Denise and me to participate.

In 2014, CTBA lobbyist Robyn Black convinced several California lawmakers to author a resolution honoring California Chrome, his connections and the California racing industry at large. It passed unanimously through the State Senate and Assembly.

As part of the announcement, there was a mid-August visit scheduled for Dumb Ass Partners to bring Chrome's Kentucky Derby and Preakness Stakes trophies to the floor of the state capitol in Sacramento; imagine the clerk typing that name up on the lawmakers' formal agenda for the day!

We received a warm reception from the legislators, many of whom wore touches of our purple and green silks colors and declared themselves "Chromies." We posed alongside our trophies for photos with various state representatives and senators so the politicians could generate some positive publicity. There was a short ceremony, during which we received formal copies of the resolution.

The morning festivities complete, we traveled the short distance over to the California Museum, where we loaned the trophies and various other California Chrome mementos to the facility for their California Chrome exhibit which, after being developed that fall, would be on display for an entire year. This was a project I had set up, promoted and paid for with a $20,000 donation to the museum.

The California Museum is the official state history museum of California, located in the capital city of Sacramento. It is dedicated to Californian history and the stories of California. As home to the California Hall of Fame, the museum has more than 20,000 square feet of exhibition space.

For one year, it was home to The California Chrome Exhibit. This display featured a life-sized plastic replica of Chrome with his official Kentucky Derby saddle cloth, the Kentucky Derby and Preakness trophies, the horseshoes worn by Chrome in the Derby and many personal pictures taken of Chrome. I believe many of the fourth grade classes in the state of California take a field trip to visit the California Museum, so I was pleased that these youngsters would learn about the equine industry in California through the Chrome exhibit.

One of the four walls was dedicated to California racing and the equine industry; all the others were dedicated to Chrome. As the regular custodian of many Depression-era trophies and memorabilia items from the late, California-based Seabiscuit owner Charles Howard's estate, the CTBA loaned several of these very special artifacts to the exhibit and provided a display that featured industry statistics.

Along with the Coburns, we were invited to the California Museum's 2014 California Hall of Fame inauguration and reception, where I was able to meet and talk with someone who was one of my childhood heroes, General Chuck Yeager. There were Rap artists and basketball players and movie stars all around us, but I do not remember their names. I got to have a personal conversation with Chuck Yeager—the first pilot to break the sound barrier—and his granddaughter for 10 whole minutes. How cool is that?!

There were many, many honors that we received on California Chrome's behalf, and we were proud of each and every one.

Denise and I received a plaque with a copy of a U.S. Congress resolution recognizing Chrome that was sponsored by California congressman Jim Costa. We received the "key to the city" for our adopted hometown of Yuba City. We were feted at The Big Fresno Fair with a California Chrome Day and a private viewing of the California Chrome exhibit in the Fair's museum.

It was a hectic period, and a little overwhelming at times. But we did our best to attend each event that was graciously hosted as a tribute to Chrome and to shake each hand that was extended to us in congratulations, since we were very honored and glad to share in the success of our California-bred colt.

My Call To Rommy

During the whirlwind Triple Crown run, I received a countless number of requests for my time. I would quite often have to say "no thank you" or postpone these appointments to a later date. One such request I put off was with pedigree analyst Rommy Faversham, who wanted to discuss California Chrome's breeding.

A couple of weeks after the Belmont Stakes, Denise and I were returning from one of our visits to Harris Farms. We stopped at a restaurant for a cup of coffee, and I decided this was a good time to keep my promise and call Mr. Faversham. We ended up having a two-hour conversation, and I would have been happy to make it four. He was knowledgeable and delightful, and had shared many of the same horse owner experiences. It was fun to talk to him!

A few days after our conversation, Rommy sent me a copy of the book "Racehorse Breeding Theories," which he had co-authored with

Frank Mitchell and other pedigree experts. I immediately turned to Chapter 12, the section on Female Family Inbreeding, and read it in full. Wow, why couldn't I have come across this sooner? It would have saved me a lot of research!

The one part I will never forget was at the end, where he asked, "What female family inbreeding lines will determine the champions 10 years from now?" At the top of his list was Numbered Account.

Love the Chase is inbred 3x3 to Numbered Account and her first foal, California Chrome, was a Kentucky Derby-winning champion! I quickly turned to the front of the book and looked at the copyright date: 2004. Wow, 10 years exactly! Safe to say that there just may be something to Rommy's analysis.

After Chrome shot to fame, I wrote a series of three articles for the racing industry's "BloodHorse" magazine, as the individual who had planned his breeding.

In these, I speculated about setting up a futures bet for the Kentucky Derby that would be 10 years out, and based on breeding. It was meant as a joke, because the racing industry argues that it is competing for gambling dollars with casinos that offer quick-action games of chance. Some believe these fast-moving games are more exciting and enticing for gamblers than live horse races, which occur about every 25-30 minutes at the racetrack. My thought process was: If gamblers have a hard time waiting 30 minutes between races, who will wait 10 whole years to collect a bet?

It was about a year after my articles were published when a Kentucky Derby futures bet was created to allow wagers on the sire of the forthcoming winner: the Kentucky Derby Sire Future Wager. I am sure it was just coincidence, and nobody got the idea from my article. Although if they ever introduce a futures bet on female families, I might get suspicious.

I was asked once if there were any positive benefits to having the large number of stallions that we do competing for mares in the U.S. I could not think of any reason at the time. Now I can say that a positive benefit of having so many stallions is the offering of higher odds on the

Kentucky Derby breeding futures bet. I would not exactly call that a silver lining; maybe some out-of-sight silver embroidery.

Kentucky Derby Rings

Perry & Denise's Kentucky Derby Rings Inscribed inside with
"Partners Forever"

14

DEL MAR DUST-UP

You would think, with Chrome being between races after a farm rest, that the late summer months of 2014 would be a quiet time for his owners as well. That was not to be.

I was kept very busy with my day job at Martin Testing Laboratories while keeping tabs on Chrome's progress by phone with Art at his new home, Los Alamitos. Every few days, I would Google "California Chrome" to read whatever news was circulating in the media about our horse.

When Chrome was back in training in Southern California, his name would come up quite often in the San Diego media. I clicked on a few of these online links to find interviews with the president and chief executive officer of Del Mar Thoroughbred Club, Joe Harper. Joe was name-dropping Chrome as a potential competitor for the Grade 1 Pacific Classic, Del Mar's premier race. I knew Chrome would be nowhere near race condition by the time the Pacific Classic was scheduled to run that August, so I called Art just to verify.

Art confirmed what I already knew. He was thinking that Chrome's first race back would be the Grade 1 Awesome Again Stakes at Santa Anita in late September, but only if everything went to plan. No worries, then; I decided to just ignore the San Diego rumors.

In interviews that Art would give the media, he let it be known that we were pointing to the Awesome Again. This declaration spurred two different chains of events on opposite sides of the country.

One was in the San Diego media again, as Joe Harper did a pivot; he was now saying that he was in contact with Art about having Chrome honored and paraded at Del Mar on the day of the Pacific Classic.

The second was brewing at the Parx racetrack in Pennsylvania, where racing secretary Sal Sinatra was hatching a plan to get "America's Horse"—as Chrome had been dubbed—to compete in the track's Grade 2 Pennsylvania Derby, which was scheduled to run the same week as the Awesome Again in California. Sal just wasn't sure how to get it done. His inspiration would be revealed to him via the Del Mar Dust-up.

I wasn't surprised when the call came.

Del Mar representatives had been talking to Art about shipping Chrome to Del Mar to make a public appearance on Pacific Classic day. Art told them they would need to talk to me.

The media person for Del Mar called me and said they would like to honor Chrome on Pacific Classic day. I said that Chrome was in training at Los Alamitos for the Awesome Again and I would not break his training regimen to haul him to Del Mar to parade; he is not a parade horse, he is a racehorse. I was asked if there was anything they could do to change my mind.

I thought about it a bit, then replied, "This is a business. If you provide $25,000 to Chrome's trainer and his team for their trouble, and $25,000 to the owners to cover our expenses, we'll send him."

In response, I was told Del Mar didn't have $50,000 in discretionary funds, so we were done. I hung up the phone, never expecting to hear another thing about it.

Ten minutes later, I got a call from a reporter with "The San Diego Union-Tribune" who asked me how I could let my greed get in the way of Chrome being honored. The newspaper published a story about Chrome's greedy owner the next day. I sent out a press release explaining my reasoning which was published in whole by some news outlets; however, the public response was very anti-Martin.

Getting Flayed In The Press

I had to laugh when I read that celebrity chef Bobby Flay had weighed into the situation, offering to counsel me on how to be a "good" Thoroughbred owner and how to deal with the media properly.

I told Denise, "Who does this guy think he is? He had his personal life, marriage and divorce dragged through the media mud and he's going to give me advice on being an owner and dealing with the media? I should be giving him advice on how to conduct his marriage; that is much more important!"

I then said something about him being a skinny little twerp and he probably wasn't a good cook, and I should challenge him to a throwdown.

Denise pleaded, "Please don't!"

So, I forgot about the whole thing—until now!

Racetracks' and horse owners' business interests have a common thread, but if you look at it objectively, we are basically competitors. This sport is far away from baseball, football or any of the major sports in which the owners form a league to control their common business interests. In those sports, the owners bargain for and receive the income from media contracts, ticket sales, concessions and even parking. In horse racing, these income-generators are all controlled by the tracks, who own all rights and intellectual property concerning the major races.

Take a well-known horse race like the Kentucky Derby which, by the way, is sponsored in a multi-year and multi-million-dollar deal by Yum! Brands, a major fast-food restaurant corporation whose brands include Pizza Hut, KFC and Taco Bell.

In the year we ran, the purse for the Kentucky Derby Presented by Yum! Brands (yes, that is the race's official name, exclamation point and all) was $2 million guaranteed. There were 19 runners, whose owners each paid in at minimum $50,000 in entry and starter fees, so nearly half of the race's purse was covered by the owners running in the race. All the owners who nominated their horses along the way for the Triple Crown also paid into the purse.

As the co-owner of the Kentucky Derby morning-line favorite, I received one small box of six seats to watch the race at Churchill Downs. I had to purchase additional seats for my family, who certainly did not want to miss this once-in-a-lifetime experience, at $400 a pop.

So, when a track wants to honor my horse, and increase their attendance and accompanying ticket, parking, racing program, food and beverage and souvenir sales, not to mention their on-track handle, because of his fame, they damn well are going to pay for it. Bobby Flay is free to run his life and business any way he wants.

After reading about the Del Mar Dust-up, Sal Sinatra called me and asked what it would take for us to bring Chrome to Parx Racing for the track's Grade 2 Pennsylvania Derby. I told him if we could get a cash guarantee which exceeded what we would earn if we won the $300,000 guaranteed Awesome Again Stakes, we would make the trip.

A few days later, it was announced that the winners of the 2014 editions of the Kentucky Derby, Preakness Stakes, Belmont Stakes, Haskell Invitational Stakes (G1) and Travers Stakes (G1) would each receive $100,000 guaranteed to be split between the owners and the trainer if the horse started in the 2014 Pennsylvania Derby. The announcement explained that California Chrome, having won two of that year's Triple Crown races, would receive $200,000 if he made it to the starting gate.

I called Art and explained our windfall. We would get more money—$200,000—for just starting against a restricted field of 3-year-olds in the Pennsylvania Derby than we would get for Chrome winning the Awesome Again while facing older horses for the first time, which would mean a $180,000 payday. The 50/50 split between the owners and the trainer meant Art would receive $100,000. The bonus would be if Chrome performed well, since the purse for the Pennsylvania Derby was $1 million. Art was in!

This was definitely a verification of the axiom: Any publicity is good publicity.

15

THREE RACES: MORE THAN $6 MILLION ON THE LINE

Oh well. For that kind of money, it was worth a shot.

The Pennsylvania Derby

Tex Sutton flew Chrome from California to Pennsylvania on their Boeing 727 cargo aircraft nicknamed Air Horse One. We had used the equine air transportation company previously, at the start and end of our Triple Crown run, and Chrome behaved as an experienced flyer.

Denise and I made the cross-country trip without family this time.

Everything was pretty uneventful. I was able to continue my tradition of speaking with Raul before the race, but this time I could get no commitment from him. Chrome was just so-so, not yet at the top of his game after the three-month layoff. I only made a token bet.

We watched the race from the rail at mid-stretch. Chrome broke well and was able to remain forwardly positioned until the stretch run. But where he usually kicked for home, opening lengths between himself and the competition, on this day he stayed flat, tiring to finish sixth of eight behind the untested front-runner, Bayern, whom Chrome had bested by 21 lengths in their only previous match-up in the Preakness.

With their runner performing much the best on this occasion, even breaking a 40-year-old track record for 1 1/8 miles in the process, Bayern's connections collected the $100,000 Haskell bonus on top of the $562,000 Pennsylvania Derby winner's purse for his facile victory.

The racing secretary's concept to lure the country's best sophomores to Parx Racing for his track's marquee event had worked; not only did he attract a top-class field to his modest facility, the track's all-source handle for the 13-race card smashed the previous record by a whopping 88%, proving that race bonus incentives work for all parties involved. This includes racing fans, who benefit by being treated to the rare opportunity of seeing elite horses actually compete against each other, rather than continually dodge the toughest competition until a single championship event.

For Chrome, it was a highly paid workout, upon which we could build.

Getting Away From It All

It was about this time that Denise and I purchased our new permanent residence in Alpine, Wyoming: a 2,500-square-foot getaway that offered peace and tranquility amidst some pretty darn breathtaking views of nature.

We were spending so much time away from our Martin Testing Laboratories in Sacramento anyway, because of our horse racing endeavors, that it made sense to make the move. Our new base would be Alpine, and we would travel back to California for short stays at work and the races.

For work purposes, I could write all of the testing and analysis quotes from my computer in Wyoming. The lab in California had trained technicians who could perform the testing and email me the results. I could write the testing reports and email back to the lab for sign-offs and report distribution.

A Mugging In Broad Daylight: The 2014 Breeders' Cup Classic

When we got Chrome home to Los Alamitos, Art had the entire month of October to turn the screws and sharpen him up for the Breeders' Cup Classic (G1), the most elite race for Thoroughbreds on the annual U.S. calendar. Featuring a guaranteed purse of $5 million, the 1 1/4-mile championship test would be held at Santa Anita on November 1, and would mark California Chrome's debut against older runners.

Our colt did not win a Breeders' Cup Challenge Series race that year, so we would need to pay a $50,000 pre-entry fee plus a $50,000 entry fee in order to participate. I kept a close eye on his progress to assure we were not going to waste our money. Every weekend, Chrome worked stronger and stronger. I was gaining confidence as the race approached.

We could not get reservations for our regular Embassy Suites hotel in Arcadia, as it had sold out well in advance of the Breeders' Cup. We ended up staying a good distance away at the Pacific Palms Resort in the city of Industry, about 17 miles southeast of Santa Anita.

Denise and I found this to be a special place situated on top of a hill near the center of a golf course, which provides isolation from the noise of the city. The golf course landscaping, with its palm trees and many water features, made for lovely morning walks. Eating breakfast from the restaurant outdoor patio overlooking a vast expanse of Los Angeles was special.

We enjoyed our stay so much that we made it our new default hotel in Los Angeles. If you catch the traffic right, the drive to Santa Anita is only 20 minutes. But catch it wrong, and it's two hours. Such is life in the big city.

The day of the race, we had a slight change in our regular routine, as the races were conducted by the Breeders' Cup and I needed to pick up our tickets and passes in the temporary trailers that had been set up in the Santa Anita owners' parking lot. At Santa Anita, you can almost never park in the designated owners' parking lot since it is so small; with two large trailers parked there, it was even smaller. As always, we parked in the regular lot and walked over to the trailers.

Denise's brother Andrew and his family and my brother Roy and his family joined us for this race, so I purchased an additional box of seats to accommodate almost everyone. We always had someone away from the box, so not having quite enough seats did not matter. Besides, if it began to feel too crowded in the box, I would just go for a walk with Denise to help calm our nerves.

We only had a few walking ring passes. The Breeders' Cup folks are pretty strict about that, so Denise and I went to greet Chrome prior to his race as his co-owners and the others in our group were left to sort out who got the remaining passes.

After the horses were saddled and led by their handlers around the walking ring, the call for riders to mount up rang out and we followed the field of runners through the tunnel to the track. As the post parade began, we made our way to the track apron to find our usual viewing spot.

Always too nervous to sit for Chrome's races, we would either pace or rock in place if it was too crowded. We did both before the Classic. Chrome had drawn post position 13 out of 14, so we would have a good view of our boy both times he ran by in the stretch.

They were off! Well, sort of...

Emerging out of the seven-hole with jockey Martin Garcia aboard, our old rival Bayern immediately veered sharply to the left, bumping hard into the diminutive—and undefeated—5-2 race favorite and reigning Champion 2-Year-Old, Shared Belief, and causing a chain reaction which affected every horse to his inside. Coming one lane over in a horse race is considered a foul; coming over three lanes like Bayern did is usually considered assault and battery.

The rough stuff wasn't over yet.

An eighth of a mile in, the nine-horse, Toast of New York, squeezed off a resurgent Shared Belief again, causing the latter's rider, Mike Smith, to pull up. Two obvious fouls that the stewards reviewed for 10 minutes after the race was completed only to rule that the fouls occurred at points of the race where they did not affect the final order of finish. The fact that the Santa Anita stewards could essentially say that there is a part of the race where the safety of horse and rider does not matter is astonishing to me!

For his part, California Chrome stayed out of the scuffles and ran valiantly throughout from his outside position, largely keeping up with the pace and just missing by a neck at the wire in a three-way photo finish that went Bayern's way on top, with Toast of New York second and Chrome third, 3 1/2 lengths clear of the unlucky fourth-place finisher, Shared Belief. As it turned out, the eight older horses may have just as well not been entered in the race after all; the first six finishers were all 3-year-olds, which set up an interesting battle for end-of-the-year divisional championships.

Under his regular rider, Victor Espinoza, our colt ran wide the entire race, keeping out of trouble but giving up a lot of ground in the process.

If you have ever watched sprint races in the Olympics, you have seen the runners positioned in a staggered start. Human athletes must stay in their designated running lane the whole race; therefore, the outer lanes start farther up so that everyone runs the same mathematical distance.

In any Thoroughbred race, however, the horses run slightly different distances depending on race positioning and strategy. If you check the Trakus figures for the 2014 Breeders' Cup Classic, you will see that Chrome ran 41 feet farther than Bayern, yet he lost the race by approximately a few dozen inches. Those inches were the difference between a $2.75 million paycheck for first and a $500,000 paycheck for third, not to mention future stallion valuations and other consequences for young Thoroughbreds at this level of the game.

I always take a lot of heat for pointing out how this ride could have been better. People say I am not appreciating Victor enough. I do appreciate a perfect ride! If the ride is not perfect, I point out how to do better. Doing better improves performance, which is what it takes to make a champion.

Remember my professional background: failure analysis. It is my life's work to seek perfection, and to adjust what can be adjusted if perfection is not achieved.

I really do not care if people do not like it. I especially do not care if the media says it is without class. Most of the media thinks not vomiting on their own shoes is class, while they vomit on other people's shoes for a living.

Surface Switch: The 2014 Hollywood Derby

I had been looking for a grass race for Chrome for a long time. His pedigree has a lot of turf influence, so I thought he would manage it just fine. As they say, the good ones can run on anything!

I mentioned Del Mar's Grade 1 Hollywood Derby on November 29 to Art as a possibility for his next race. I also offered the Group 1 Japan Cup as an alternate, knowing from our previous discussions that this international option was distasteful to Art. As I had hoped, Art announced to the media that Chrome was pointing to the Hollywood Derby.

The media went a little wild. There were many articles on both sides of the issue. One school of thought stated that we were stupid to chance running our horse on a surface new to him. If he were shown to dislike the turf, we would reduce his breeding value and end any chance for the Horse of the Year title. The other side said that our savvy trainer was very shrewd, noting that Chrome had not performed his best since the Triple Crown and a Grade 1 win on the grass at the end of the year would guarantee a Horse of the Year title.

Exciting! I can't wait to see what happens.

As you know from an earlier chapter, Denise and I did not attend this race, which Chrome mastered by two lengths under mild urging from Espinoza, obviously relishing the surface switch to capture his sixth of nine starts—and fourth Grade 1 trophy—as a sophomore. The runner-up in the $300,250 race, Queen's Plate Stakes winner Lexie Lou, went on to be named 2014 Horse of the Year and Champion Grass Mare in Canada.

At post time, we were on the way to my mom's memorial service in Michigan. While driving through Wisconsin, we pulled over to watch the race on Denise's iPhone. We marveled at the ease with which he won, then set back to our task at hand.

The second school of thought had prevailed, and Chrome was honored with Eclipse Awards as 2014 Horse of the Year and 2014 Champion 3-Year-Old Colt. Denise and I did not attend the Eclipse Awards ceremony in Florida the following January. By this time, we were cherishing any time we could spend in our Wyoming oasis.

"Voice Of The People"

A Christmas present for Chrome was announced on December 25: he was selected by fans to receive the 2014 Secretariat Vox Populi Award, a relatively new annual honor that was created by Secretariat's owner, Penny Chenery, as a way to recognize racehorses who best capture the public's affection and gain recognition for the sport.

Previous recipients of the Vox Populi, or "Voice of the People," Award were Breeders' Cup Classic winner Mucho Macho Man in 2013, laminitis survivor Paynter in 2012, blue-collar racing hero Rapid Redux in 2011 and the wildly popular 2009 Breeders' Cup Classic-winning mare Zenyatta, who won the inaugural Vox Populi Award in 2010.

The media release accompanying the announcement summed up Chrome's spectacular season quite succinctly.

"Everyone loves a Cinderella story, and this one was no exception," Mrs. Chenery was quoted as saying. "California Chrome, a proven champion and formidable competitor, reminded us that it doesn't matter from whence we came, but rather how we dance when we get to the ball. Furthermore, his inspiring story and engaging popularity reached beyond the racetrack stands and into the conversation of a nation."

We were honored to receive a custom-made bust of Secretariat from Team Secretariat during a special award ceremony at Santa Anita in January 2015. The evening prior to the presentation, our group enjoyed a special dinner with Mrs. Chenery's children.

It's a good thing we were well-fueled. The following day, Denise and I, along with the Coburns, Art, Victor and Chrome's regular exercise rider, Willie Delgado, were stationed at an autograph table inside the Santa Anita grandstand, where we signed everything that was put in front of us for hours, including a small poster depicting an artist's portrait of California Chrome that was given to the first 2,000 fans in attendance. We started at 11 a.m. with an extremely long line of fans that snaked through the ground floor to the fountain area outside, and the crowd of well-wishers finally dissipated before our trophy presentation in the winner's circle after the fifth race on the card, which was broadcast live on HRTV.

In conjunction with the award, Dumb Ass Partners donated autographed, race-worn silks from Chrome's winning effort in the 2014 San Felipe Stakes for auction, with proceeds to benefit The Secretariat Foundation and other equine charities. The winning bid was $2,476.

It was a hopeful way to start the new year. Chrome had worked six furlongs in 1:11.60 that morning at Los Alamitos as he prepared to make his 2015 racing debut.

16

THE LOST YEAR

In 2015, California Chrome made more than $2 million and finished second in two graded / group stakes races. For most horses, that would be considered an exceptionally good career. For California Chrome, however, it is considered a "lost year."

At A Crossroad

On the heels of his remarkable Horse of the Year campaign in the U.S. in 2014, California Chrome received an invitation to run in the Dubai World Cup, an international Group 1 race which, at the time, was contested for a purse of $10 million—the richest race in the world!

After Chrome's season-ending win in the Hollywood Derby, I wanted to ship to Dubai early to let Chrome have time to get over the stress of the long trip, and to get him a race over the host track prior to the Dubai World Cup in late March. This was the successful approach that had been taken by Racing Hall of Fame trainer Steve Asmussen with Curlin in 2008.

Up to this point in Chrome's career, I had pretty much gotten my way on everything by explaining the reasons for the actions I was recommending. Who the media gave credit to was not important to me; I just wanted to do what was best for the horse and for our horse business. If the business does not make money, we would be unable to run the horse.

Every story about Chrome during this time period went one of two ways: If he was successful, it was because of his cunning old trainer; if he failed, it was due to his neophyte owners. I understood that, unless I acquiesced to my trainer, that was how it was going to be portrayed. Luckily, I did not care.

I thought I had given excellent reasons for wanting to travel overseas early, but this time I was greeted with a unified resistance.

Art did not want to go early, because he had a small stable and could not part with the workers Chrome would need to support him for the two months he would be in Dubai. Our trainer wanted to fly in, race, then fly out.

Steve wanted to run against Shared Belief in Santa Anita's Grade 2 San Antonio Invitational Stakes in early February. The press was talking up the possibility of the match-up as the start of a great rivalry. Steve felt that by establishing this great rivalry, we would save racing in the U.S.

I was at a crossroad. As the majority owner, I could do whatever I wanted, but I would have to change trainers and piss off my minority owner in order to do so. After much consideration, I made my first mistake in managing Chrome and agreed to let him run in the San Antonio.

Royal Invitation

For the San Antonio, Denise and I again stayed at the Pacific Palms Resort. There is just something about that place. Note that the restaurant there does something special with ahi tuna.

I was not happy about not preparing the horse in Dubai, but I was going to make the best of it. We showed up at the track all smiles, greeting everyone who would stop to wish us good luck as we found our way to the luxury suite that Santa Anita had graciously supplied our ownership group. We enjoyed the wine and shrimp cocktails that were provided while we waited for our race.

Many interesting people dropped in to our luxury suite to visit with us. Particularly interesting were the two gentlemen representing Royal Ascot.

After introducing themselves and giving me their business cards, they asked me if I had given much thought to attending Royal Ascot. When I said no, they appeared a bit puzzled. They explained that they had visited Art often and had discussed over breakfast with him The Queen's invitation to participate in the glamorous annual race meet in England. I informed them that this was the first I was hearing about it.

They filled me in on the invitation, the travel allowance and several other details. I gave them my business card and asked them to communicate directly with me going forward. I requested them to email me all the details, and said I would make a decision after the Dubai World Cup.

But first, back to the business at hand.

In the $590,000 San Antonio, Chrome broke well under Victor, and started to establish a good early position on the lead until he was quickly passed by the speedy longshot Alfa Bird. Our colt sat in second for most of the trip with his new rival, Shared Belief, glued to his outside flank throughout. After six furlongs, Chrome wrested the lead from the quickly fading front-runner, but he did not have enough to hold off Shared Belief, who passed him in late stretch to win by 1 1/2 lengths. Frequent opponent Hoppertunity from Hall of Famer Bob Baffert's barn clocked in third, more than six lengths behind our runner-up.

Not only was this result disappointing, it was perplexing as well. The final time for the 1 1/8-mile race was 1:48.45, nearly a full second slower than Chrome had run on the same track in winning the 1 1/8-mile Santa Anita Derby the previous year. Something was off, but it would take a couple months to figure out what it was.

We extended our stay at the Pacific Palms, as we needed to attend the 2015 California Thoroughbred Breeders Association awards dinner at another hotel in Pasadena a few days later. That event turned into a virtual Chrome Family Fest!

In addition to being named 2014 California Horse of the Year, California Chrome earned trophies as the California Champion Turf Horse and California Champion 3-Year-Old Male. His sire, Lucky Pulpit, was honored as Champion Sire of California-Conceived Foals by Earnings, while his dam, Love the Chase, was named California Broodmare of the Year.

His humans walked away with some pretty nice hardware that evening as well.

Art was selected as Trainer of the Year and Steve and I received accolades as Champion Breeders of California-Foaled Thoroughbreds by Earnings. That's right; we bred one horse and he earned more money racing in his nine starts in 2014—a grand total of $4,007,800—than each of the state's largest breeders had amassed with their vast stables. Number two on the list was Tommy Town Thoroughbreds, whose runners had earned $2,512,981 from 749 starts. Talk about putting things into perspective!

Most notable for me at this event, however, was an impromptu meeting I had with Victor as the dinner attendees were leaving the ballroom. I pointed out to him that the more he whipped Chrome in a race, the worse Chrome performed. Let's just say I encouraged him with a loud voice to show some restraint in the future.

Desert Delights

Contested since 1996, the Dubai World Cup (G1) is one of several high-dollar races conducted on a single-day program every March in the United Arab Emirates (UAE). This lavish event regularly attracts international competition to Meydan Racecourse which, in Arabic, suggests a place where people congregate and compete.

Before we left on our journey for the Dubai World Cup, I tried several times to wire the $100,000 entry fee for California Chrome per the provided instructions, but it kept getting kicked back. Apparently, our government in the U.S. had set up safeguards to prevent large sums of money from being sent to the Middle East. Something about funding terrorism.

I called the Dubai Racing Club and informed them of my problem. They had not yet set up a U.S. destination to wire the money, so I suggested that I could bring a cashier's check with me. They gave me the name of the person I should contact and give the check to upon our arrival. They would need to take it back to the United States to deposit it, but they would trust me.

The Dubai Racing Club and His Highness Sheikh Mohammed bin Rashid Al Maktoum, the vice president and prime minister of UAE and ruler of Dubai, were very generous to the California Chrome connections. They provided round-trip transportation for Chrome and first-class round-trip seating on Emirates Airline for our group, which included his owners, trainer, selected family members and our support team.

The first-class airline accommodations were superb. I ate like a king. I was able to walk to the bar to stretch my legs and enjoy the complimentary beverages which included the very best spirits available. I returned to configure my mini-apartment in order to sleep lying down and, in the morning, I awoke to enjoy a five-minute shower before breakfast. At the end of the 16-hour flight, I was refreshed, alert and ready to explore the new world we were entering. We had finally found a better way to travel, but could we afford it if it was not subsidized?

Upon landing, we ran into more people that we knew in the Dubai airport than we had at Los Angeles International Airport (LAX). We knew jockeys, members of the media, celebrities and, yes, Chromies. We talked at length about our trip while waiting in line at Customs.

Outside Customs, we were met by our personal driver, Shiraz, who was assigned to us for the duration of our trip. He loaded our luggage into the Land Rover, and we were off.

After checking in at the front desk, we were escorted to our four-room suite, where we were greeted by a welcome tray of figs and cheeses in addition to a chilled bottle of champagne. It took us 10 minutes to tour our suite, pressing every button that worked automatic doors, drapes, air temperature and lighting. We ended our tour on the balcony which overlooked the racetrack. I would spend several mornings there, watching horses exercise below while drinking my morning coffee.

We used our driver's knowledge of the area to assist us in planning our days touring Dubai. We spent a morning out on Palm Jumeirah, the man-made islands of sand shaped like a palm tree, and visited the unique hotel at its center, which featured deluxe shopping.

In fact, shopping is one of the most popular activities in Dubai. We visited many souks, which are a type of outdoor shopping mall or marketplace, each with its own theme. There was the gold souk, the spice souk and a very large souk located by the port which featured many goods imported from Iran.

At this souk, Denise and I had a special encounter with a salesperson who promised to offer us the best prices available. I was about to tell him to buzz off when Denise said, "Please show us."

We were asked to follow him as he led us away from the outdoor tents into the narrow passages between dilapidated brick buildings. After a couple blocks, I couldn't believe Denise was still following him with me in close pursuit. We finally found our destination and were led through a small (for me) door that entered into a small foyer. The foyer continued the trend, having one very small elevator. The three of us had to squeeze together to let the door close. We went up one floor and exited the elevator to find a closed door. Our guide gave a secret knock, and the door was opened by a large man who was guarding the door. I was gratified that the man was not as large as me; I am not sure he felt the same.

Denise was escorted over to the handbags, and I followed. The walls were filled with packed shelves and the shelves were labeled Dior, Gucci, Kors and a whole bunch I didn't recognize. As Denise perused the bags, I made my way over to the watch counter, where the clerk asked me in perfect English what I was interested in seeing.

I asked to see the gold Rolex and he handed it to me. The first thing I looked at was the price tag, which read $1,750. Then I looked at the face of the watch to see that it was running five minutes slow and the second hand was not sweeping, per Rolex design, but instead incrementally ticking. I asked what was the best he could do for price. He made a show that he would have to ask the manager and left me with the watch as he entered the back. I was thinking that I could always use a fake Rolex if the price was right. When he came back and told me $500, I said, "No thank you." I can get a fake Rolex in Mexico for $20.

Denise did buy a fake Gucci bag and matching wallet for $80, then we were on our way.

We found our way back to the souk and bought a half-pound of saffron, along with some mint tea to bring back to the states. Saffron is hard to fake, and awfully expensive in the states, so we purchased a lifetime supply for $100. The mint tea only lasted a couple of months after we got back, and we barely dented the saffron.

On other excursions, we visited the famous Burj Khalifa, the world's largest mall and an indoor snow skiing facility, next to the world's tallest building at the time. We would often pass the black Ferrari police cars as we traveled to and from each destination. You're not going to get away from the cops if you're speeding in Dubai!

The best feature of this exotic trip, other than the racing, was the Dubai World Cup outdoors reception hosted by Sheikh Mohammed, who greeted us himself and shook our hands. After this warm welcome, we were treated to a world-class buffet accompanied by a superlative dinner show featuring orchestra music, singers, skydivers and animal acts and topped off by a wonderful fireworks display. Best party I have ever been to!

With Chrome's late arrival, we had to conduct all training from the quarantine barn, which was a 45-minute walk to the track. The quarantine horses were all allotted different times on the track, and we had to be alert not to miss our window. Chrome really took to this new routine and environment; it was a pity his exposure to it would be so short.

The day of the race, our group was given a large table in the clubhouse. The clubhouse featured an expansive, complimentary buffet, and we could purchase wine for our table. Buffets are common in

Dubai, as the populace seems to enjoy sampling a little of everything, rather than being limited to a menu.

When experiencing a buffet meal in Dubai, we would usually start by visiting the cheese, fig and fruit bar to populate a sample plate we could enjoy with a glass of wine. Later, depending on our taste, we would visit a seafood bar, a steak and roast bar or a vegetable bar. The only thing we couldn't find was pork in any way, shape or form. Even the breakfast sausages were beef.

Race For $10 Million: The 2015 Dubai World Cup

As darkness fell on the 2015 Dubai World Cup program, we walked down to the extremely large saddling paddock prior to our race. This paddock was so huge you could almost run the race in it. I am not kidding, as it took me three minutes to walk from the entry to our horse's assigned area.

After the saddling and call for riders up, we followed the horses out of the paddock and diverted to find a spot on the track apron to watch the 2,000-meter race.

Partnered again with Victor, Chrome broke from the outside post of the nine-horse field, and floated up slowly on the outside into fourth to race in contention with the early leaders. He was four wide on the first turn, giving up valuable ground to remain in the clear. On the backstretch, he continued floating up on the outside into third, and remained four wide in the final turn as he ranged up into second for the drive home.

Chrome did not have his usual kick again in this race, and was not able to put up much of a fight when Sheikh Mohammed's seasoned colorbearer Prince Bishop (Ire) drove past him on the outside to take a commanding lead. Chrome managed to hold on for second, 2 3/4 lengths behind the 8-year-old winner and 1 1/4 lengths in front of his fellow American Grade 1 winner Lea, who finished third.

Our champ was not himself again, but in this case, I was blaming it on him still being weary from travel. We would not find out the root cause until returning home to the states.

Denise and I returned to our clubhouse table to meet with the rest of the group. I was disappointed, of course, but how disappointed can you be collecting $2 million for second place? We had earned more money finishing second in this race than we had winning the Kentucky Derby.

My thoughts immediately turned to the next phase in Chrome's career. We had just competed fairly well in a truly international race, without the use of Lasix, against the best classic-distance horses from Europe, Japan and the U.S. This was still March, and Royal Ascot was not until June.

If we went straight to England, the flight distance would be half of that to the U.S., putting less stress on Chrome. And he would have plenty of time to recuperate and train over the gallops in England in order to get accommodated to running over a terrain that was not flat.

I had already talked to the Dubai Racing Club, and they would transport Chrome to England for free. I had negotiated a $55,000 travel allowance for Chrome from Royal Ascot with the two representatives who had sought me out at Santa Anita the previous month; this amount would cover our additional training expenses in England and Chrome's subsequent flight back to the states.

I had done all the groundwork, and was enthusiastic about the decision to compete on one of the world's grandest stages for horse racing. So I announced to the group that was assembled in Dubai that we were going to England next.

To say the shit hit the fan would be an understatement. I was in the middle, getting pummeled from both sides.

On one side, Art was repeating that he had a stable in California he had to attend to, and he didn't have the resources to support a trip to England, and he didn't know how to train in the English style. On the other side, I was getting a high-volume dissertation of everything I apparently cannot do.

When I was finally allowed to get a word in, I said, "First, we are drawing a lot of attention and we need to keep it down. Second, seventy percent of the shareholders vote to take this trip, so unless you are willing to buy them out, which will be very expensive, we are going. Get used to it and start making plans."

I feel it's best to just rip the bandage off.

European Vacation

The next morning, Denise and I went down to breakfast, where we saw Art at one of the tables. He stood up and waved us over. When we got there, he introduced us to Rae Guest, a trainer in England whom Art had worked with before, having allowed one of Rae's employees to perform an internship with his barn in California. Rae had brought one of his horses to the Dubai Racing Carnival, and met up with Art at breakfast. This turn of events seemed serendipitous indeed.

We arranged a plan for Chrome to train out of Rae's yard in Newmarket. Art would remain the trainer of record, while Rae would be his assistant. Rae would receive his regular day rate to train the horse and would share any purse money earned with Art. Royal Ascot signed off on the agreement while we were still eating breakfast.

Before we had left the U.S., I had used our return tickets from Dubai to book a flight from Dubai to Rome, and from London to Los Angeles. Although the U.S. Air Force had sent me around the world for work during that phase of my life, Denise had never been to Europe, and of course we could not be sure if we would ever have such an opportunity for a trip like this again. So, we decided to take inspiration from the Roman poet Horace and "seize the day!"

After two days in Rome, we would take the train to Milan. After two days in Milan, we would take the train to Geneva. After two days in Geneva, we would take the train to Paris. After two days in Paris, we would take the train through the Chunnel to London. After two days in London, we would take the train to Edinburgh. After two days in Edinburgh, we would take the train back to London.

We had some excellent adventures during these excursions. I had planned the trip, and every hotel we would stay at was a short walk to the train station, which put us near the center of town in every case.

First up was Italy.

After taking a taxi from the Rome airport to our hotel, we could walk or take public transportation everywhere we wanted to visit. The neat thing about Rome is that all of the big attractions are within walking distance of each other. We always had breakfast at the hotel as part of our package stay. For lunch, we would pick a neighborhood restaurant near whatever famous site we were visiting. Both of our dinners in Rome were at a small family restaurant near our hotel. Our waiter, a son of the restaurant's owner, had gone to college in the U.S., and he was always happy to recommend the best choice for that evening's meal.

The high-speed train ride from Rome to Milan was very scenic, as more than half the trip was along the ocean. There are many trains available each day, so we selected one around our hotel check-out time. Our 300-mile train trip took approximately four hours, allowing us to arrive at our Milan hotel at the proper time to check in.

We dropped off our luggage and explored the local neighborhood to find the perfect place for dinner. Milan's grand churches and cathedrals are among the top draws to the city, especially the historic Duomo. Again, small neighborhood restaurants would provide us with a magnificent sampling of Northern Italian cooking, which is much different from that of Southern Italy.

We considered making the 67-mile bus trip to Brescia to see the city where my mom's parents were born, but that would have to wait for another time, as we were on a tight schedule.

Our Rome to Milan trip was a pattern we would follow throughout our European adventures.

It was another 4 1/2-hour train ride from Milan to Geneva, Switzerland. A 3 1/2-hour train ride from Geneva to Paris. A 2 1/2-hour train ride to London through the undersea Channel Tunnel. A 5 1/2-hour train ride from London to Edinburgh.

I'll condense our travelogue a bit and only discuss this last stop, as it was by far our favorite.

Exploring Edinburgh Castle, dinner every night at the Magnum Restaurant & Bar and, of course, touring The Scotch Whisky Experience. The end of this tour was a tasting bar where we enjoyed a sample flight of scotches from the various regions of Scotland. We lingered after the tour to do a bit more sampling of our favorites, after which we were done for the day. Good thing this was a walking tour.

After our brief visits to these beautiful and intriguing cities of Europe, we took the train back to London to complete the most important part of our international trip.

Visiting The Gallops

Upon our arrival back in London, Royal Ascot provided us a car to visit California Chrome, who had shipped to Rae Guest's yard at Newmarket two days after his runner-up finish in the Dubai World Cup.

Denise and I arrived in the early morning, and the yard was void of humans. We let ourselves through the gate and into view of the yard inhabitants. We heard a familiar whinny as Chrome had spotted his people, and had let us know where he was. We looked toward the sound and saw the familiar white blaze sticking out of a barn door, looking in our direction.

We walked over and greeted Chrome by feeding him some cookies we had brought in our pockets. Once we had said our proper hellos to our Horse of the Year, we set out to find one of the crew members, who were busy with their morning duties.

We spent an entire day visiting with Chrome and experiencing what Chrome was experiencing. We were told that, after he arrived at Newmarket, he spent a week sleeping. The only exercise he was asked to do during that quiet first week was a short walk in his turnout each day. He was just starting his new normal routine, which meant he would take a 45-minute walk under a rider to the gallops, where he would then train on the selected course.

We took a car and were at the gallops when Chrome arrived. He stopped at the edge of the gallops and surveyed the area. Nothing but green grass-covered hills as far as the eye could see. Chrome had never seen anything like this, and I could only imagine what he was thinking while he stood there for about 10 minutes, slowly scanning from left to right then back again.

While Chrome was sent out to his assigned gallop, Rae took us for a walk to explain what was occurring. It did not take long to realize we were in a completely different environment from the flat, speed-favoring dirt training strips of Southern California.

The gallops at Newmarket reproduce the major turf courses in all of Europe. They reproduce the terrain, the type of turf and the depth of the turf in different areas. To emphasize his point, Rae used his turf walking stick to note the turf depth in different spots. He handed it to me, and I noted the changes in effort that it would take to penetrate the turf on different gallops. Rae explained that, on the morning of a race, a trainer would walk the actual course with the jockey to locate areas to avoid during the race, as well as the best path forward.

We met up again with Chrome at his stall after his post-exercise bath. He was being treated to a triple-wide stall, suitable for a distinguished guest of honor and accomplished by removing the shutters between three regular stalls. Chrome had his feed bucket for grain and his hay net on one end and a heat lamp at the other end.

On chilly Newmarket mornings, you could find Chrome lying under his heat lamp. Once warm, he had plenty of room to pace while waiting to begin his morning training.

At this moment, it was time for breakfast. Chrome was up to his old tricks: burying his head in the bucket for a few bites of grain before sticking his muzzle out the stall door to munch hay and watch the goings-on in the yard.

What a cool customer he was. For Chrome, it always seemed that wherever his halter would hang, that was his home—California, Kentucky, Maryland, Dubai, England. It mattered not; he was at ease with himself, and his surroundings. That kind of behavior really instills confidence in an owner.

We visited with Chrome until the morning duties were done. Then Rae took us on a tour of Newmarket, pointing out all of the famous yards and sites of historical interest.

As we parted ways, we gave Rae our email address so he could send us regular photos and updates on Chrome's progress.

While Chrome was in England, we were also treated to updates and photos from a self-described Chromie named Margaret whom we had met many times at Art's Los Alamitos barn. Margaret and her husband had a summer house in Newmarket, and she visited our colt often during this period.

Our trip back to London took a few sightseeing detours, but we made it back in plenty of time for dinner.

The next day, we took the London Underground subway (famously known as the "Tube") to Heathrow Airport, then a long flight home. We had been traveling for three weeks, starting with Dubai, and we were appropriately spent, but it was one of the most memorable trips of our lives and I am so grateful now that we took the time for it.

My wife and I left England in mid-April, confident that Chrome was in good hands for his Royal Ascot tilt in mid-June. Our minds were at ease. I was also hopeful that he would benefit greatly from his works over the hilly gallops. This is a type of conditioning that few U.S.-based horses get.

Hope For The Future

California Chrome's full sister, Hope's Love, was now a 2-year-old and was in training with Steve Sherman at Golden Gate Fields. We selected Northern California because Hope was a bit small, and we felt starting her in easier company was the safer bet than the tougher competition in Southern California.

When in California, we would try to visit on weekends when she would usually have her works. She was progressing nicely, and it was looking more and more like she would be ready to debut at about the same time as her brother's race at Royal Ascot. We had our plane and hotel reservations for England booked far in advance of Royal Ascot so as not to lose out and have to stay far away.

Unfortunately, I had waited too long to reserve a tuxedo in London, as all of the rental companies had sold out in advance of the very posh

Royal Ascot meet. So I rented from a company in the U.S. and would take the tux and top hat with me.

Evaluating Kentucky Stallion Farms

For two months after the Dubai World Cup, I received calls from representatives of Kentucky farms that had been contacted by Steve Coburn about selling his interest in California Chrome. In every case, I was asked if I would stand Chrome at their farm if they purchased Mr. Coburn's 30% ownership share. In every case, I told them that Denise and I were going to visit Lexington during the first week of June to select a farm to stand Chrome, and we would schedule a visit with them if they desired.

Denise and I visited seven farms that were interested in Chrome: two per day for 3 1/2 days. The remainder of our time in Kentucky was used to visit the horses and friends we have there.

Our routine at each farm was the same. We would tour the farm and take mental notes about the condition of the farm, condition of the mares and condition of the stallions. We would ask how many mares the farm was willing to send to Chrome. We asked about their ability to develop a syndicate group and their plan for marketing. At the end of each day, Denise and I would have dinner and compare notes.

I am not naming any of these farms publicly except for the farm we selected, Taylor Made. The reason I am not naming the other candidates is because our opinion of them was very low and I do not wish to embarrass them.

If some Kentucky stallions are garnering all of the top mares, it is because their farms have a business plan to capture those mares. Most of the farms we talked with seemed to have a general business plan of, "You give us a boatload of money and we spend it and hope something happens."

Taylor Made had a long list of potential syndicate members and a plan to bring them aboard. The facility and care of the mares, stallions, foals and yearlings were exceptional.

We told Taylor Made we would stand Chrome there if they would have us. They set out to purchase Mr. Coburn's 30% ownership share.

Chrome Misses Royal Ascot

All of our preparations were complete to attend the races at Royal Ascot. I had been receiving weekly updates from Rae, and Chrome was progressing nicely.

We got a bit of a curveball thrown at us when Victor Espinoza called Art and declined to ride Chrome at Ascot. We were told that Victor felt that the Royal Ascot course would not fit his style of riding. I took that to mean that the course got a bit narrow at the turns, and Victor would not be able to take Chrome as wide as he was used to doing.

With Royal Ascot's help, we were able to secure William Buick for the ride in the Group 1 Prince of Wales's Stakes. He was the jockey who had guided Prince Bishop past Chrome and Victor in the Dubai World Cup. William agreed to work Chrome in advance of the race so the two could get acquainted. Art attended the work, but spent most of his time talking to the media and disparaging my insistence to run at Ascot.

Chrome walked the mile from Rae's stables to the Newmarket racecourse under his regular work rider, Robbie Mills, before William took to the saddle to work Chrome a little over 1,200 meters on the Watered Gallop. Halfway through the work, California Chrome cruised up alongside his work partner then, in a matter of just a few strides, went past with ease and finished the routine with gusto.

William reported that Chrome felt very good under him and only needed one reminder to change leads while taking a right-hand turn. All systems were go. Our American horse was handling the deep turf well, was unfazed by right-hand turns and was not chemically dependent on Lasix. We had anticipated everything and had worked to solve every problem. What could stop us?

Rae called me about two days before we were scheduled to fly to England. Alan Sherman had arrived two weeks early to take over Chrome's race preparations and had galloped Chrome over the woodchip path to the gallops. Chrome had bruised his foot and developed an abscess. The vet was going to drain the abscess, but it was doubtful that Chrome would be better in time to race.

It was a very bitter disappointment.

The media had touted Spielberg (Jpn) as the horse to beat that year in the Prince of Wales's Stakes, and I felt the race had been very winnable for Chrome.

Edward Stanley, the 17th Earl of Derby, was my guide in planning Chrome's breeding, and he held the record for most wins of the Prince of Wales's Stakes, with five. His winning horses were Stedfast (1911), Sansovino (1924), Caissot (1926), Hyperion (1933) and Heliopolis (1939). I just wanted to win once, and I know I had the horse to do it. But, it was not to be.

I sent word to Rae that we would be there for the race anyway. We had airline tickets, tickets for Ascot, hotel reservations and I'd rented a tuxedo which was already packed in my luggage. It was a shame that we would have to miss Hope's Love's first race, but life is all about making choices.

The Martins Also Miss Royal Ascot

Denise, Kelly and I were booked on a Southwest Airlines flight from Sacramento to Boston's Logan International Airport, where we would catch our direct flight to Ireland. From Ireland, we would take the train into London. I had selected flights that would arrive in Boston six hours before our scheduled departure to Ireland, thinking that would leave plenty of time to collect our bags and check in at the international terminal. Our travel plan included a leisurely dinner at Logan Airport before we took off.

The flight to Boston was in two segments. The first leg of the flight out of Sacramento went off without a hitch, but when we landed to transfer to the second leg of our trip, we were informed that the flight was delayed due to maintenance issues. This original 30-minute delay turned into a one-hour delay. Sometime after an hour, Southwest Airlines texted me instructions to check in with gate personnel. We were told they were routing another aircraft to fly this leg of the trip and we should check back in another hour to find our new gate assignment.

To make a long story short, we finally got to Logan Airport, collected our luggage and ran to the international terminal. When we arrived, we were told that we could not check in, as our flight was leaving in 45 minutes. International flight rules at that time required passengers to check in at least one hour prior to departure. There were no other overseas flights available until the next day, and none of those would allow us to arrive in time for the races at Ascot.

Although we were dejected, to say the least, we tried to salvage what we could out of a bad situation.

We still had our bags. So we went back to Southwest to see if we could return to Sacramento in time to drive to Golden Gate Fields to see Hope's Love make her racing debut. Southwest was able to accommodate us, so we spent the evening traversing the U.S. in the other direction.

Our flight landed in Sacramento in the early morning hours of race day. I took my luggage into the men's room, where I put on the tuxedo I was going to wear for Royal Ascot. I decided to leave the top hat in its box until we arrived at the track. Denise and Kelly took their luggage to the ladies' room and changed into their Ascot best. Dressed to the nines, we got the truck out of long-term airport parking and started off to Golden Gate.

When we arrived at Golden Gate Fields, we hung out on the track apron, which garnered a lot of finger-pointing in our direction. We were apparently quite the attraction in our Ascot finery.

I had chosen a green waistcoat to go with a purple bow tie to honor the DAP color scheme. It looked very sharp with the black tux and grey top hat. The girls wore fine dresses along with large hats typical of those worn by women at the races even here in the U.S., so they did not look nearly as out of place as I did, standing in my sophisticated togs amidst the t-shirts-and-jeans bottom-floor racing crowd on a Golden Gate Saturday afternoon. This must have been sort of what it felt like for some of the "Chromies" who showed up to our champ's races wearing sequin-covered costumes in his honor.

Hope's race was an open-company maiden special weight test carded at 4 1/2 furlongs for 2-year-old fillies. The race went off, but our filly missed the break and was suddenly dawdling at the back of the nine-horse field. In such a short race, this would be very difficult for her to overcome, especially as a first-timer, so I immediately let out a moan. All that cross-country effort to make the race, and this is how we were going to be rewarded? I continued to watch in silence.

Like a light switch being flipped on, Hope swiftly rose to the occasion as a 6-5 wagering favorite should. After finally getting into full gear, she managed to catch the field and was now passing horses in the turn. I had never seen such a small horse with such a long stride!

She continued stretching way out down the stretch; her four legs looked like about 160 degrees front to back when fully extended. I thought, "She might do it!"

There was a photo snapped at the wire, but Hope wasn't in it for long. She quickly moved out eight lengths past it before jockey Ricardo Gonzalez could pull her up. We finished second, a neck behind the winner, but what a horse we had. This was going to be exciting.

After the race, Hope's Love went lame. Three days of diagnostic tests, including nuclear magnetic resonance (NMR) at UC Davis, revealed a small fracture in her shoulder. That long stride of hers had localized too much stress at her shoulder.

It took six months for her to recover, without surgery, and train up to her next race in January of her 3-year-old season. But Chrome's little sister was never able to move past that injury, and she retired a maiden in May 2016 after five starts with just the single placing and $8,562 in earnings to her credit.

Quarantine Quandary

Every horse race in the United Kingdom is run without Lasix. Rather than pumping diuretic drugs into a horse so that it will excrete

60 to 80 pounds of body weight through urination before a race to help control exercise-induced pulmonary hemorrhage, trainers in the United Kingdom use diet and exercise to do the same thing. This takes more work and requires additional knowledge and horsemanship, but it results in a healthier animal.

The very few Thoroughbreds that do not respond to this regimen are either retired or shipped to race in the United States. Either way, they are removed from the UK's gene pool so that the breed there does not become weakened.

Am I saying that U.S.-based trainers are lazy because they depend on chemicals such as GastroGard and Lasix to treat how they misfeed horses? Am I saying trainers in the U.S. have delegated their responsibilities to veterinarians? I would never say that! I am simply laying out the facts you never read or hear in the media to give you the knowledge to make your own informed decision. With the industry trying to reinvent itself, and focusing on the health and safety of its stars, I'm just doing my part to help.

Arlington Park in Illinois is a quarantine facility for horses who are imported into the United States. As I wrote earlier in these pages, the historic Arlington Heights facility is also the first track I ever visited, where I gained my love and appreciation for horse racing, and where I took my future bride on our first date.

As former locals, Denise and I still had family in the Chicago area in the summer of 2015, so if my Royal Ascot dreams were dashed, it was on to the next dream—the Arlington Million! I made plans to bring California Chrome back from England for a start in this venerable Grade 1 turf event, scheduled for mid-August.

As Chrome was en route to the U.S., I received four phone updates. He was usually a very good traveler, as indicated by his outstanding race record as a shipper, but on this occasion, he was agitated and was not drinking enough water during the overseas flight. Perhaps they encountered some rough air.

I was informed that the veterinarian who was accompanying Chrome had to give him mild sedation and had started IV fluids to address the dehydration. I was assured that he was in no danger, but remember that Chrome had been training for months in the English style and his body weight was about 75 pounds less than normal. When you add dehydration, sedation and a still-sore foot, Chrome did not look like a champion coming off the plane after the long journey from England to Illinois.

As Chrome was paraded for the media in the Arlington quarantine facility, they were able to get multiple "bad" pictures of him and multiple statements from "reputable equine experts" that Chrome would never be the same again if he was even able to recover. All of the "knowledgeable social media equine experts," you know them, avatar folks who claim they have owned nothing but undefeated Grade 1 champions, stated that Chrome was definitely abused.

Not knowing the whole story behind the photos, the ever-growing army of Chromies was aghast! Social media went on full alert. I rolled my eyes, thinking, "Here we go again!"

Meanwhile, Taylor Made had begun discussions with Mr. Coburn to purchase his 30% ownership share in Chrome. There was a tentative agreement for $2 million, but it was dependent on Chrome passing a physical exam.

While Chrome was in the quarantine facility, he was being vetted for sale. The veterinary exam showed that his joints looked like a 2-year-old's, with little to no damage. However, there was a problem found with his cannon bones: bone bruising.

"Bone bruising" is a misnomer. Everyone knows that bruising is caused by trauma, so people think that it is caused by the pounding on the track. Incorrect. Bone bruising is actually a reduction in bone density which shows up on x-rays. It is caused by the way horses are trained in the U.S., spending 23 hours each day inactive in their stalls. Horses are grazing animals, and need to walk a lot for circulation, their general physical health, and digestive system, to work the way nature intended.

In one famous example, bone bruising is what caused the premature retirement of another Kentucky Derby and Preakness Stakes winner, 2004 hero Smarty Jones. He was sent to stud at 3 with chronic bruising of the bottom of the cannon bone in all four of his fetlock joints, never having faced his elders on the track after running second in the Belmont Stakes in his Triple Crown attempt, which was 10 years ahead of Chrome's.

It is my feeling that Chrome's time in Dubai and England under different training routines actually mitigated the condition somewhat. If only he had gone to Dubai earlier.

With the bone bruising diagnosis, Mr. Coburn ended up selling his share of California Chrome to Taylor Made for $1.5 million, thereby valuing the horse at $5 million.

I was called by my new partners and told the news about Chrome's condition. I was told he could still race in this condition; in fact, he probably had done so when running less than par in the Breeders' Cup Classic, San Antonio and Dubai World Cup over the previous eight months!

I had found my root cause, which gave me closure on his substandard performances in those races. For the sake of the horse, I would let my second dream of winning the Arlington Million die as well.

I asked Taylor Made to turn him out at their Kentucky farm, where he could recover and be evaluated monthly by the experts at Rood & Riddle Equine Hospital. With luck, we could bring him back to the races at 5—a rarity for any Kentucky Derby winner in the modern era.

17

CALIFORNIA CHROME LLC

The sales contract that Taylor Made had used was written specifically for the state of Illinois, where California Chrome was located when 30% of him was sold. The contract stipulated that Chrome was being sold for racing purposes. At that time in Illinois, horses sold for racing purposes were exempt from sales tax.

Our earlier evaluation of Taylor Made was spot-on; they had a great deal of equine business savvy. There was no way Chrome's new co-owners could ever be considered Dumb Ass Partners, so we would need to change the name for their sake.

The estimated recovery rate from bone bruising was 95%. Chrome only had a mild case, so it was fairly certain he would return to racing after some well-deserved time off.

Team Approach

During the fall of 2015, Denise and I met with Taylor Made leadership at their expansive farm in Nicholasville, Kentucky.

We decided to run our operation out of an LLC composed of 50 shares. Each share would be equal to 2% of the horse. This configuration allowed for great flexibility in optimizing operations for the remaining racing phase of Chrome's career, and later for the breeding phase of his career.

Taylor Made was named as the stallion farm that would stand California Chrome, and Duncan Taylor, the farm's founder and president, was named the breeding manager of the LLC. Duncan would need to consult all shareholders on major issues, but he would run day-to-day breeding operations and have the final say on all breeding-related matters.

I was named racing manager of the LLC. As such, I would need to consult all shareholders on major issues, but I would run day-to-day racing operations and have the final say on all racing-related matters.

Per the business plan proposed by Taylor Made, we would begin taking on partners that would help us to solidify Chrome's future breeding career. In-house, we called this our "super syndicate." These were premium Taylor Made customers who would promise to breed one of their top mares to Chrome each of the first two years of his stallion career.

I would sell five shares (10%) and Taylor Made would sell five shares. These would be full shares, which would receive racing income and have two breeding rights per season going forward. These shares were offered for the special price of $150,000 each. Chrome's new valuation was $7.5 million. These shares would sell out very quickly.

I knew this initial offering price was very low, but I needed to think about this in the terms of the TV show "Shark Tank," in which fledgling business owners sell parts of their companies for a lower valuation in order to bring in investors with desired skill sets.

A quick side-story. I offered a share of California Chrome to John Harris, the owner of Harris Farms in California, because I thought he would be a perfect addition to our super syndicate. John had several high-value mares that would be perfect for Chrome, and this would solidify the California connection by having the farm which was his birthplace participating. John passed on the offer, believing the price was too high. It didn't bother me, since I ended up selling the share for much more, but I always thought it was strange.

Chrome ended up earning an additional $8 million in his subsequent races. That alone is $160,000 per share. The breeding income, sale of yearlings and ultimate sale to Japan added up to many multiples of the acquisition price for all who shrewdly came in at $150,000 each.

We concluded our organizational meeting in Kentucky by agreeing to our primary racing goal for the upcoming year: to capture the world's richest race, the Dubai World Cup.

I insisted, and it was agreed, that we would go to Dubai two months early to get Chrome situated and get a race into him over the host track. We would offer the training job to Art Sherman, but if he would not commit to supporting the horse in Dubai, we would ask Steve Asmussen to train Chrome going forward.

I had one additional request for Taylor Made: I wanted them to provide a point person to interface with Art, should he decide to continue training the horse. I would discuss matters with the point person, and he or she would relate the information to Art. The group selected Frank Taylor to perform this task.

Skipping ahead a bit, Frank enjoyed this role immensely. The trips to California, interfacing with the Shermans and being around Chrome, was great fun for him. I think he enjoyed the media attention as well.

As for me, I basked in the shadows reading the interviews that Art would give about how brilliant the decisions concerning the horse were now that Taylor Made was involved. Even going to Dubai early was now considered a magnificent move.

I kept optimizing the team around Chrome. A good manager needs to know when to delegate.

Our Partial Distribution

Almost immediately after the opening of the super syndicate, the available shares were sold out. Demand was still high, and as Chrome eventually began winning races on his comeback, demand grew even faster.

When the formation of a new "world's richest race," the Pegasus World Cup Invitational Stakes (G1), was announced in early 2016 with a proposed purse of $12 million for its January 2017 inaugural running at Gulfstream Park in Florida, and it was revealed that California Chrome LLC had invested $1 million to obtain one of the 12 limited spots in the starting gate, demand skyrocketed.

If you look at the potential earnings from competing in just three of the lucrative races we had targeted for Chrome's comeback—the $10 million Dubai World Cup and $6 million Breeders' Cup Classic in 2016 and the $12 million Pegasus World Cup in 2017, you can understand why folks wanted in, and wanted in badly. Chrome could earn in excess of $16 million by winning all three of these races. He was very highly regarded as a racehorse, so the opportunity was real, and this did not even consider his accompanying increase in value as a breeding stallion if he were to win one, two or all three of these elite races.

Because of this tremendous demand, I agreed to sell another 30%, or 15 shares, of our Martin Racing ownership in Chrome during this time period. Full shares were now $400,000 each, with any sales fees or commissions paid by the buyer. I would sell only a few shares at this level, as it led to a valuation of Chrome at $20 million, which is higher than the big stallion farms and media were estimating for Chrome's value.

Early in the sales process, limited shares were available for $250,000 plus commission; this price rose to $275,000 near the end. The remainder of the available shares sold for this latter unit price, creating a Chrome valuation of $13.75 million.

Limited shares were for breeding purposes only. Denise and I would pay all expenses on these Martin Racing shares while Chrome was racing, but we would also receive our designated percentage of all racetrack earnings.

When Chrome was retired from racing, the limited shares would become full shares, so Denise and I were ultimately left with 15 shares, or 30%, of Chrome. As small breeders ourselves, this was a higher ownership stake than we felt we could support for his breeding career, but a super majority of LLC shares was required for any major changes, such as a sale, so maintaining this ownership level gave us veto power. This would be a very important asset to us when assessing and negotiating any sale offers in the future.

The Dissolution Of DAP

As you can imagine, during California Chrome's career, there were many contracts and agreements that I signed concerning Chrome. Many of these agreements contained non-disclosure components; some did not. If an agreement was signed by me and it contained a non-disclosure component, I will not talk about it, as I keep my agreements. I will, however, talk around the agreement details and limit my discussion to open public knowledge.

Around this time, the Dumb Ass Partners horses Love the Chase, her 2013 filly Hope's Love and her 2015 colt subsequently named Faversham officially became the property of Perry and Denise Martin. Love the Chase's 2014 filly R Sunday Surprise, originally named California Chromet, became the property of Steve and Carolyn Coburn. This is public knowledge, as you can research these horses on the internet and learn this information.

Each of the horses we retained would play a part in our breeding and racing program and also enrich our lives.

18

BACK ON TRACK

It was early January 2016, and the main goal was a return run in the Dubai World Cup at the end of March. Still, we needed an assessment of where we were with Chrome's conditioning, and a Grade 2 race at a track our horse obviously liked was a good place to start.

We had a nine-month respite from racing, which felt really good after the whirlwind Triple Crown campaign and our following frustrations, but it was time to get back to it.

For his highly anticipated comeback as a 5-year-old, our champ would carry the newly designed silver silks of California Chrome LLC, along with matching silver blinkers. A new look for a fresh start.

New Silver Silks Strike Gold

Our base for Santa Anita's 1 1/16-mile San Pasqual Stakes (G2) was again the Pacific Palms resort. At this point, Denise and I would seek out any relaxation we could get, and being away from the racetrack meant less media scrutiny. This hotel had less noise, walking trails along the manicured fairways with beautiful landscape and water features; a little slice of heaven awaited us, so we could decompress no matter the outcome of the highly anticipated comeback race.

The early morning was a little overcast as we negotiated the highways to the racetrack.

At Santa Anita, it was as if our horse had not had any time away from the track. There was much excitement about his return, and we received well wishes and requests for autographs from many Chromies. Several of our new syndicate partners were able to join us for this race, and their excitement was contagious. I was enjoying this fresh start.

The race went very much as planned. Reunited with Victor, Chrome broke quickly and went to the lead, but was quickly passed by the speedy longshot Alfa Bird. Victor was content to settle in second and did not press the pace, which resulted in fairly pedestrian fractions. He and Chrome simply waited for the final turn and made their move, joined by a fast-closing Imperative. Chrome was able to separate himself and held sway for a 1 1/4-length victory as the 3-5 favorite. Not his best race, but it was a Grade 2 win with an accompanying $120,000 purse, and something to build on.

We joined our partners and fans in the winner's circle for a group photo and the start of a rousing celebration of Chrome's comeback. The celebration moved to the clubhouse bar. A little later, we met up with Team Chrome at the famous Derby restaurant in Arcadia for dinner.

As we were leaving the restaurant, I happened to look into one of the private rooms and spotted Mrs. Penny Chenery having dinner with the American Pharoah team, whose wonderful colt had won the Triple Crown and her organization's Vox Populi Award in 2015. We dropped in and said hello to everyone. Imagine the collective racing auras bouncing off the walls of the room that evening, as the connections of two Triple Crown winners and one near-miss Triple Crown hopeful mingled and congratulated each other on their champions' successes.

That chance encounter was the only time we would meet Mrs. Chenery.

Our evening walk at the Pacific Palms would be very pleasant.

Double In The Desert

Denise and I made two trips to Dubai in February and March 2016: one for Chrome's prep race and one for the World Cup. We enjoyed the adventures this new world presented to us, as we found the people of Dubai to be friendly and very happy.

On the first trip over to watch the prep, we flew in economy class on Emirates Airline. Let's just say this was a completely different experience from our first-class accommodations the year before. When we traveled for the big race, we upgraded to business class tickets that were provided to all World Cup runners' connections by the Dubai Racing Club.

Chrome departed for Dubai on January 22, with plans to live and train in that emirate for just over two months. We believed this would allow him plenty of time to adjust to the new time zone and acclimate to the new environment.

He would again train from the quarantine barn, but at this point, I knew it was providing a positive benefit to Chrome's health. On our first 2016 visit before Chrome's prep race, Denise and I actually made the long, 45-minute walk to the track once ourselves to experience what our horse and team were going through, as well as to gain the benefits of a workout. We did not make the walk back, preferring instead to have breakfast on the track patio.

On the evening of February 25, Chrome ran in the Trans Gulf Electromechanical Trophy Handicap at Meydan as a primer for the Dubai World Cup. He carried 132 pounds, giving up 14 pounds or greater to his seven opponents in this race. This was a handicap reminiscent of days long past, in which the champions would be tested by carrying significantly more weight. In all of Chrome's U.S. races, he seldom carried more than 5 pounds more than his competitors.

As usual, Denise and I watched the race from the track apron. Chrome broke from the rail into a crowded start, but Victor promptly angled him out for a comfortable, three-wide running position while stalking close behind two battling early leaders. He coasted through much of the race, despite being challenged by several horses along the way. Chrome took control at the top of the stretch, ran clear of the pacesetters while on a tight rein and crossed the wire after about 1 1/4 miles as an easy, two-length winner. He was expected to win the prep, and he did in fine style, under a hand ride and with plenty left in the tank.

We could see Chrome was a confident horse coming out of this race, but the world would throw their best at him in the next!

The prep added a nice purse to our horseman's account at Meydan, but we would still need to add to the funds to pay for the Dubai World Cup entry fee. Luckily, the small amount we would need to wire would not be challenged this time.

Many of our new partners made the trip overseas to watch Chrome run in the world's richest race, as did our daughter, Kelly, who loves to travel and experience new cultures. Taylor Made organized several get-togethers for the syndicate members, and Denise and I were becoming very familiar with the partners who chose to attend the races. It was a good group that emanated positivity.

The 2016 Dubai World Cup reception was again a standout, coming in as the second-best party I would ever attend. My favorite thing, though, was getting up early to attend the morning works and talk to the trainers who were there representing so many different countries. It was like a mini-United Nations of horse racing. The training techniques were as varied as the countries represented, and I would take a lot of information away from this incredible experience.

The races of the Dubai Racing Carnival are held in the evening to avoid the heat of the day. The darkness of the desert also provides for a dramatic setting.

It was a pleasant night in Dubai on March 26, with a cool wind coming off the ocean. Our group was too large for one table, so we had several tables in the Meydan clubhouse. The now-familiar buffet presented numerous tempting offerings to satiate our hunger and fill the time until our headline race. Some food, a little wine and some pleasant conversation would help us to ignore the building stress as the $10 million race got closer. Finally, the race previous to ours was over and we stood up to walk to the enormous saddling paddock.

We showed our passes and entered the paddock, which was isolated from the excited crowd. That was probably a very good idea, as some of the horses, especially Godolphin's homebred Wood Memorial (G1) winner Frosted, were showing signs of being nervous. Frosted had two handlers, one on each side holding a tight lead rope; the gray colt, who had also won his local prep for the Dubai World Cup a month earlier, was tugging against both of them while his owner, His Highness Sheikh Mohammed, and his wife looked on in admiration.

California Chrome was his normal, composed self, content to follow Raul along his oval walking path in his assigned area. No nervous behavior here. It seemed a longer delay between races than normal, but I was hoping it would drag out even longer, as the agitated horses were expending their energy on their handlers. Better for them to use their mojo here than on the racetrack.

With the call of "Riders up!," Denise and I followed the horses out to the track, diverting our path before we hit the dirt track surface. We found a less congested area on the track apron from which to watch the race. As the horses paraded, we surveyed our surroundings.

We spotted Kelly standing down by the rail. Sheikh Hamdan bin Mohammed bin Rashid Al Maktoum, the Crown Prince of Dubai, was standing next to her. Earlier in the day, Kelly had wandered into the Royal Enclosure and Sheikh Hamdan had befriended her when the Royal Guards had surrounded her after discovering their and her mistake. We also saw Art, the Taylors and several syndicate members in a nearby group. Everyone wanted to be close to the action.

Mere seconds after loading into the 11th stall out of the 12-full starting gate, Chrome broke like a rocket when the metal doors opened. He was instantly able to put all of that energy he had conserved in the paddock to use when Victor shook the reins leaving the gate. He hustled quickly to be up among the leaders on the outside, then Victor seemed happy to bide his time there, remaining four-wide on the first turn.

I remember thinking to myself, "Damn, Victor; four-wide, really?" We would need to run much faster than the other horses, since we were running further.

When asked in the post-race news conference what I was thinking during the race, I made the mistake of telling the truth. Here's a tip for you if you ever find yourself in a situation like this: Don't ever do that;

always have some polite lie ready in advance. The unsocial media pages really let me have it after I made my honest comments about Victor's ride. Whatever!

Throughout most of the 2,000-meter race, Chrome stayed in his outside path among the leaders, where he could avoid any kickback or trouble that might stem from the closely packed field. Running four-wide as he entered the stretch, Chrome found another gear and kicked for home. Frosted approached Chrome on the outside and tried to go with him, to no avail.

With the Meydan crowd going wild in the desert night, Chrome burst into the lead as the track announcer exclaimed, "California Chrome has gone into overdrive!"

When our horse flew past us, I suddenly noticed his girth strap had not been tightened properly, and his saddle had slipped back to his flank. Oh no. I crossed my fingers and squeezed my fists very tightly while hoping Victor would not fall off or that Chrome would start bucking in irritation. In my fog of immediate worries, I vaguely remember hearing the announcer calling, "It's alchemy in Dubai; Chrome turns to gold!"

With a clear lead now secured, Victor eased up and coasted Chrome past the wire for a comfortable win margin. I saw Sheikh Hamdan congratulating Kelly as she excitedly jumped up about two feet in the air.

We had won the world's richest race, and the $6 million paycheck allowed California Chrome to surpass 2007-2008 Horse of the Year Curlin as North America's highest-earning Thoroughbred in history! In addition, we had beat the best the world had to offer, and set a new track record of 2:01.83 despite a wide gate draw, a wide trip and just coasting home at the end. The plan was coming together.

For future audiences who were unable to watch this race live, or who perhaps were not old enough or even fans of horse racing at the time, I recommend you find and watch a replay of the 2016 Dubai World Cup online to see for yourself the qualities that made California Chrome a multiple champion, fan favorite and indeed the horse of a lifetime. His talent and professionalism were on full display that night, as his chestnut coat glistened confidently past the best classic-distance dirt rivals in the world.

Overjoyed, our group met on the outdoor terrace of The Meydan Hotel bar on the opposite end of the facility, away from the post-race festivities. We sat on the terrace and listened to the world-class musical acts performing on the outdoor stage while consuming our celebratory beverages of choice. Janet Jackson was the headliner, but, to our group, Chrome was the real star of the show.

Most of the guys were drinking Kentucky bourbon; very fitting. Most of the ladies were drinking California wine; again, very fitting. I was drinking scotch, a lyrical gesture to the international nature of the event, certainly not just because I like scotch. I will never forget sitting on the terrace and sipping my scotch while watching the moon shimmer over the Dubai skyline.

Later, we enjoyed a massive fireworks display. Before the pyrotechnics began, all of the racehorses on the grounds of Meydan were led into the vast underground tunnels which service the large facility. There, the horses were immune from the noise above.

Chrome would need to be quarantined for a couple weeks after flying back to the states. We had learned from our previous trip to Dubai that this long journey was taxing on the horse, so he would get a short break at Taylor Made's Kentucky farm, where he could not only rest, but show off for potential breeders in advance of his forthcoming stallion career. It was the end of March, and he would not race again until late July.

Surfing The Skies

We were kept informed of Chrome's springtime recuperation at Taylor Made and his transfer back to Art's Los Alamitos barn in May. After his well-deserved layoff, he was refreshed and would have eight weeks to sharpen up for our next target, the Grade 2 San Diego Handicap at Del Mar.

In the meantime, Denise and I had found a better way to travel. We signed up for a new private air travel service called Surf Air which was flying out of a private terminal at McClellan Business Park, the former U.S. Air Force base in Sacramento where our laboratory was located. They took our pictures, we completed a Federal Aviation Administration form and, two weeks later, we were approved as certified travelers.

For a set monthly fee, the two of us could fly anywhere Surf Air went, as often as we wanted. This is very handy if you have an active, champion racehorse. We called it "Surfing up and down the state of California."

We could walk from the lab to the terminal if needed, but we usually drove over to take our bags. We could show up 10 minutes before our scheduled departure, check in at the counter where they would call up our file and match us with our computer photos, then we would place our bags on the luggage cart and enjoy a complimentary beverage before our flight.

Surf Air's private planes are configured for eight passengers. The turboprop made our frequent trip from Sacramento to Hawthorne Airport in Los Angeles County (located across from SpaceX) in 45 to 50 minutes, depending on which way the wind was blowing. We would collect our bags at the bottom of the aircraft steps, walk to our rental car that was waiting outside the terminal door and, within two minutes, we were en route to the racetrack. We could attend morning works at Santa Anita or Los Al, then go back to the lab after losing only a morning rather than a whole day.

This was great! Together with our Pacific Palms hideaway, we were finally experiencing pleasurable travel. All it took was spending a lot of money.

San Diego Showdown

One of the most thrilling races of California Chrome's career was the 2016 San Diego Handicap, which pitted him for the first time against the strapping up-and-comer Dortmund, Bob Baffert's 2015 Santa Anita Derby winner. This match-up between two chestnut titans is so popular that you can regularly catch a half-hour special broadcast about it, including a replay of the race itself, in after-hours programming on TVG.

For our journey down to Del Mar, Denise and I took a 60-minute Surf Air flight from McClellan Airfield in Sacramento to San Diego International Airport on the morning of the race, July 23. We rented a convertible and put the top down for our ride to the racetrack.

We were excited to see our champ back in action in his home state. It had been nearly two years since he had raced at Del Mar, winning the track's Grade 1 Hollywood Derby in his only career start on grass in November 2014.

With two defections from the $200,000 San Diego, only five runners were left to compete in the 1 1/16-mile race. As the oldest and, by far, most accomplished horse in the field, Chrome was tasked with carrying 126 pounds as the 4-5 wagering favorite, 5 more pounds than 6-5 second choice Dortmund and 10 more pounds than a pair of double-digit longshots.

The two favorites bookended the break, with Dortmund on the rail and Chrome on the far outside. Victor gunned Chrome from the gate, but soon took a follow-the-leader position just behind and outside the front-running Dortmund.

Just as billed, it was a two-horse race.

Early on, Victor let Dortmund get a full length ahead of Chrome, but he slowly applied pressure and closed the gap to just a half-length behind the leader. At the top of the stretch, the two warriors hooked up for a battle royale, moving in unison, and remained separated by just a head throughout the run home.

In this scenario, experience triumphed over youth. Running full out in the final yards, Chrome gained a half-length advantage which he carried to the wire, stopping the clock in 1:40.84, just four-fifths of a second off Del Mar's 54-year-old track record for the distance. The hapless third-place finisher, Win the Space, completed the test 7 1/4 lengths behind Dortmund, with the remaining two entrants another zip code behind.

Some pundits claimed that Chrome broke Dortmund's heart in this gritty contest. I'm not sure I believe in such racetrack colloquialisms, but I will note that Chrome's gallant rival on that day never did win another race.

Chrome, meanwhile, was four-for-four while wearing his sparkling new silks, and had Del Mar's premier race, the $1 million TVG Pacific Classic Stakes (G1), within his sights.

Spirit Of Collaboration

After the 2014 Del Mar dust-up, and having had Chrome eschew the West Coast to try his luck back east instead, the Del Mar folks decided to strap down the loose cannon.

They got together with the Santa Anita folks and offered a $1 million bonus to any horse that could win the 2016 runnings of the Pacific Classic, the Awesome Again Stakes and the Breeders' Cup Classic, the former at Del Mar and the latter two at Santa Anita. That certainly got our attention.

In addition, Del Mar representatives reached out to both me and our ownership group, offering luxury accommodations at the Fairmont Grand Del Mar Resort for both the San Diego Handicap and the Pacific Classic. Plus, I was given the opportunity to work with the Del Mar marketing team to build up momentum for two appearances by our wildly popular horse at the seaside oval.

One fun thing we did on the day of the San Diego Handicap was to host an on-site contest between approximately 20 gourmet food trucks to determine the best California Chrome-themed food item. Kelly and her friend, Robin, judged the contest as its official taste-testers.

Winning the California Chrome food truck superfecta were the California Chrome Pork Belly Burger by Monster Crafts Truck, the Cajun Cali Chrome Bisque by Ragin Cajun Truck, the Cali Chrome Double Bacon and Steak Derby Fries by Seoul Man Food Truck and the California Chrome Sloppy Joe by Hacks Food Truck. The top finisher was awarded an engraved silver serving tray, which I provided.

This collaborative approach toward racetrack/horse owner communications worked much better than our previous war of words that was waged in the local San Diego media. We even added a little Bobby Flay throwdown influence to our food truck challenge, all in good fun.

Another nice example of our industry working together—instead of apart—was our group's donation of the California Chrome LLC silks Victor wore to victory in the San Diego Handicap, which were offered up for bidding during a Barretts Sales auction of horses of racing age conducted in Del Mar's paddock after the races that evening. The silks sold in a package with Chrome's halter and his horseshoes to a New Jersey handicapper for $20,000, with all proceeds going to the V Foundation for cancer research. The winning bidder, Mark Stanton, was a fan of Chrome whose mother had died of breast cancer, and who was at Del Mar that day to participate in a handicapping challenge.

Like they say, teamwork makes the dream work.

Cheers!

Riding high from this newfound cooperation and Chrome's ongoing win streak, Denise and I headed back to Del Mar in August for the Pacific Classic. It was going to be a competitive race featuring familiar rivals Chrome had previously vanquished, including Dortmund and Hoppertunity, as well as one very talented horse he had never faced: the three-time Eclipse Award-winning champion mare Beholder, 8 1/4-length winner of the race's 2015 rendition.

The evening before the race, I entered the bar at the Grand Del Mar and joined a group of California Chrome LLC members spread across two tables. I asked one of the guys what he was drinking, and he replied, "Oban 18." I had never had that, but I like scotch, so I thought I'd give it a try.

I called over the barman and asked for an Oban 18, then told him to get something for everyone at our two tables. To a person, they all ordered Oban 18. I thought to myself that it must be good stuff. The drinks were distributed, and we toasted to good luck to Chrome in the next day's race.

The barman handed me the bill: $816. Must be good stuff indeed!

Trying not to show surprise, I reached into my pocket and pulled out my betting money. I counted out nine $100 bills, gave them to the barman and told him, "Keep the change."

Staying philosophical, I figured I would just have a little less to bet.

It was good scotch, though. I still treat myself to a bottle every Christmas.

Coasting In The Pacific Classic

The next morning, our group met outside the hotel's front entrance at 11 a.m. to board the shuttle bus Taylor Made had rented to take us to the racetrack.

With Beholder returning to try to reclaim her crown after dominating the Pacific Classic the previous year, the cheers of "Girl Power!" from the fans were almost as loud as the "Go Chrome!" shouts.

Denise and I stopped by the barn to see how Chrome was feeling. Raul gave us a strong two thumbs up. When I saw Victor, I told him not to win by more than six lengths, as I didn't want to embarrass the mare. Her owner was B. Wayne Hughes of Spendthrift Farm, and I was greatly influenced and impressed by his business acumen across multiple industries.

Chrome was ready to rumble that day. When the starting gate opened, he popped like a cork from the inside stall and immediately took control of the race. He quickly cleared the field but, instead of utilizing a ground-saving trip for the 1 1/4-mile test from his rail position, Victor moved him out to the middle of the track, choosing to lead the proceedings and dictate the pace from approximately the eight path.

Later, when I would watch the TVG analysts describe the race, they would refer to this maneuver as a brilliant strategic move, because it confused and froze the other jockeys. My thoughts were that weaving added to the total distance run in the race, whereas running in a straight line would have put him two lengths further ahead. I guess I'll never understand this game as well as the media.

Back to the live race, which turned out to be not much of a race at all, since the result was never in doubt.

Chrome was in high cruise mode now and easily stayed more than a length in front of Beholder through the early going, with Dortmund in third and Hoppertunity in fourth. The top four stayed in this order for the remainder of the race, with the only change being the spacing of the horses as they approached the finish.

With Victor's whip confidently tucked away, Chrome coasted home in the stretch and eased up to a gallop approaching the wire as a five-length winner ahead of Beholder, in what track announcer Trevor Denman dubbed, "One of the greatest performances you'll ever see."

The final time, 2:00.13, was a shade off the 1:59.11 track record for the distance that had been set during the great Candy Ride (Arg)-Medaglia d'Oro Pacific Classic showdown in 2003.

Chrome had won $600,000 along with the Pacific Classic trophy, and captured the first race required for the $1 million Del Mar/Santa Anita bonus. But this was the last thing on our minds as we boarded the shuttle back to our hotel.

We were very tired. There is always the long, strenuous wait to the feature race, the adrenalin rush during and after the race and now the coming down.

Maybe an Oban would help? I decided beer would work just as well.

Awesome...Again

Denise and I were at a party at a house belonging to one of our Alpine, Wyoming neighbors when the talk, as usual, turned to California Chrome. How is he doing? What is his next race? We talked about him for awhile, then discussed his upcoming race: the $300,000 Awesome Again Stakes, a Grade 1 event that would serve as a local Breeders' Cup prep race at the 2016 host track, Santa Anita.

We invited everyone to come and meet Chrome and watch his race. We told them we would be staying at the Pacific Palms, and we could meet up there.

The Awesome Again trip was a lot of fun for us.

Using our Surf Air membership to fly privately, Denise and I arrived in Los Angeles the morning before the October 1 race to meet up with our Wyoming friends and take them to watch Chrome jog and get a bath. That evening, we attended a dinner with our California Chrome LLC colleagues.

Everybody watched the race from a luxury suite provided by Santa Anita. Two horses scratched out of the field, so only five would compete in the 1 1/8-mile race. One of them was our old pal Dortmund. As 3-year-olds in 2015, Dortmund and Frosted found themselves running behind American Pharoah. As 4-year-olds in 2016, they were now running behind California Chrome.

I wish California Chrome and American Pharoah would have hooked up. But the 2015 Triple Crown winner's entire career spanned less than 15 months, and he was retired at 3. Shame the racing community never got to see that match-up.

For the Awesome Again, Chrome had again drawn the number one post position. This time, though, Victor stuck to the inside rail like glue.

After a sharp break from the gate, Chrome took to the lead, with Dortmund's huge frame looming just behind him and applying pressure to Chrome's outside. The crowd's two favorites, Chrome at 2-5 and Dortmund at 8-5, hooked up for their own private battle, distancing themselves from the other three hopefuls by more than 10 lengths at one point on the backstretch.

Dortmund managed to keep up with Chrome for a half-mile, but could not sustain his effort and started to fall back, leaving Chrome alone with an extremely comfortable lead. With nobody closing in the stretch, Victor was content to let Chrome canter to the finish in another hand ride, the margin of victory officially recorded at 2 1/4 lengths. Dortmund lumbered up for second, more than four lengths clear of the third-place finisher in a drawn-out field.

Another huge winner's circle crowd of at least 70 well-wishers was waiting for us when we got there. Who were all of these people?

The Pacific Classic and the Awesome Again were each designated as Breeders' Cup "Win and You're In" races, so we had double-punched our ticket to the $6 million Breeders' Cup Classic on November 5. Best of all, our horse had now won six races in a row, and two of the three races needed for the $1 million bonus.

The hotly contested federal elections pitting Donald Trump against Hillary Clinton for president were scheduled for November 8 that year, and the Breeders' Cup was being held just a few days earlier. We decided to have some fun, so we had 1,000 "Vote Chrome For President" campaign-style buttons created to hand out on the day of the Awesome Again.

I had two pockets full of buttons, and limited my hand-outs to kids. Who was the one adult I gave one to?

We were going up the Santa Anita escalator and, on the other side, Bob Baffert was coming down. As we came closer to Dortmund's trainer, I grabbed a button out of my pocket and reached it over toward Bob.

"Hey Bob, this is for you!" I said.

He took it as we passed. I wonder what he did with it. Probably worth a pretty penny on eBay right about now.

After the race, I gave an interview to reporter Art Wilson which was published as below:

ARCADIA—Perry Martin, majority owner of the best North American horse in training, was sporting a red, white and blue "California Chrome For President" button in the winner's circle at Santa Anita on Saturday.

Hey, why not?

"We're very serious about running him for president," Martin said after California Chrome improved to 6-0 this year and strengthened his candidacy for Horse of the Year with a 2 1/4-length victory over Dortmund in the $300,000 Awesome Again Stakes, one of five "Win and You're In" Breeders' Cup Challenge races on the warm afternoon.

"I think the two major candidates between them don't have one good leg to stand on, and we proved today we've got four. I think it could be a much improved country if we could have Chromeyism rather than cronyism.

"And our slogan of course, as he proved here today, is 'Let's Make America Awesome Again.'"

Of course, he'd also need a running mate.

"It's gotta be Victor (winning jockey Victor Espinoza)," Martin said. "I mean, they're a team."

Hey, what can I say, I was ON that day!

A New Rivalry Is Born

Denise and I invited our siblings, Andrew and Roy, to the two-day Breeders' Cup championship event at Santa Anita on November 4-5. We stayed, of course, at the relaxing Pacific Palms, where we enjoyed some visiting time together, as well as meals out on the patio. It was nice to squeeze in a little family time when we could.

Our California Chrome group again intermingled in a luxury suite at Santa Anita on the day of our race, but we couldn't watch it from there. My wife and I just had to watch from our usual spot on the apron.

All I could think about as post time drew near was: What could go wrong? The last time our horse had won six races in a row, there was disaster in the Belmont Stakes when a Triple Crown was on the line.

The main tactic for the 1 1/4-mile Breeders' Cup Classic was that Chrome needed to get away clean from the starting gate. That's exactly what happened, and everything almost went perfectly to plan for our champ's undefeated comeback season, except for one newcomer fly in the ointment named Arrogate.

Making just the sixth start of his career and brazenly entered against his elders in the Breeders' Cup Classic by trainer Bob Baffert, the brilliant Arrogate was coming into the championship match on his own four-race win streak, which included most recently a jaw-dropping,

13 1/2-length score against some very good fellow sophomores in the 2016 Travers Stakes (G1) at Saratoga, his graded stakes debut. The Breeders' Cup bettors duly respected his chances at 8-5.

As we had mapped out pre-race, Chrome broke fastest among the nine-horse field and took an early lead as the group passed by the grandstand of 72,811 fans for the first time. Although 2016 Santa Anita Handicap (G1) winner Melatonin was at his outside hip, Chrome was moving in medium cruise speed, with the early fractions a bit slower than usual: the opening quarter-mile in :23.28 and the opening half-mile in :47.15. Arrogate, with Hall of Famer Mike Smith in the irons, loomed on the outside in third, sitting pretty within his comfort zone and always within four lengths of Chrome.

No one was pushing, so Victor felt safe. I was nervous, however, as we were not running Chrome's optimum race. It would have been much better to run at high cruise—either the others would have to work harder to keep up or Chrome would widen the gap to his advantage. But that's not what transpired.

As Chrome exited the final turn while still running on the lead, Victor was not urging him home; instead, he stood up and casually looked back on his left toward the rail, where Smith had maneuvered Arrogate while passing Melatonin for second in the turn. Not seeing Arrogate or any other threat there where he expected them to be, Victor kept his hands quiet on Chrome while he glanced to his right. Guess who was there staring right back at him, like a great white shark approaching an unsuspecting, lonely seal?

Obviously startled by Arrogate's sudden appearance at Chrome's outside flank, Victor started pumping the reins frantically and finally reached for his whip. But it was too late. Chrome put up a valiant effort in responding to his rider's cues in a heated stretch drive, but his late burst of speed while toting 126 pounds was unable to separate him from Arrogate, who carried his momentum and his 4-pound weight allowance as a 3-year-old to a half-length victory in 2:00.11.

Mike Smith had run a much smarter race, and deservedly collected his record 25th career Breeders' Cup trophy. Meanwhile, Chrome finished second as the crowd's 4-5 favorite, nearly 11 lengths in front of 2015 Travers winner Keen Ice in third.

That's horse racing!

Farewell, Love

As the end of his 5-year-old campaign approached, California Chrome's breeding career was getting closer and closer, and the Martin Racing mare portfolio was about to get significantly tweaked.

From Chrome's 2-year-old season onward, Denise and I were always thinking and planning for his breeding career. We knew we had a champion, even if it would take a while for that champion to develop. For that reason, we had been slowly acquiring mares and breeding them along lines so that, if a filly was produced, she would be a perfect match by pedigree standards for Chrome.

This was the same line of reason that got us into breeding Thoroughbreds in the first place. We couldn't afford to buy a champion, so we would breed one ourselves. This approach takes patience, as you must wait 11 months after the breeding to see what you get, then wait years to see how that develops.

As Chrome began distinguishing himself from the others in his foal crop, I remember people saying how lucky we were to have bred him. Luck runs both ways. The first five mares we bred to produce fillies for Chrome all produced colts that first year! How lucky is that?

We entered Love the Chase in the 2016 Fasig-Tipton Kentucky November Sale, with Taylor Made's sale division as consignor. This was a business move we were planning to make for a long time.

In fact, we bred California Chrome's dam to the prominent Kentucky stallion Tapit in mid-February that year. He was a more fashionable choice than Lucky Pulpit but, like Chrome's California-based sire, he was a son of the late A.P. Indy stallion Pulpit; in fact, both successful stallions were from Pulpit's 2001 foal crop, born just 17 days apart.

We bred Love the Chase to Tapit on a very early cover date in order to potentially raise her price in the auction ring. Sending her to this leading sire was an expensive gamble, as we were required to pay his

$300,000 stud fee in advance of the sale. With Taylor Made's guidance, we set a reserve of $1.9 million.

Denise and I flew to Lexington right after the Breeders' Cup in order to attend the sale on November 7. I was a nervous wreck as Love the Chase entered the auction ring. There was our most valuable mare who had conceived our champion horse standing calmly in front of us.

As the bidding started, Denise leaned over and whispered, "I hope she doesn't make reserve."

I was silent, but smiled back at her, thinking to myself, "Me too!"

Still, the plan was to sell her so we could afford to purchase top-quality mares for Chrome at the upcoming Keeneland November Breeding Stock Sale.

The bidding was going quickly, and the price was approaching our reserve. It now seemed like an eternity between bids as she reached $1.9 million. One more bid, and we would lose her.

As the seconds clicked on, I thought we were going to keep her. I started to think ahead to her Tapit yearling in the sales ring. Just then, the price on the board clicked up to $1.95 million. That was as high as it would go, but it was just enough. Our first broodmare was gone!

Investing $2 Million In Mares For Chrome

In order to acquire mares for California Chrome in the most sensible manner, we hired a company to facilitate a like-kind exchange. Also known as a 1031 exchange, this is a part of U.S. tax law that is used mostly by real estate investors.

When you sell a property and purchase a similar property within a close period of time, you carry forward the gain on the new property and do not have to immediately pay the capital gains tax. This offered us the benefit of being able to use all of the proceeds from the sale of Love the Chase to purchase mares for Chrome. These funds were directed to an escrow account as we awaited the start of the 2016 Keeneland November Breeding Stock Sale.

California Chrome LLC was looking to purchase quite a few mares to support Chrome as a new stallion, so we coordinated our efforts in order to prevent syndicate members from bidding against each other and driving the prices up.

Taylor Made developed a master list of potential mares who were entered in the sale and suitable for Chrome. The mares on this list were vetted using heart capacity evaluations, conformation evaluations, genetic evaluations and, finally, pedigree evaluations. The master list also had price limit guidelines.

The LLC members basically split up the list to decide who would bid on each mare. If there was overlap, we would either trade off or flip a coin.

One mare I traded off was Hotlantic. A dual stakes winner and graded stakes producer by Stormy Atlantic, she was owned by California breeders John Harris and Don Valpredo, who had purchased her for $47,000 from Taylor Made's consignment at the 2011 Keeneland November sale. I had called John a couple months before the 2016 sale to try and purchase her privately. I was prepared to offer up to $225,000. I didn't want to go that high if I didn't need to, but that was my limit.

When I inquired, John told me they were planning to sell her at the Keeneland November sale, and they expected she might go as high as $600,000. That stopped me in my tracks. I didn't want to insult anybody, so I just kept my offer to myself and wished him luck. I traded Hotlantic off to another LLC member; she sold in the ring for $115,000. This is a tough business.

Denise and I were able to purchase six high-quality mares for Chrome at that sale. We had to throw in a little extra money to seal the deal, but that was fine.

We ended up spending just over $2 million to acquire Theworldweknow, a Speightstown half-sister to Grade 1 winner Marylebone in foal to American Pharoah; Roughing, an Eskendereya half-sister to Grade 1 winner Diplomat Lady in foal to Uncle Mo; Our Biggest Fan, a Distorted Humor half-sister to graded stakes winners Gottcha Gold and American Freedom in foal to Tapizar; Evasion, a daughter of Empire Maker and Hall of Fame champion Inside Information in foal to Super Saver; Decennial, a stakes-placed winner by Trippi in foal to

Majesticperfection; and the broodmare prospect Right There, a Grade 1-placed stakes winner by Eskendereya.

Putting together a good broodmare band is not that difficult. It's training them to each play a different instrument that is the problem!

Once More, For The Fans

The Pegasus World Cup Invitational Stakes in January 2017 was the new goal. California Chrome LLC had invested $1 million to purchase a spot in the inaugural edition of this $12 million race in Florida, which was positioned on the calendar just a few weeks prior to the start of the 2017 breeding season.

Between the Breeders' Cup Classic in early November and the Pegasus World Cup in late January, we needed a race to keep Chrome sharp.

The Winter Challenge Stakes at Los Alamitos was a concept that was put together to accomplish two things: first, to get a prep race into Chrome and second, to reward his fans for their support and loyalty.

Chrome had been stabled at Los Alamitos and worked in the mornings at the modest Orange County oval since the move over from Hollywood Park, but he had never run at Los Al in the afternoon. That would be corrected soon.

The Winter Challenge carried a total purse of $180,000; however, the winner would only receive $50,000, which was significantly less than the standard 60% winner's share of the overall purse. The Los Al racing office was having difficulty finding horses to fill the race and line up against Chrome, so we agreed to allow this deviation. With the race now not so top-heavy, Los Al was able to guarantee that at least $10,000 would be paid out to any horse who ran in it.

As an additional inducement, Chrome was assigned number 10 for the 1 1/16-mile race, which would require him to break from the far outside stall of the starting gate. The other nine competitors drew for position.

The script for California Chrome's final start in his home state wrote itself.

"This is not about anything other than one thing—the fans; this is for the Chromies," TVG personality Todd Schrupp said on the live broadcast as the horses broke from the Los Al starting gate.

Chrome emerged sharply, and treated the crowd to a good look at him as he ran four-wide and unhurried past the small grandstand on the first pass and into the clubhouse turn. Victor kept Chrome away from trouble, placing him on the outside and in mid-pack of the condensed field until he was caught as wide as six paths out from the rail going into the final turn.

Without ever feeling Victor's whip, Chrome accelerated smoothly and swept the field from the outside, then began piling lengths onto his lead as he showed off for his fans, untested and unequaled in the long Los Alamitos stretch. His margin of victory as the overwhelming 1-20 favorite was a dozen lengths. Despite the wide trip under a hand ride, he also set a new track record: 1:40.03.

There were smiles everywhere we looked. The Chromies were proud and wished Chrome the best going into his last race.

Worldwide Appeal

The day after Chrome received a hero's welcome at his home track, his fans spoke loudly and clearly for him yet again. He became the first horse in the history of the publicly voted Secretariat Vox Populi Award to win the honor twice—and, in fact, he remains the only one to do so to this day.

The press release announcing the 2016 honor summed it up nicely, stating, in part:

"California Chrome's celebrated comeback in 2016 was highlighted by seven wins in eight starts, including commanding performances in the Dubai World Cup and TVG Pacific Classic, a sensational second-place effort in the Breeders' Cup Classic and a record-breaking finish in his most recent start, the Winter Challenge at Los Alamitos Race Course...In the online poll, California Chrome's international appeal translated into widespread support from Vox Populi voters in more than 40 countries."

The announcement also included some meaningful words from Secretariat's famous owner, Penny Chenery.

"The far-reaching participation we received from this year's Vox Populi voters has been quite thrilling," said Mrs. Chenery. "This global enthusiasm and California Chrome's repeat selection are testament to both his athletic excellence and his abiding appeal among racing fans. In both the sports and entertainment realms, we have seen some names repeatedly receive honors, and it is those stars who typically become the all-time greats in their field. I think we are seeing California Chrome's emergence as an enduring racing celebrity propelling him to a new level of stardom."

In response to the accolade, I was pleased to contribute the following comments to the official news release as well.

"This horse has given us one stratospheric ride," I said. "I continue to be amazed by his courage, athleticism and his will to win. Mostly though, I'm proud to witness the love and devotion of Chrome's fans. They've always seen what I've seen in him. Winning the Vox Populi Award two years ago was an incredible honor, and it is just as terrific the second time around."

On January 14, 2017, the Chenery family graciously presented us with our second Vox Populi trophy in another special ceremony at Santa Anita. Art, Victor and I met with fans and autographed another beautiful poster of Chrome that had been created especially for this occasion and given to track patrons in attendance that day.

As was the tradition, we enjoyed dinner the night before the ceremony with Mrs. Chenery's children, Kate Chenery Tweedy and Christopher Tweedy. Mrs. Chenery was again too ill to attend.

Secretariat's owner, who did so much for the sport of horse racing in her lifetime, passed away later that year at 95. It was an honor not only to meet her and be recognized by her, but to campaign a champion worthy of being mentioned in the same breath as her beloved "Big Red."

Fan Mail

This seems like an appropriate place to address the instant fame that comes along with having a popular racehorse.

I know the origin of the word "fan" comes from "fanatic"—a person exhibiting excessive enthusiasm and intense, uncritical devotion toward some controversial matter. I don't think that quite covers what we have with California Chrome.

When Denise and I returned home after our Kentucky Derby trip in 2014, we had about five letters waiting in our mailbox. Most of these were from neighbors congratulating us on our Derby win. Denise answered these with thank you cards or letters that night.

When we got to work the next morning, we were not prepared for the mountain of mail that had been piled on our desks. The NBC prerace special had featured our place of business, Martin Testing Laboratories, and it seems people thought this would be a good place to write to us. We could not work with our desks covered with mail, so we sorted through the stacks quickly, tossing anything that looked personal into one of four large cardboard cartons we put on the floor. The business mail we immediately opened and addressed.

With our desks clear, we began catching up on delayed work. The cartons of mail sat on the floor, getting a little fuller each day after the mail arrived.

As I wrote about in an earlier chapter, Denise and I had a wedding anniversary trip to Vegas planned during Preakness weekend, and we needed to get caught up on work before we could leave. We asked a colleague to sort our mail while we were gone, putting only the business mail on our desk. The "horse mail," as we called it, continued to accumulate until the four cartons were overflowing onto the floor.

We did not open any of the horse mail until about two weeks after the Belmont. We had finally caught up with our work and our horse was getting a breather at the farm, so he was out of the spotlight for now. Mail inflow fell to a trickle, so we felt we could address the massive pile of letters in a reasonable manner.

Denise and I would open and read five letters a day each. Our method was to just grab off the top, even though those were the last to arrive. We compared notes after the first day.

Most of the authors of these letters were telling us about themselves and their hopes, dreams, aspirations and problems and their need for money. In fact, about half of the letters were a plea for money. We were so lucky, they were not, so we should give some of our money to them. This was not a compelling argument to me.

All of the first-week letters were tossed in the round file on the floor next to my desk. Some call this a trash can. Some might feel that you should not throw away fan mail; however, we have received unsolicited requests for money forever, and I always throw those out, no matter who they are from.

This was not encouraging. It was looking like a complete waste of time, but we decided to continue until we had addressed all of the horse mail that was on the floor and heaped over the top edge of the cartons.

We stopped reading and sealed the cartons once we could close them. We put the boxes in storage, and planned to take them out in order to read their contents after we were retired and had time to do so.

I estimate there are about 4,800 letters in those boxes.

Being scientists, Denise and I did an analysis of the approximately 600 letters we did open: 54% were a direct plea for money, 8% were an indirect plea for money, 34% were letters of encouragement and the remaining 4% we classified as "other." We answered only the mail classified in this latter category.

If the statistics hold, then 4% of 4,800 equals 192 letters that I regret not yet answering. I doubt that I'll get to them; maybe my kids will.

Most of the "others" we opened were from children, although two letters contained not only a personal note, but a $5 bill in each. These letters just instructed to buy Chrome some cookies. As Chrome never suffered from lack of cookies, the fivers went into my pocket and we sent thank you notes to the senders.

One reason I still hold on to those boxes of unsolicited mail we received from strangers is that, statistically speaking, 0.333% of the letters will have $5 in them, or potentially a total of about $80. The way the horse market goes, I might just be forced to go through those letters for pizza money some day!

CALIFORNIA CHROME

OWNER - STEVE COBURN & PERRY MARTIN, DAP RACING
TRAINER - ART SHERMAN · JOCKEY - VICTOR ESPINOZA
2014 SECRETARIAT "VOX POPULI" AWARD

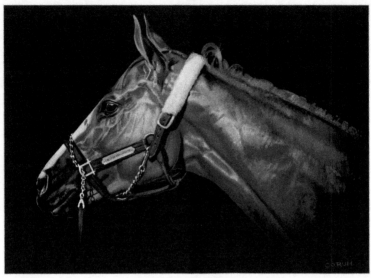

CALIFORNIA CHROME

OWNER - CALIFORNIA CHROME, LLC
TRAINER - ART SHERMAN · JOCKEY - VICTOR ESPINOZA
NORTH AMERICA RACING'S ALL-TIME LEADING EARNER
2016 SECRETARIAT "VOX POPULI" AWARD

19

THE LAST RACE

For a short time, I had a definite passion for the Pegasus World Cup concept, which was announced in early 2016 by Frank Stronach, visionary and founder of The Stronach Group, as a way to generate excitement for his company's newly refurbished Gulfstream Park in Florida.

The horse owners buying into the race were told they would own the race. As the race owners, we would receive the media contract proceeds, a major portion of the wagering takeout and other benefits of ownership. I felt this was the future of racing, moving toward the model of other professional sports. That was not to be, but this passion explains why I gave the media one last chance.

Media Circus

From my home in Wyoming, I gave a reporter a 40-minute telephone interview discussing the Pegasus World Cup prior to the race. I was asked what I liked about the concept, and I gave a long list of things I liked and explained why I liked them. When asked what I didn't like, I had another long list and I explained why I didn't like those features. I even provided suggestions on ways to fix the perceived flaws. I gave a balanced analysis of the Pegasus concept.

When the article came out, my name was featured with a list of things I found wrong with the Pegasus concept. That was it, only un-balanced, cherry-picked quotes. I had said those things, yes, but, taken out of context, I was made to sound like I hated the Pegasus and was whining about it.

I understand that with the decline of horse racing, some media outlets have dropped staff and prefer to purchase independent content not subject to fact-checking. It's just cost-effective. Independent "journalists" now must compete to sell content. The more salacious you can make your content, the easier it is to sell. That is just the unfortunate new way of the world. Throw in the commie bias of these supposedly university-educated fiction writers against anyone successful in the business, and you have a recipe for fake news. It now permeates all media facets.

So now you have my mindset going into the 2017 Eclipse Awards ceremony on January 21.

I didn't attend the first Eclipse Awards ceremony in January 2015, during which California Chrome won awards for Champion 3-Year-Old Colt and Horse of the Year. I probably would not have gone to the second show either, if not for the fact we were already in Miami to attend the Pegasus World Cup program at Gulfstream the following weekend.

Our daughter, Kelly, and her lifelong friend Robin represented us at the Longines World's Best Racehorse Rankings ceremony which was in Paris that year, and conducted the same week as the Eclipse Awards ceremony. They were able to fly from Miami to Paris and back in time for both the Eclipse Awards and the Pegasus. It's good to be young!

During the Eclipse Awards dinner gala, I spoke from the podium twice, but only my Horse of the Year speech is acknowledged by the media. They do not think that my first speech, in which I addressed Chrome's 2016 Champion Older Horse award, is important.

It's worth noting here that the Eclipse Awards are voted upon annually by the members of three groups: the National Thoroughbred Racing Association, "Daily Racing Form" and National Turf Writers and Broadcasters (NTWAB). And it is these groups who join together to host the awards ceremony.

I was not sure that Chrome would win the 2016 Horse of the Year balloting, but I was informed in advance of the ceremony that he had won the Older Horse division. Thus, I spoke about the important things that needed to be said in my first speech. I thanked everyone I could think of: Art, Alan, Victor, Raul and his wife, Florentina, exercise riders Dihigi Gladney and Anna Wells and the Taylors.

Frank Taylor followed me at the podium, and added to the list of contributors Gilberto Terrazas, Taylor Made's stallion manager who had taken great care of Chrome upon his return to the U.S. and respite at the Kentucky farm. In my defense, I had not yet met Gilberto, so his mention had slipped my mind.

If you would like to see and hear the speech that the media will not acknowledge, we keep it posted online at martinracing.us.

The other speech, for Horse of the Year, I am quite proud of also, but we didn't feel the need to post it on our website, as it is all over the internet; you can just Google it. The original speech I wrote for this spot would have been better; it was a kick to the media's gut. I revised it several times in consideration of the audience, down to a mild slap in the face. It was meant as a wake-up call.

Still, it worked its magic, perfectly eliciting the vile, rambling response I was hoping for. They can dish it out, but they can't take it. Hell, they can't even understand it.

These are the people who use the term "horse rescue" instead of "retraining" or "repurposing centers," implying that horses need to be rescued from racing. Then they wonder about why the popularity of horse racing is falling.

The Pegasus World Cup

Denise and I spent a week in Miami, soaking up the sun while seeing the sights.

We watched a wild manatee for about an hour at a local harbor. That manatee never gave us too much to look at; mostly we would spot its snout come up out of the water to catch a breath every five minutes;

occasionally, we would glimpse its tail as it flipped to move locations. After the novelty wore off, we moved on.

We took one day to drive down the Florida Keys, stopping occasionally to eat the local seafood or shop for souvenirs.

We stayed at one of those chic Miami hotels one block away from the beach. There was a great seafood place about a 10-minute walk away. I think we ate there almost every night, then walked back to our hotel along the beach. The whole vacation leading up to the race on January 28 was very relaxing.

Denise and I did not visit the track backside at all during this trip. Knowing this was the last race for Chrome, it was easier to just listen to the on-site reports from Art and Frank. During this week leading up to the Pegasus, Frank told Art, Alan and Victor that the syndicate had voted to give each of them a lifetime breeding right for Chrome's U.S. breeding career.

What this meant was they could breed one of their own mares to Chrome each year he stood in the U.S., or they could take a share of the pool payout. The pool payout is a concept we created for Chrome's syndicate, which I will explain in detail in my next chapter.

The day of the race, we took a long morning walk on the beach. After cleaning up and changing clothes, we got our group together for brunch. After brunch, we enlisted two Uber drivers to take us to the track. We skipped the red carpet BS and entered the Gulfstream clubhouse, where we were shown to our table.

You must remember that this was the inaugural running of the Pegasus World Cup, so the host track officials naturally decided to employ the same abominable style to the clubhouse party décor as was applied to the concrete, colossus Pegasus statue soiling the landscape outside. "Celebrities" were paid to make an appearance, and they were spotted around the clubhouse taking selfies with attendees.

There was a buffet, but this was not reminiscent of the expansive and exotic Dubai World Cup buffet. Denise and I sampled some offerings, but I ultimately chose a hot dog I purchased from a vendor on the track apron.

Scantily clad young women dressed like Vegas showgirls paraded around the clubhouse with their large headwear, stopping at each table and offering to take pictures with those who desired it. This was going to be a long wait to our race, which was carded as the 12th and final event on the day's program.

This Grade 1 race, his finale, would be a hard one for Chrome.

We had drawn the bookends with Arrogate, the newly minted 2016 Champion 3-Year-Old Colt. As our 4-5 main competition, he had drawn the one post on the far inside, where the racing surface was compacted and lightning fast. Chrome, on the other hand, had drawn post 12 on the far outside, where the rarely tilled sand dunes provided very poor footing. In addition, NBC had placed a cameraman just outside of Chrome, ostensibly to film the race start from a unique angle, as distracting to our horse as it was.

When the starting gate opened, Chrome twisted his right knee in the deep sand. The adrenalin boost allowed him to range up on the outside and keep pace with the first flight of runners through the opening half-mile, but his race was essentially over at the beginning. With the pain from his throbbing knee, Chrome slowed; Victor got the message and rode him home evenly.

Arrogate proved his championship mettle with a runaway, 4 3/4-length victory in a track-record time of 1:46.83 for the 1 1/8-mile distance, earning a $7 million paycheck in the process.

Chrome's ninth-place finish, nearly 30 lengths behind the winner, was by far the worst effort of his racing career on paper. But we were not thinking about that anomaly at that moment.

We stayed in the clubhouse sulking over our drinks while the crowds diminished, and we got updates from the barn on our phones. A photo of Chrome's swollen knee was texted to Denise's phone, along with a message of hope.

"The vet thinks it's not too bad. We'll ice it all night and let you know in the morning."

Once the coast was clear, we took an Uber back to our hotel.

The next morning, over coffee, a text message came in with a new picture. Chrome's knee was down to almost normal size, and Frank Taylor was giving us a thumbs up.

We told Frank we would see him and Chrome back in Kentucky. We needed to make a quick trip to California first to attend the CTBA awards ceremony.

Chrome Shines One Last Time

The California Thoroughbred Breeders Association hosted its 2017 annual meeting and awards dinner on February 8 at the posh Langham Huntington hotel in Pasadena. It was another "California Chrome Family Fest," as our champion earned a multitude of awards for himself and his connections.

Chrome was named 2016 California Horse of the Year and Champion Older Male. Lucky Pulpit was recognized as Champion Sire of California-Conceived Foals by Earnings, as well as by Number of Winners. Love the Chase received her second California Broodmare of the Year title. Mr. Coburn and I again were honored as Champion Breeders of California-Foaled Thoroughbreds by Earnings.

Art did not win the Trainer of the Year title again this year, but he did receive a more esteemed honor: He was inducted into the California Thoroughbred Breeders Association Hall of Fame along with trainer Bob Baffert and owner/breeder Don Valpredo.

As if to strike home the sense of finality that was hitting us with the conclusion of Chrome's racing career, we were sorry to hear the news just five days after the awards ceremony that his sire, Lucky Pulpit, had died of an apparent cardiac arrest while covering his first mare of the 2017 breeding season at Harris Farms. He had stood his entire stallion career in California, rather than being whisked away to Kentucky as the sire of a two-time North American Horse of the Year, and his fee was just a modest $7,500 at the time of his death at 16.

It was indeed the end of an era.

20

THE BUSINESS OF BREEDING

California Chrome is a remarkably intelligent horse.

The Pegasus World Cup was held in Florida on January 28, and Chrome was shipped to Taylor Made Farm in Nicholasville, Kentucky the next day. Now a hardy 6-year-old, he was scheduled to begin his breeding career in two weeks—an unprecedented short period of time to adapt to his life as a stallion.

Embarking On A New Career

We were able to visit Chrome soon after he arrived at the farm. He learned his new duties as though he had performed them his whole life.

During our visit, stallion manager Gilberto Terrazas brought Chrome down to the stallion complex viewing ring, where Chrome put on a show for us. He posed majestically, responding to Gilberto's cues without hesitation. His polished leather halter, rich copper-colored coat and manicured, lacquered hooves gleamed in the sun at all angles. Everything screamed that this was a happy, healthy horse; even novice breeders would have been able to appreciate his athletic physique and overall appeal.

We followed Chrome to the breeding shed, where a test mare was waiting for him. We climbed the stairs to the elevated viewing platform and test laboratory. Once we were situated, a large timer was started and the signal was given for Chrome to mount the mare.

The seconds accumulated on the display as Chrome performed his duties. He finished and dismounted the mare. The timer was stopped: 51 seconds! I was going to make a funny comment, but Denise gave me a look that hinted it would not be appreciated.

A microscope slide was used to collect a sample of Chrome's semen. It was brought up to the lab, where a cover plate was applied and the slide was viewed under the microscope. Thousands of sperm were swimming vigorously; I could not identify any that were not moving. The future looked bright!

As Chrome was led back to his stall, we walked to the Taylor Made conference room for a short meeting.

We decided to set Chrome's first year stud fee at $40,000. This meant that he would not have the highest stud fee among all the 2017 first-year stallions; that honor would go to Darley's multiple Grade 1 winner Frosted, whose initial fee was $50,000. Even though Chrome earned almost four times more on the racetrack and Frosted never finished in front of Chrome in any of their races together, Frosted boasts a blue-blooded pedigree, being by Tapit and out of a graded stakes-winning dam. This was the nature of the business; Darley has many high-level mares and client mares who would mostly fill Frosted's book.

The remaining breedings sold to the market could sustain a higher market price due to the low supply.

Our structure for California Chrome's syndicate was: For each of the 50 shares, the shareholder would have two breeding seasons and breed one mare of their own each year. In theory, that would guarantee a 50-mare base for each year. The other breeding would be sold to the market, and the proceeds from that external stud fee would go into an internal pool, with each share receiving 1/50th of the pool.

This is different from many syndicates in which the owner's share, say number 37, is sold and if that mare aborts, the shareholder gets nothing since the contract has a "live foal stands and nurses" guarantee.

I think the pool payout method is much better, having all shareholders share the risk.

For the record, California Chrome covered 145 mares in 2017, a solid figure for a young, Kentucky-based stallion. Our year one pool payout was more than $38,000 per share.

The last thing we reviewed with Taylor Made during that early 2017 visit was the ongoing discussions for Chrome to shuttle during the Southern Hemisphere breeding seasons to Oussama Aboughazale's Haras Sumaya Stud near Santiago, Chile. A trip to Australia to market Chrome for a shuttle season there did not prove fruitful, so a three-year deal was brokered by Chile's Sullivan Bloodstock in conjunction with Taylor Made Bloodstock.

Marshall Taylor, Duncan Taylor's son who was taking on a larger role within his family's Thoroughbred business at the time, had met Sullivan Bloodstock partners Juan Pablo Sullivan and Cristian Benavente during the time he worked in Chile.

Everything just came together as an opportunity to improve California Chrome's chances of becoming a successful sire.

The decision to shuttle was not taken lightly. Ben and Duncan Taylor flew to Chile to visit several potential farms and did an extensive amount of due diligence, evaluating whether there was a situation that would meet a very high set of standards established by Rood & Riddle's Dr. Charlie Scoggin and Dr. Rolf Embertson, our entire advisory team and our shareholders. The health and safety of California Chrome was paramount, so the quality of facilities, experience of staff and reputation of the farm were very important factors to be considered.

We decided that Taylor Made personnel would accompany California Chrome during his time at Sumaya Stud to assure our established protocols would be followed. They would have the assistance of two on-site veterinarians at Sumaya Stud, led by Dr. Carolina Rojas, who would monitor Chrome's physical condition and attitude continuously.

Our syndicate would receive $1 million for each shuttle season, equaling $20,000 per share, with Sumaya picking up all expenses on the horse.

Despite owning 15 shares, Denise and I only sent eight mares to Chrome in Kentucky that first year. We gave our other seven breeding seasons away as gifts.

John Harris and four key employees of Harris Farms were each given one slot in appreciation of their help in bringing Chrome into the world. John did provide a mare for Chrome, while the others took the pool payout.

The other two gifts were to family members, who also took the pool payout.

Denise and I did not yet have the quantity or quality of broodmares available to pull our weight that first season, but Chrome still attracted a very respectable, full book, thanks to his syndicate members and outside breeders.

He was a novel stallion at an affordable price who breeders were willing to give a shot. The big question was how long that novelty would last.

Expanding To Standardbreds

Standardbred breeder Mike Gulotta of Deo Volente Farms in New Jersey took a share in California Chrome and offered Denise and I a share of his 2014 Hambletonian winner, Trixton, through Taylor Made. We accepted, and became part owners of the two horses who won the 3-year-old championship races in their respective sports in 2014. Kind of cool, I think.

We partnered with Mike on two Standardbred mares, and have been partners ever since, each year offering one or two yearlings for sale at the auctions for that breed. Our interest in the sport of harness racing continued to expand in subsequent years.

Since we bought in, Trixton moved to Ontario, Canada. We've purchased a mare named Girl Talk who will be bred to him in 2022. Our other two Standardbred mares will remain in New Jersey. The New Jersey-breds will go to auction and we will race the horses by Trixton.

Sumaya Stud

Denise and I liked to maintain contact with all our horses, but as the first horse we had ever bred, Junior was always very special to us.

Once the deal with Sumaya Stud was complete, we started making plans to visit his new winter home. Chrome had taken us to the Middle East and to Europe; now he was taking us to South America. Kelly, always the adventurer, wanted to go with us, so we booked three tickets for an October 2017 trip to Santiago, Chile. We would spend a leisurely two weeks in that country to get the full experience.

After a few days in Chile acclimating to the culture, we planned to drive to Sumaya Stud. Apparently, our downtown hotel had a heliport on the roof, because, before we left, we were called by Mr. Aboughazale, the farm's owner, who kindly offered to send his helicopter to shuttle us to the farm since the roads outside the city were quite rough. I politely declined, saying we wanted to experience the drive in the country. I didn't mention what a crash investigator from Canada had once told me, "Helicopters are 25,000 spare parts flying in formation!"

Having made their fortune in agriculture, the Aboughazale family is a majority shareholder of the fresh produce division of Del Monte Fruit Company. Oussama Aboughazale, a native of Jerusalem who now lives in Chile, campaigns a string of Thoroughbreds in North America as Sumaya U.S. Stable; his North American breeding interests are based at the former Belvedere Farm in Kentucky. His mother, Sumaya, inspired the names of both his racing stable and his farm in Chile.

We made it out to the gated farm in Pirque, south of Santiago, about mid-morning, and were met by two guard dogs at the main gate. They continued barking at us as we spoke into the intercom to introduce ourselves. Dr. Rojas came to meet us at the gate and took us on a tour of the facility.

The pinnacle of the tour was, of course, California Chrome himself. He was out in his private paddock, looking like the chiseled champion that he was. We met Chrome's handler and full-time companion for his time in Chile, Sebastian Angelillo. Sebastian showed us Chrome's large stall, then his own apartment right next door, which had a closed-circuit video feed from Chrome's stall.

Just as our tour was ending, Oussama had walked down from the farmhouse to meet us. We introduced ourselves and discussed Chrome and his possibilities in Chile. Then we were invited for lunch up at the house, which we happily accepted. Oussama is a very pleasant and outgoing man who made for delightful company.

His cook was a middle-aged, local woman who had prepared multiple dishes inspired by the regional culture. We were joined for lunch by his helicopter pilot, Sebastian and Carolina. We ate in the dining room, and I sampled a bit of everything while the conversation at the table revolved around Oussama's early days in Chile, and then to the horse farm and his future plans.

Upon the completion of lunch, we moved outside to the covered garden patio, where we were served a local fruit juice-based energy drink, hot coffee and an assortment of cakes and cookies. Here, the conversation turned to the Martins for the next few hours.

We were offered, and accepted, a tour of the helicopter by the pilot. It was an executive model, in which the passengers sit in a noise-reduced compartment behind the pilot seats. Two facing white leather couches were draped by leather upholstered doors with triple-pane windows. Very nice. We said our goodbyes to everyone, exchanged business cards, then made our way back to Santiago.

Our hotel was a city block away from a large mall which we visited frequently. It seemed every other morning I would walk down to the Starbucks to purchase a venti mocha in my perfect Starbucks Spanish. I would sit in the courtyard watching passersby while the girls completed their showers back at the hotel.

One morning, I got an urgent call from Denise.

"Hurry back," she pleaded. "Kelly fell on the wet bathroom tile and broke her ankle!"

Kelly had broken her ankle on a previous occasion. I can't go into details, but it had something to do with dancing on an elevated platform in high heels and falling off.

I immediately assumed it was the ankle she had broken previously, which had a replacement tendon. When I got back to the hotel, I found out it was the other ankle.

Denise and I helped Kelly to the rental car, and we used Denise's phone GPS to locate the local hospital. The GPS worked perfectly, so I dropped the girls off at the emergency entrance, then I went to park the car. It took me 15 minutes to find a spot to park, then another 10 minutes to find my way back to the emergency entrance.

When I got inside, I found that Kelly had already been admitted. The lady at the desk spoke English and gave me directions to the orthopedics department, where Kelly had been directed. When I got there, I found Denise sitting outside the department. She told me that Kelly had been x-rayed, but the orthopedist needed higher contrast, so she was getting an MRI.

Denise and I waited in the hospital's Starbucks café while Kelly discussed the results of her tests with an orthopedist who spoke English. When our daughter was ready to check out, they sent a lady to find us, and we went to the out-processing center. Kelly was waiting there.

We were led to a desk to review findings and pay our bill. There was a two-page list of charges which we went through: Emergency Admitting, CT scan, MRI, ankle wrap and brace, crutches, consultation with an English-speaking doctor and prescription pain medication. All done in less than two hours for a grand total of $357 U.S. I was impressed. If I ever need medical care, I may travel to Chile again.

During our time in South America, we also spent two days with Sullivan Bloodstock's partners, Juan Pablo and Cristian. On the first day, they escorted us to several farms, where we viewed multiple stallions, broodmares and yearlings. The first evening, we went to Cristian's home for dinner. We met his lovely wife and kids and, after dinner, spent hours out on the patio enjoying their company.

The next day, we went to Valparaiso Sporting Club, which is a Thoroughbred racecourse in Viña del Mar, located in the Valparaiso Region of Chile near the Pacific Coast. We stopped to get lunch on the way at a very good steakhouse. While we were at the track, it was fun to imagine Chrome's Chilean-bred foals possibly racing there someday.

California Chrome attracted top-quality mares during his first two Southern Hemisphere shuttling stints at Haras Sumaya Stud, with his book in Chile hovering just above 100 mares each year. We enjoyed our visit to that country, and the wonderful hospitality that was shown to us, as well as to our horse. But when Chrome appeared weary after returning to the U.S. from his second shuttle season in 2018, we decided to pull the plug, as per our option.

The results of Chrome's time spent in Chile have been impressive to date. At the time of this writing in mid-December 2021, he is already represented by 31 winners—including three stakes winners—from his initial Chilean foal crop. Not surprisingly, he ranks at the top of his class as the leading first-crop sire in that country by number of winners and by 2021 progeny earnings.

Haras Sumaya posts regular updates and photos of their California Chrome homebreds on their Facebook page, if you would like to follow along on their progress.

We have every hope that his South American-sired offspring will continue to add to Chrome's legacy.

The Starbucks Connection

I mentioned above spending time at two different Starbucks locations in Santiago, Chile. With more than 33,000 stores located across the world, this wildly popular coffeehouse chain offers a sense of familiarity and comfort for frequent travelers such as myself, no matter their destination. For our family, though, it offers even more.

Our daughter, Kelly, has worked as a Starbucks barista since she was 19 years old. With her friendly, engaging personality, she is perfectly suited for her job interfacing with the public on a daily basis. Based in of one of the company's Northern California locations, she is a loyal and dedicated member of the Starbucks workforce.

During California Chrome's unprecedented racing career, Kelly was fortunate to have understanding supervisors who allowed her flexibility in her schedule, so she could travel with us to many events throughout California, the U.S. and even to other continents. I believe these experiences of learning and briefly living in other cultures have helped our daughter become a more well-rounded individual and, undoubtedly, a better employee, and I am grateful for that.

If you follow our naming patterns for our horses, you'll notice a lot of Starbucks references. For example, Cold Brew Kelly and Majestic Blend, both winners out of our stakes-placed Trippi mare Decennial.

Passion Tango is the name of a Starbucks tea flavor, as well as our 2020 California Chrome homebred filly out of Berryessa (Ire), a 2014 Dandy Man (Ire) mare who won under our Martin Racing silks for trainer Rae Guest in England and, after we imported her to the U.S. in 2018, for trainer Steve Sherman in California.

Passion Tango is being broke in the U.S., but she will eventually ship to Rae's training yard in Newmarket. We are hoping she will find the success there that Chrome could not.

Perry Jr.

As I've been writing this story, I noticed that our son, Perry Jr., does not get a lot of attention. This is because he is just not that into horses and only rarely accompanies us to the Chrome events. One reason for this is his aversion to flying, which I talked about earlier. However, he can overcome this aversion if the travel destination is appealing enough.

Perry Jr. did accompany the family on a salmon fishing trip to Bob's Cabin in Soldotna, Alaska. He also made Chrome-related trips when he did not have to fly.

I mentioned that he went to the 2014 Kentucky Derby. He bought himself a new suit to wear to the Derby, which I thought was a bit strange. He had been coordinating the trip with his cousin Andrew. If you ever see the iconic Kentucky Derby 140 winner's circle photo, the two guys dressed like the Blues Brothers are PJ and Andrew.

I know it isn't a fear of horses. PJ has traveled with us to horse farms and will jump the fence to mingle with and pet the horses. Horses can sense fear and get nervous if a person displays anxiety, but PJ is fearless. Denise always said he should have been a veterinarian.

I can only think of one possible story that explains his aversion.

One time when PJ was about 8 years old, Kelly and Denise had a girls' night out. I don't remember what they were doing, but I do know PJ wanted no part of it. Thus, we would have a boys' night out.

I asked him what he wanted to do, and his reply was, "I don't know."

I suggested bowling and he shook his head no.

He asked me what I wanted to do, so I told him to grab his jacket and follow me. We jumped in the truck and started toward Sacramento.

The whole trip, he kept asking, "Where are we going?"

I kept saying, "You'll see!"

As we arrived at Cal Expo, I heard a muffled, "Oh."

He had been here before maybe four or five times, and had played in the grassy area at the top of the stretch while either Denise or I watched him.

On this occasion, we went inside, purchased a program and found our spot to watch the races. We decided on the Cal Expo theater, which displayed the harness races on a large, elevated screen, below which there was a row of automated betting terminals. The padded seats were comfortable, the view unobscured and food services, betting and bathrooms were only a few steps away. I let PJ review the program while I went to get us some hot dogs, garlic fries and sodas.

I returned with the food and PJ dug right in. I took the opportunity to borrow the program back and handicap the first couple races before eating. After we finished eating and had settled in, the business of betting was at hand.

At his young age, PJ could not legally place any bets himself, so I would do it for him. I told him I would bet $2 for him on whichever horse he liked.

The first race, he decided to bet along with Dad, so I purchased a separate $2 ticket on my selection that he could hold in his hand. Our first wager hit, paying $6.

The second race, PJ decided to go along with Dad again, so when I returned from the machines, I handed him a $4 voucher and a $2 win ticket. He looked at them, then up at me and asked, "Our horse paid $6; why is the voucher only for $4?"

I told him that the other $2 was in his win ticket and that he should not expect me to advance him more money every race while he was ahead. He thought that was reasonable, so we focused on the upcoming race. Dad's pick did not do so well in the second race, so PJ decided to study up in order to make his own selection in race three.

I had already made my selection in advance and had circled the post number on the program, so I was ready when PJ was and could afford to sit quietly. He was studying intently, and I remember thinking, "If he would only study that hard in school."

I was keeping an eye on the betting machines. They were all occupied, with several having more than one person in line, so with four minutes to post, I nudged PJ and asked him for a selection. He decided on number four and handed me his voucher.

I walked down to the row of betting machines and waited behind one person. As the announcer called two minutes to post, I continued waiting. Each of the machines now had a small line of people waiting. The person in front of me seemed frozen in the light of the terminal, no movement, as the announcer declared one minute to post.

I was getting nervous that I would be frozen out. Then I heard PJ calling, "Dad, Dad!"

I looked back and he was waving and calling out, "Six, six."

Just then, the guy in front of me finally finished and moved away from the terminal. I quicky moved in and made the bets my son and I had agreed on earlier. As I finished up, the announcer called out, "The starter calls the field."

I walked back up to PJ, sat next to him and handed him his tickets.

PJ looked at the voucher and the $2 win ticket on number four. He said, "But I wanted you to bet the six horse for me?"

I said, "You told me number four."

He said, "Yeah, but I wanted to change to the six. Didn't you hear me yelling?"

I told him I did hear him yelling, but I wasn't sure exactly what he was talking about and I needed to act quickly while it was my turn at the terminal. I told him that if there is a race delay, I can change the bet, but the horses were already pacing toward the start.

We sat back and watched.

The race ended up being a photo finish between the four and the six, with the six-horse prevailing at 60-1! PJ was devastated. I felt a bit sick myself.

I tried to console him with stories of all the big ones I had missed for various reasons. All my stories of shoulda, woulda, coulda. Nothing I could say would make him feel better. He didn't want to bet anymore and I was a bit tired, so we hit the road for the 45-minute drive back home.

What could have been a very good boys' night out with a father/son story that would be told for years to come was now just a disappointing trip to Sacramento.

Hopefully the balance of the universe has now been restored.

Cash Flow

Through our fast-growing Martin Racing, Denise and I continued to purchase mares privately and at auctions as we headed toward the 2018 breeding season in North America. Some of the fillies we had bred became broodmare prospects for Chrome as well. With the help of two foal share mares, we were able to pull our weight by providing 15 mares in total for Chrome's second year in the breeding shed.

For year two, the California Chrome LLC syndicate maintained his advertised stud fee at $40,000. As is common in our industry, his appeal as a new stallion began to fade a bit, leading to 133 mares on his second-year dance card—still a respectable number, albeit lower than during his inaugural year of availability.

The second year bump down is due, in part, to the commercial market waiting to see what a stallion's foals look like.

Chrome's very first foals began to hit the ground in January 2018, with more and more coming as the months advanced. There were 98 total first-year foals, and they were all over the board, looks-wise. I would guess that a little more than half were chestnuts with the familiar chrome markings similar to dad. The other half resembled the mares.

Later in the year, the national market reacted somewhat positively to Chrome's first-crop weanlings who sold at auction. From eight offered, seven sold for an average price of $116,714 and a median of $130,000. Not too shabby; still, no sale-toppers. Denise and I did not offer any weanlings at public auction, electing instead to wait for the 2019 yearling sales to unveil our Chrome babies.

Many of the mares we had purchased for Chrome in 2016 foaled in 2017, and those resulting foals were now yearlings in 2018. We had been breed-to-race people, but with so many mares, we had to adopt a breed-to-sell program. We decided to offer all of our yearlings on the market, setting fair reserves in the process. If the market would not pay a fair price, we would keep the yearling and hope to race him or her ourselves.

One of our better Martin Racing yearlings in 2018 was an Uncle Mo colt out of our mare Roughing, a daughter of Eskendereya out of the excellent producer Playcaller whom we had purchased for $500,000 during the 2016 Keeneland November sale. We entered him in the 2018 Keeneland September Yearling Sale and set a reserve of $349,000, so he would sell if someone bid to $350,000. The bidding stopped at $335,000, so he was ours to keep and race.

We named him Mo Mosa. Kelly likes mimosas, the cocktail drink that mixes champagne with orange juice. We were thinking that Uncle Mo was kind of a champagne stallion. Later on, we also decided to keep Mo Mosa's 2020 California Chrome half-brother out of Roughing. We named him Beer Mosa because California Chrome is kind of a beer stallion, at least in the U.S.

The horse business was still going well for us, with California Chrome driving the revenue. With fewer mares bred, the pool payout did drop some, but, overall, money was coming in. We would also receive the Southern Hemisphere breeding funds, and we did sell some yearlings. Even with increased expenses for the additional mares and having to train and race more horses, we had positive cash flow.

California-Bred Foal Share Program

As Chrome's largest shareholders, Denise and I were in constant communication with Taylor Made and had regular input regarding his management. Taylor Made advised us that year three of his stallion career would be the toughest in terms of attracting quality mares, and in maintaining his book size. This is the nature of the stallion business in general; the situation was not specific to Chrome.

Chrome's fee for each of his first two years at stud was $40,000. In our discussions about setting his 2019 fee, I suggested to Taylor Made that we should give his syndicate members an additional season for each one they would use for breeding to him.

In addition to reducing his 2019 fee to $35,000 as an incentive to outside mare owners, Taylor Made adopted my bonus season idea and announced the news to syndicate members in advance of the 2018 fall mixed sales, allowing everyone plenty of time to purchase additional mares for the extra seasons if they so wished.

But that's where Denise and I ran into a problem of our own. We had already acquired mares to use all 15 of our shares in Chrome, but now we suddenly had 15 more seasons to him, and we needed quality broodmares to fill those spots. We decided to reach back to our Golden State roots to develop a unique program that would work for the California market, and to bring a little of Chrome's magic touch to his home state.

Denise and I were originally drawn into breeding by the benefits offered through the California-Bred Incentive Award Program administered by the CTBA, the very program that we used to produce California Chrome. We decided to base our expanded 2019 breeding strategy on that same proven path. The result was our California Chrome Foal Share Program, which we instituted for the 2019 breeding season in hopes of attracting top mares through various incentives.

In this invitation-only program, each mare that we accepted through a nomination process was bred to California Chrome in Kentucky in 2019, dropped her 2020 Chrome foal in California, then was subsequently bred back to a California stallion of the owner's choice in 2020 in order to satisfy the state's breed-back rule and qualify her 2020 Chrome foal to become a registered California-bred, with Denise and me listed as co-breeders of the Chrome foal alongside the mare owner. In fairness to ourselves as the stallion season providers, as well as to the mare owners who undertook the bulk of expenses in raising the Chrome foals, we created several financial incentives for the program, including waiving his $35,000 fee for accepted mares and splitting evenly any transportation costs to ship the mares to Kentucky and then to California for foaling.

The end goal of the program was to sell these California-bred California Chrome foals of 2020 as either weanlings or yearlings at any West Coast auction, with each mare owner choosing the sale, consignor and reserve price that best adhered to their own business model.

Sale proceeds were used to reimburse mare owners for their expenses in consigning their foals to auction, as well as any California-bred or Breeders' Cup registration fees. After all sale commissions were paid from any net proceeds, the mare owner was also entitled to the first $4,000 from the sale of a weanling or the first $9,500 from the sale of a yearling. Any remaining proceeds were split 50/50 between the mare owner and Martin Racing.

Conversely, if a foal did not meet its reserve or otherwise failed to sell, the mare owner would be responsible for all foal and mare expenses, as in a normal foal share agreement. From that point forward, we would split costs on the foal 50/50.

Our thought process was that, beyond the sales ring, the likelihood of a good mare producing a good runner would provide us with California breeders' awards down the line to help offset our costs of the incentives we provided to mare owners in the foal share program.

After we developed our foal share initiative during the fall months of 2018, the California-based bloodstock consultant Lisa Groothedde started working to recruit high-quality West Coast mares to the program. We were overwhelmed with the positive response from breeders.

Lisa enlisted 17 mares in our inaugural California Chrome Foal Share Program, nearly each of whom was a stakes winner, stakes producer or stakes-placed winner. This impressive group comprised the earners of a combined $2.5 million whose foals to race had banked more than $5 million collectively at the time.

Through Lisa's efforts, we were excited to partner with many new friends in California, Arizona, Washington, Oregon and Nevada to produce and sell California-bred offspring of the richest California-bred runner in history. We also received many rewarding cards and comments from the participants.

In 2019, Chrome was bred to 143 mares overall, with Denise and I responsible for 41 of them using our own mares or foal share mares. We actually needed to purchase additional shares, but were able to do so at a discount.

This process was very expensive and time-consuming for us, but we wanted to give Chrome every chance we possibly could to make it as a stallion. We were going to leave nothing on the table.

Cottage Industry

Concurrent with the business of breeding, there seemed to be no end to Chrome's popularity among racing fans, even well after his retirement.

In recognition of his status as a cultural phenomenon, Taylor Made held regular tours and fan events centered around the farm's most famous resident, and sold branded California Chrome merchandise in its online gift shop. We're talking everything from polo shirts, photos and calendars to blankets, stickers and baby bibs.

Chrome was also honored with his own Breyer horse model, which, as of 2021, retails for $50 on Taylor Made's website.

Breyer offers a paltry 2.5% commission to the owner on sales of its model horse collectibles, so I never signed Chrome up while he was racing. After he was retired, we signed him up for the program and sold the model through the Taylor Made store, receiving 55% of the sale price for each unit sold.

Having Some Fun Along The Way

In 2014, both Denise and I stopped taking paychecks from Martin Testing Labs. I would have a notebook computer with me and would try to stay on top of the lab quotes for services while we were traveling with Chrome. When we were home, we were in the lab every day, though most of that time was spent catching up, rather than getting out with customers to sell services. Still, the momentum from my earlier sales efforts was enough to keep the lab afloat through the California Chrome years.

It certainly didn't help that I would take on new projects which would also soak up large amounts of my time.

For example, during the Dumb Ass Partners days, I developed DAP Hot Sauce. I believed that the hats, shirts and other Chrome merchandise would eventually fade, so I was looking for something that would generate continuous revenue long after Chrome was retired.

I worked with a commercial kitchen to develop the sauce, and I thought it was an exceptional product. It was not vinegary like other hot sauces, but instead had a distinct pepper flavor. Yes, there was some heat from the Scotch bonnet peppers, but it was very manageable. I also spent a lot of time with a graphic designer to get the label for the bottles perfect. Our catch phrase was, "A little DAP will do ya!"

Television host Ken Rudulph would always ask me for more hot sauce every time I saw him, so you know it must have been good, because Ken is a hot sauce expert!

We never recovered the production costs for DAP Hot Sauce, as we ended up giving most of the product away. I didn't have time to promote the lab, let alone develop a hot sauce business. I am slowly eating through the six cases I have left while I anguish over not hiring a promotion manager.

Another side project was less publicized than the hot sauce, but no less fun to work on.

During the California Chrome LLC years, I worked with a company that sells mascot costumes to develop a California Chrome mascot costume.

The company had a standard horse mascot costume, but it was not offered in chestnut. I found an appropriate color that they offered with a cow costume so, for a small additional fee, they were able to use that model to sew a custom horse costume.

The four white feet and large white blaze (with freckle) were all designed into the costume. For whatever reason, Chrome was not naked, but wore a baseball jersey with his name on the back.

We paid young adults some very good money to wear the costume at events. If I would have fit into it, I probably would have worn it, because it looked like great fun!

Chrome, the mascot, only appeared at two races and a couple of California Chrome LLC dinner functions. Usually we provided the mascot with "Chrome Buttons" to hand out at the races. This was mostly designed for kids, but the mascot would never refuse any adult Chromies who just had to have the buttons.

The costume was stored in a heavy-duty garbage bag which unfortunately disappeared after being left in a racetrack bathroom for a short time. It was either stolen or mistaken for garbage and thrown away.

It was fun while it lasted, but I wasn't about to replace the costume, even though Taylor Made was nice enough to reimburse me for its loss from LLC funds.

First Yearlings Sell

For me, the most fascinating aspect of yearling sale season is the introduction of youngsters by first-crop sires to the market.

The fall of 2019 was Chrome's first time at the yearling sales, and we would get our first look at how the Thoroughbred commercial market would accept him as a sire. If the market was warm to him, commercial breeders would then flock to him, making our business a lot easier. If cold to him, the reverse was true.

The highest price paid in the sales ring for a Martin Racing yearling by California Chrome was $180,000 for a very nicely put together dark bay filly who was the first foal out of the Grade 1-placed stakes winner Right There, by Eskendereya. She was purchased during the 2019 Keeneland September Yearling Sale by leading Japanese owner and breeder Teruya Yoshida of Shadai Farm. Subsequently named Cal Fragrance, she has won three races as a 3-year-old in that country, as of this writing.

Let me point out that the sales price for this filly was 4 1/2 times Chrome's advertised stud fee. This means that, after raising the filly, we made about 2 1/2 times what we put in. Positive cash flow for sure, but far from a home run. This did not get us excited, and it certainly would not get commercial breeders excited.

Again, this was our best-performing yearling in the sales ring, so you can be sure the others also did not get us excited.

Overall, 45 of California Chrome's first-crop yearlings sold in 2019 for an average price of $85,756 and a median of $52,000. He did achieve a single-day session-topping colt at Keeneland September, but only at $85,000 on the 11th day of the marathon sale.

In the case of our $180,000 filly, her buyer may have recognized that her third dam produced the North American Hall of Fame champion Silver Charm. Similar to California Chrome, Silver Charm was a regionally bred runner who was able to defeat international competition in the 1998 Dubai World Cup after capturing both the Kentucky Derby and Preakness Stakes. As a stallion, the Florida-bred originally stood in Kentucky before he was purchased by Japanese interests and relocated to stand in that country, where he remained for several years until he was pensioned and returned to the U.S. in 2014.

This sincere interest in Chrome from the Far East may have foretold what was to happen next.

9 PHOTOS FROM A MAGICAL DAY IN SEPTEMBER 2019

A MAGICAL DAY IN SEPTEMBER 2019 #1
JennyPhoto

A MAGICAL DAY IN SEPTEMBER 2019 #2
JennyPhoto

A MAGICAL DAY IN SEPTEMBER 2019 #3
JennyPhoto

A MAGICAL DAY IN SEPTEMBER 2019 #4
JennyPhoto

A MAGICAL DAY IN SEPTEMBER 2019 #5
JennyPhoto

A MAGICAL DAY IN SEPTEMBER 2019 #6
JennyPhoto

A MAGICAL DAY IN SEPTEMBER 2019 #7
JennyPhoto

A MAGICAL DAY IN SEPTEMBER 2019 #8
JennyPhoto

A MAGICAL DAY IN SEPTEMBER 2019 #9
JennyPhoto

21

SELLING TO JAPAN

In year three of California Chrome's stallion career, Denise and I had fought like hell to keep Chrome's stud fee at $40,000. We felt that we had shown through the early bookings in our foal share program that regional breeders were amicable to sending Chrome their best mares in a foal sharing scenario. If his advertised fee was to drop too steeply, the value just would not be there.

We ended up with a minor fee reduction to $35,000 for 2019, which was sufficient for us to close on many mares. He ended up covering a book of 143—a very respectable number that was actually an increase of 10 mares compared to his 2018 book.

Back To The Negotiation Table

As Chrome's syndicate members again collaborated during the fall of 2019 to discuss strategies for the 2020 breeding season, Denise and I found ourselves fighting again to hold the line for year four.

We argued that Taylor Made could always offer discounts to achieve any price point needed to fill Chrome's book. We were pre-selling foal shares through our Martin Racing program before the 2020 stud fee announcement, and making good inroads. We were hopeful this would impress Taylor Made and help bring them over to our side of the fence.

In return, Taylor Made pointed out the poor yearling sale results from the 2019 Keeneland September Yearling Sale, during which 30 colts and fillies from California Chrome's initial foal crop sold for an average price of $92,833 and a median price of $57,500. As mentioned earlier, four of his six top-selling individuals, priced from $260,000 to $180,000, were purchased by Japanese interests. But U.S. commercial breeders, who had supported Chrome with healthy book sizes during his first three breeding seasons, would be a tough sell going forward.

Taylor Made felt that if we really dropped Chrome's stud fee for 2020 to, say, $15,000, that would represent real value based on sales results, as a commercial breeder might get a 20-time return with his or her Chrome yearling in 2022.

Believe me, we went back and forth for several days. We told them they could offer big discounts to target commercial breeders if they thought they could make the sale. We felt we could get the job done by attracting regional breeders through foal sharing. Our first foal share effort was focused on the West Coast. If we targeted additional regions, I was sure it would work.

I believe we settled on an announced 2020 stud fee of $30,000. Another good compromise. Taylor Made was authorized to offer 50% discounts to preferred customers, and their marketing efforts began to trickle out.

Soon after our discussions, I got a call from Taylor Made to inform me that a bloodstock agent representing Japanese interests had made an offer to buy Chrome. When told the amount, I paused, then said, "Tell them that is a very flattering offer, but it's not enough."

Before ending the call, the question arose as to what would be enough? Perry, what is everything you would want? I laid it out, and we hung up. I think it was two days later before the phone rang again.

What do you do when someone offers you everything you want to make a deal happen? I said yes.

Making Plans For Japan

Back when I was buying mares for California Chrome during the 2016 Keeneland November sale, I was quoted as saying, "I hope and expect that he's going to displace **Tapit** as the top United States sire!"

Obviously, with only three North American seasons at stud, that would now be a stretch. With his change in jurisdiction, I've made a change in my expectations: I now hope and expect that California Chrome will top the world rankings for sires by progeny earnings!

Why not? As of this writing in December 2021, nine of the top 10 international sires are, or have been, based in Japan. Leading the list with more than $72 million in international earnings this year is the late Deep Impact (Jpn). America's only representative among the top 10 is Into Mischief, whose nearly $25 million in 2021 international progeny earnings rank him fifth.

The offspring of Japan-based stallions race mostly in Japan, where purse levels are significantly higher than in the U.S. Although Japan has far fewer people than the United States, they bet four times as much money on the races each year. Since that country uses a betting-driven purse schedule like the U.S., the purses are much higher than they are here.

This purse disparity is one reason I was happy to see our horse move there as a stallion. When Chrome's Japan-conceived progeny hit the tracks in that country in 2023, he should quickly move up the international sire rankings. For Martin Racing, doing business in a healthy business environment will also help our bottom line.

Part of the "everything we wanted" package that we required through the syndicate in order to approve the sale of California Chrome to Japan was five lifetime breeding rights to him at his new home: Arrow Stud in Hokkaido. As a result, Denise and I exported five of our "A" team mares to Japan for him in two shipments, with a plan to breed to sell, or to race if the market in that country valued our horses too low.

Our first shipment was our top four open mares, as the Japanese import regulations charged a high tax on imported pregnant mares.

Composing the initial group of mares we exported for Chrome prior to the 2020 breeding season were our dual Grade 1-placed Grade 3 winner Wildcat Lily, our multiple stakes winner Lake Ponchatrain and two mares with strong pedigree ties to Japan: Evasion, a daughter of Japan's former stallion Empire Maker out of 1995 Champion Older Mare Inside Information, and the Grade 1-placed stakes winner Right There, a daughter of the Japan-based stallion Eskendereya out of a half-sister to U.S. Hall of Famer and longtime Japan sire Silver Charm.

The move for Right There was especially on target: her first foal, Cal Fragrance, is the California Chrome filly whom we bred and sold as a yearling for $180,000 to Shadai Farm, as I mentioned earlier. Cal Fragrance has won or placed in six of her 11 starts in Japan to date at 3.

We were going to purchase another mare in Japan to fulfill our fifth breeding right, but before we could do that, the regulations changed and the tax on pregnant mares was reduced. So, we decided to make a second shipment, sending our stakes-placed winner Decennial, who was already pregnant to Chrome.

Decennial foaled a beautiful chestnut colt in April 2020—the first Japanese-bred Thoroughbred for Martin Racing. We liked him so much that we decided right off that we would keep him and race him in Japan. As of this writing, he is just going into training to be broke and to get his early lessons.

He has been named "Komorebi no Omoide." Do you know how when you walk in the forest and look up to see the sunlight coming through the trees? The Japanese have a word for that: "Komorebi." Denise always loved that word, but the name was taken. However, the Japan Racing Association approved the longer name we submitted, which translates as: A Remembrance of Komorebi. This colt should start racing in 2022, and our expectations are high.

We will continue to support Chrome in Japan with five Martin Racing mares, upgrading our broodmare band when we can. The U.S. Grade 1 winner Discreet Cat, by Forestry, preceded Chrome to Japan as a sire and has four crops on the ground in that country. This is a strong pedigree match for Chrome, so we will add some of his good daughters to our Japan holdings when they become available.

When our Japan-bred California Chrome foals go to auction in that country as yearlings, we will set fair reserves for them; if any reserves are not met, we will race those horses ourselves. Our main goal is to help Chrome become the number one sire in Japan and, thus, number one in the world. These are by far our grandest plans.

I started the process of becoming a licensed racehorse owner in Japan early on. Good thing I did, because, as of this writing in late 2021, I am still filing paperwork, more than eight months after my first application.

It is very difficult as an outsider to become a licensed owner in Japan, but the rewards can be great. After all, in America, horse racing is the sport of kings. In Japan, horse racing is the king of sports!

Launching In Louisiana

After our syndicate inked the deal to sell Chrome to the JS Company of Japan, Denise and I needed to make a quick pivot with many of our horse business plans.

One option would be a quick dispersal at a sale. We chose another route.

One day in late 2019, as we were visiting Daehling Ranch, a Thoroughbred breeding farm in Elk Grove, California, where we keep many of our pensioned horses, it was mentioned that the owner of the farm's veteran stallion Peppered Cat wanted to sell the graded stakes-siring grandson of Storm Cat to raise funds in order to help send his daughter to college.

At the time, we had a handsome, homebred Peppered Cat 2-year-old named Major Wager who had impressed us in his early training. And, on top of that, I had always thought Peppered Cat had punched above his weight despite being a lightly supported California sire, with average earnings per starter of more than $50,000 and a significant percentage of black-type runners from his limited opportunities.

Denise and I made the deal to purchase Peppered Cat at an equitable price that would give us a ready-made option to breed back our Kentucky-based mares who had been covered by California Chrome, and to extend Martin Racing to another regional program, which we were initially hoping to do with a planned expansion of our foal share program in 2020. Instead of California, however, we sent Peppered Cat to Clear Creek Stud in Louisiana, where the state's breeding incentives were growing, unlike back in California.

We decided to ship our "C" team of mares to Clear Creek to support our new acquisition, who turned 20 in 2020—a relatively advanced age for a breeding stallion. Our goal for Peppered Cat was rather humble: We hoped to breed enough mares so that his Louisiana offspring would generate enough stallion awards to fund Peppered Cat's pension.

In 2021, our decision to acquire Peppered Cat resulted in a fine crop of 9 Martin Racing Louisiana-bred foals, some of which we have already sold and some of which we will retain for racing.

Blood Brothers

California Chrome's only full brother, Faversham, is a homebred for Martin Racing. As such, we tried to follow in his big brother's footsteps when it came to his racing career.

Chrome was born in February 2011 and started his racing career in April 2013, as an early 2-year-old. Faversham was born in April 2015 and was scheduled to debut in June 2017, also as an early 2-year-old. He was entered in a maiden special weight race for California-breds at Santa Anita, but a tendon tear forced us to scratch. That soft-tissue injury would continue to plague him throughout his career.

Faversham was rested and given Platelet Rich Plasma treatments in order to recover, which meant he could not start in a race until mid-January of his 3-year-old season. Platelet Rich Plasma is used as regenerative medicine, meaning it is a therapy which deals with the "process of replacing, engineering or regenerating human or animal cells, tissues or organs to restore or establish normal function."

Three-year-old Thoroughbreds who debut in January almost never make it to the Kentucky Derby four months later, and our horse was no exception. Recurring injury and soreness were the pattern for Faversham, but we were able to nurse him back to become a winner on multiple racing surfaces in California and Kentucky. He dominated a one-mile maiden special weight test by 3 1/4 lengths on Santa Anita's turf course at 3 for trainer Art Sherman, and won a 1 1/16-mile allowance at 4 on the all-weather surface at Turfway Park for the Midwest trainer Mike Maker.

We retired Faversham in the spring of his 5-year-old season after 19 starts, and placed him at Daehling Ranch in California as a stallion prospect. Because he is classified as a ridgling due to having an undescended testicle, a trait that is fairly common among A.P. Indy's male descendants, and also because of the less than desirable timing of his retirement toward the end of the 2020 breeding season, we provided him with a handful of test breedings which resulted in a very small first foal crop—one colt and one filly—born in May 2021.

For Faversham's second year at stud, and first commercial season, we listed him at a reasonable $2,000 fee to entice outside breeders. We also offered a free breeding to all of our California Chrome Foal Share Program participants, while Denise and I sent our "B" team mares to California to support him.

Faversham is now set at $2,500 for the 2022 breeding season. We believe he will catch on in California, and expect some runners.

Also at Daehling Ranch, we've obtained 25% of the well-bred stallion Pontiff, a Giant's Causeway half-brother to Pulpit out of the important matriarch Preach. This multiple winner recently moved from Washington to Northern California, and is siring some good-looking babies. His oldest foals will be 3 in 2022.

Why Not Wyoming?

Denise and I acquired Lucky Bode at the Barrett's sale at Del Mar. He is a half brother to two-time California Stallion of the year Lucky Pulpit. We will stand him for 2022 in Wyoming. Here we will experiment with Female Family Inbreeding focusing not on Numbered Account but Lucky Spell, a very good CA-Bred mare. Lucky Spell had two famous daughters, Lucky Soph, the dam of Lucky Pulpit, and Trolly Song, the dam of Unbridled Song.

We will breed Bode to several of our California Chrome sired mares and see what transpires.

Our goal is to get a Wyoming-bred graded stakes winner. A very lofty goal indeed!

Love The Chase 2.0

I'd like to circle back to the most important mare we have owned to date in order to share a brief story for the first time publicly.

Denise and I were visiting our horses at various Lexington farms in early November 2018. On November 4, we sat down in our hotel's restaurant to watch Fasig-Tipton's November mixed sale on Denise's iPad. We were going to try to purchase Love the Chase, who was in foal to Uncle Mo at the time.

Travis White of Taylor Made Farm was acting as our agent, and we had authorized him to bid to $1.1 million. We had a sample platter of the house appetizers and a pitcher of Sam Adams on the table keeping our attention while we waited for our former broodmare's hip number to arrive.

About two horses before California Chrome's dam entered the ring, Travis called my cell phone. He was set up in the back ring and had told the spotter closest to him that he would be bidding. We were ready.

When the bidding started, it was very fast as there was a lot of live action. As we approached $1 million, I instructed Travis to bid the max $1.1 million, which he did. There was a slight delay until the next bid, which had me hopeful for a few seconds, then two quick $100,000 jumps up to $1.3 million. I think the last two were the consignor bumping it up to the reserve to see if they could get a taker. They couldn't, so she walked out of the ring unsold.

Travis approached the seller after the bidding to offer our $1.1 million again. They countered with $1.25 million; we walked away.

If we would have won the day, our plans would have changed a great deal. We never would be able to support Chrome's 2019 breeding season the way we did.

For her part, Love the Chase's first foal remains her masterpiece. Since we sold her in 2016, she has produced foals of racing age by the prominent Kentucky stallions Tapit, Pioneer of the Nile and Uncle Mo.

Although these offspring have sold at auction for a combined $1.7 million, they have yielded just one win and less than $57,000 in earnings from their 15 combined starts as of this writing.

Komorebi no Omoide

Komorebi no Omoide
JS Company

22

THE NEXT GENERATION

California Chrome's foals first hit the track in 2020 during the COVID-19 pandemic. This worldwide health crisis, of course, put a damper on things and even caused the temporary suspension of live racing in the U.S., but it did provide some much-needed levity amid the day-to-day dreariness of COVID coverage to watch how these runners progressed when the tracks gradually opened back up.

Grade 1 Quality From The Get-Go

The first foal by California Chrome to race in the U.S. is, as of this writing, his highest earner to date. His Louisiana-bred filly Cilla only managed to finish third in her career debut at Delaware Park on June 29, 2020, but she quickly learned how to play the game with a follow-up, 7 1/4-length maiden special weight victory on August 13 to become her sire's first U.S. winner.

Less than two months later, she ran third in Belmont Park's $250,000 Frizette Stakes (G1) for 2-year-old fillies. Finishing second in that race was the subsequent Breeders' Cup Juvenile Fillies (G1) winner and 2020 Champion 2-Year-Old Filly, Vequist. The winner was Dayoutoftheoffice, runner-up in the Breeders' Cup Juvenile Fillies and, later, a $2.85 million purchase as a racing/broodmare prospect by Japan's Shadai Farm at the 2021 Fasig-Tipton November Sale. Top company, indeed.

In 2021, Cilla became Chrome's first black-type stakes winner and first graded stakes winner with triumphs in the $70,000 Louisiana Legends Mademoiselle Stakes at Evangeline Downs in June and in Saratoga's $242,500 Prioress Stakes (G2) in September.

Produced by the G3-placed, nine-time stakes winner Sittin At the Bar, a multiple Louisiana-bred champion by Into Mischief, Cilla herself is a three-time stakes winner and $371,000-earner through mid-December of her 3-year-old season.

Also earning graded stakes credentials for California Chrome in 2021 were a pair of juveniles from his second foal crop.

The filly California Angel, a $5,000 Keeneland November weanling, reminded many fans and media members of her sire with her own rags-to-riches tale. After upsetting Keeneland's $200,000 JPMorgan Chase Jessamine Stakes (G2) at 17-1 in October, she next contested the $920,000 Breeders' Cup Juvenile Fillies Turf (G1) at Del Mar, running 11th of 14, but only four lengths behind the winner, after a seven-wide trip as her sire's first Breeders' Cup starter.

Chrome was also represented in 2021 by his winning colt Midnight Chrome, third-place finisher in Aqueduct's longstanding Remsen Stakes (G2) for 2-year-olds.

International Male

With only a few weeks remaining on the 2021 calendar, California Chrome is represented by nearly 100 international winners from his first two crops of racing age, and collective progeny earnings of more than $3.5 million. He boasts more winners than any other stallion who entered stud in North America in 2017, and seven black-type performers among his starters in this country.

As mentioned previously, his 31 early winners in Chile make him that country's leading first-crop sire of 2021.

In addition to the United States and Chile, both in which he covered mares as a breeding stallion, California Chrome has also sent out winners in Canada, Japan, France, Russia and Saudi Arabia.

Selling MTL

Working hard to drive sales at Martin Testing Labs (MTL) finally brought us a comfortable lifestyle and the opportunity to develop our horse racing and horse breeding business. Success in horse breeding and racing brought wealth at an even greater pace, and thus demanded more of our time.

In 2020, we quickly learned there is only so much time in a day and only so many directions you can be pulled. It wore on us at many different levels. We were tired, and decided to focus on horse racing and breeding as that was where we had placed our largest investment in money and time, and it was where we received the greatest enjoyment.

Truox, a specialty oxidizer technology company I had co-founded with my brother Roy, was selling about $6 million per year in products with product margins of from 30% to 50%, depending on the product. Though we still own a large percentage of Truox stock, my direct involvement had tapered off over the years and Roy was responsible for the direct management of the company. Truox still does not provide a revenue stream for us, as profits are plowed back into research and development and new product registrations with the Environmental Protection Agency (EPA). I'm hopeful this will change after the first EPA product registration.

In 2020, the U.S. aerospace industry was growing by leaps and bounds. Companies like Aerojet Rocketdyne, Blue Origin, SpaceX, Firefly Aerospace and many others had been occasional direct customers of MTL, but had always provided us with more testing work by the testing requirements they place on their vendors and payload customers. Many of their vendors were MTL customers.

Also in 2020, an MTL customer named Precision Fluid Controls (PFC) was having us quote the qualification testing and product screening testing for a very large space program for which they would supply fluid pumps, regulators, valves and other controls. I was faced with a choice: I could use this upcoming surge in testing revenue to better position MTL for a sale down the line at a much higher price, or I could offer to sell the lab now to PFC.

Did I mention how tired we were?

During the first half of 2020, we negotiated the sale of the lab to PFC. The deal closed in June 2020, and was structured to provide the sale proceeds to MTL's employees. Denise and I only received a bill from the IRS for the taxes due.

The word I used, employees, is incorrect. Denise and I firmly believed that these good folks did not work for us, they really worked with us! Paying the taxes on the deal was a small price to pay to get to my retirement earlier.

Tragically, my one true partner in business and in life was not able to fully enjoy the fruits of our hard labor.

23

LOVE, AND LOSS

On May 31, 2021, Denise and I were thrilled to watch on television as our homebred colt Mo Mosa splashed to a 3 1/2-length victory in the $400,000 Steve Sexton Mile Stakes (G3) at a rainy Lone Star Park, scoring the most important win of his career. Although we were not able to make this Texas race in person, it was extremely rewarding to see our blue-and-yellow Martin Racing silks back in the winner's circle on such a grand scale, and at odds of 23-1 to boot.

His romp in the mud that day marked an achievement for us on multiple levels.

Not only was this Uncle Mo colt our first graded stakes winner since Chrome dominated the Awesome Again Stakes at Santa Anita in October 2016, we had purchased him in-utero when we acquired his dam, Roughing, just one month after that Grade 1 triumph, during the 2016 Keeneland November sale, using some of our proceeds from selling Chrome's dam, Love the Chase. Talk about a full-circle moment.

Just two weeks after Mo Mosa's big Memorial Day win, my beloved wife and partner suffered a sudden, massive stroke. Our children dropped everything to drive more than 800 miles together from California to be with us in her hospital room in Idaho. True to style, she fought valiantly for her life, but we ultimately had to say our final, heartbreaking goodbyes on June 14.

Denise and I had just celebrated her 61st birthday in late May. I think anyone would agree that this is far too young to lose a cherished loved one, especially a vibrant woman who is so thoughtful, intelligent and widely admired. To put it simply, she was a great Midwestern gal.

A trained chemist and California State University graduate, Denise was CEO of Martin Testing Labs from its creation in 2000 until its sale in June 2020. She previously worked for the U.S. Air Force as a civilian employee at McClellan Air Force Base.

In semi-retirement, she served her adopted Wyoming community on the North Alpine Water District Board of Directors. Just prior to her death, she had also begun taking online university courses on astronomy. Always in search of new knowledge, she was building a telescope to view the clear Wyoming night sky.

Denise was the co-founder, and heart, of Martin Racing. The one who took care of all the little details that made running our rapidly growing equine venture more than a full-time job. This included communicating daily with our farm, horse and business partners around the world, and interacting with the multitude of California Chrome fans, both in person and through his official social media channels. She always took time out for the Chromies.

She was also the heart of our close-knit family, and we have been grieving her loss together as we struggle to find a way forward without her.

Two months after my wife passed away, I set off on a pre-planned, three-week fishing trip to Montana with our son, Perry Jr. In between casting our lines for cutthroat trout and telling old yarns by campfire, this father-son expedition gave me the clarity and space I needed to help me start to heal. It also granted me the opportunity to begin writing this memoir, which Denise and I had been planning on tackling together. It was, after all, "Our Story" to tell.

Her presence is everywhere—in the wonderful children we nurtured together, in the beautiful home we shared together and in the limitless dreams we envisioned together, dreams which I am now left to pursue on my own. Fortunately, our daughter, Kelly, has decided to help pick up the reins by pursuing a more active role within Martin Racing, which I gratefully welcome.

They say life goes on. And it does, although some days are more difficult than others. Putting my thoughts down here, on the record, has thankfully helped me find at least some much-needed peace and closure as I am forced to conclude a significant chapter of my life, while continuing to plan for the future. It's yet another in a rather long list of gifts that California Chrome has given me.

Sir Winston Churchill is widely credited with penning the brilliant quote, "There is something about the outside of a horse that is good for the inside of a man."

For our flashy red horse, that oft-repeated mantra is certainly true. But it is actually what HE has inside, in his huge heart that belongs to a once-in-a-generation Thoroughbred, that has defined him as a champion for the ages.

Thank you, California Chrome.

24

EPILOGUE

This book is not a tell-all. If there is something you were expecting to read about that you didn't, it is because it is not part of "our story."

If you didn't get it from the racing partnership name I selected, Dumb Ass Partners, let me spell it out. I don't take myself that seriously; if others do, then they can deal with it. When people call me names in the media, unsocial media or otherwise, I am not hurt; I am actually entertained by it. Usually that elicits more name-calling, so thank you!

This part of the book will be a little self-serving, so I saved it until the end where I can at least consolidate it.

Over the past several years, I received many requests from Chromies, or people related to Chromies, who were gravely ill or dying. Very often, their last wish was to pet California Chrome and feed him a cookie. I simply made some phone calls; it was trainer Art Sherman and his crew who made these visits happen.

Along with both sets of our former partners, Denise and I gave the public and the media an unheard-of level of access to this great horse, and it was much appreciated by most of those people who were able to take advantage of it.

Denise was a very gracious and generous person, the light of my life and the soft cushion to mitigate my harsh edges. She handled all of the check-writing to charities and constant donations of halters, saddle cloths, jockey silks, horseshoes and other Chrome collectibles.

She was the inspiration for our partnership with The V Foundation for Cancer Research. My late wife and I both believed that it is best to try and support the greater good for all, rather than pick only one or two people to help. The V Foundation is a perfect example of this: 100% of every dollar donated to this organization goes toward the fight to cure cancer.

I am proud of the job we did in supporting our horse—before, during and after his celebrated racing career.

This book was written in advance of California Chrome's eligibility for the National Museum of Racing's Hall of Fame. Five years after a Thoroughbred retires from racing, he or she becomes eligible to be elected to the Hall of Fame, our industry's ultimate honor. Chrome's first year of eligibility is 2022, and it is my fervent hope that he will be a first-ballot inductee. The remarkable racing achievements of our two-time Horse of the Year will live on in the record books, and Denise and I were secure in our belief that his progeny will advance his legend.

What I am most proud of was our partnership with Chrome's people. I am talking about the backside team members who took such excellent care of him, despite the never-ending glare and scrutiny that were generated by an international spotlight.

Within these pages, I've already discussed the stable stakes from purses won. What I did not disclose is that stable stakes for the backside workers climbed to 5% for each of our horse's Dubai World Cup efforts in 2015 and 2016. In total, Chrome's lucrative back-to-back appearances in this $10 million race generated $400,000 for distribution to his barn crew.

In addition to the other purse funds generated, almost every sponsorship we garnered was distributed 50% to Chrome's circle of caregivers. I just felt that his people wore the hats and shirts with sponsor logos, so they should benefit from doing so. Participating in the $1 million Pennsylvania Derby in 2014 generated another $100,000 for Chrome's workers.

I don't know all the outcomes, but most of the good people who took care of Chrome on a daily basis while he was racing are now prospering, in large part because of these disbursements.

Raul and Florentina Rodriguez saved their money and purchased a farm in Mexico upon which to retire. Dihigi Gladney always had his pony ride business at Santa Anita, and has now passed his love of horses and riding to his children. His son, Jayden, works with the ponies and his daughter, London, rides bareback and competes in barrel racing events. Another of Chrome's former exercise riders, Anna Wells, is now Anna Meah, an up-and-coming, Kentucky-based trainer with whom Martin Racing has entrusted some racehorses.

This is the legacy I cherish, and that is our story.

The Author with our hero.
Photo by Denise Martin

When Perry Martin was a young boy, he had freckles and curly black hair. When the girls in his class would tell him he was cute, he would blush, the girls would giggle and the other boys in the class would become jealous and call him names.

By high school, his frame had grown to more than 6 feet in height, and he was encouraged to try out for football. He made the team and stuck with it for a year and a half, before finally deciding that an after-school job would pay better and not hurt so much. He quit the football team, and was called names.

In his career performing root cause failure analysis on high-profile U.S. Air Force "mishaps," when he determined that the root cause of a problem was design, the designers would call him names. When he determined that the root cause of a problem was manufacturing flaws, the manufacturers would call him names. When he determined that the root cause of a problem was maintenance, the maintenance personnel would call him names. When he determined that a crack had been present during inspection cycles, and had not been found by inspectors, the inspectors would call him names.

Perry Martin's life prepared him well to become a Thoroughbred racehorse breeder and owner. His motto is: "If they are not calling you names, you probably missed something!"

Acknowledgements

Editing and fact-checking by:
Lisa Groothedde
Owner & President
Thoroughbred Information Agency
www.thoroughbredinfo.com

Foreward by:
Rommy Faversham
equicross.com

Front Cover Photo by:
Dr. Jon Overholt MD

Back Cover Photo by:
Dan Dry
Managing Director Content Creation Studio

Vox Populi posters and press releases courtesy of:
Secretariat.com

Interior Photo of Komorebi no Omoide by:
JS Company

Interior Photo of The Author with California Chrome by:
Denise Martin

Interior Photos of California Chrome at Taylor Made Farm
September 2019 by:
Jenny Doyle
JennyPhoto
JennyPhoto@yahoo.com

Special Thanks to all of Chrome's People who kept him happy and healthy
and ultimately made this book possible.

Last but not least, THANK YOU CHROMIES!

CALIFORNIA CHROME: CAREER ACCOMPLISHMENTS

Winner:

- 2016 Dubai World Cup (G1) / Meydan Racecourse
- 2014 Kentucky Derby (G1) / Churchill Downs
- 2014 Preakness Stakes (G1) / Pimlico Race Course
- 2016 Pacific Classic Stakes (G1) / Del Mar
- 2014 Santa Anita Derby (G1) / Santa Anita Park
- 2014 Hollywood Derby (G1) – Turf / Hollywood Park
- 2016 Awesome Again Stakes (G1) / Santa Anita Park
- 2014 San Felipe Stakes (G2) / Santa Anita Park
- 2016 San Pasqual Stakes (G2) / Santa Anita Park
- 2016 San Diego Handicap (G2) / Del Mar
- 2014 California Cup Derby / Santa Anita Park
- 2013 King Glorious Stakes / Hollywood Park
- 2016 Winter Challenge Stakes / Los Alamitos Race Course
- 2016 Trans Gulf Electromechanical Trophy Handicap / Meydan Racecourse
- 2013 Graduation Stakes / Del Mar

Eclipse Awards:

- 2014 Horse of the Year
- 2016 Horse of the Year
- 2014 Champion 3-Year-Old Colt
- 2016 Champion Older Horse

California Thoroughbred Breeders Association Awards:

- 2014 California Horse of the Year
- 2016 California Horse of the Year

- 2014 California Champion Turf Horse
- 2014 California Champion 3-Year-Old Male
- 2015 California Champion Older Male
- 2016 California Champion Older Male

Secretariat Vox Populi ("Voice of the People") Award: 2014

Secretariat Vox Populi ("Voice of the People") Award: 2016

All-Time Leading Thoroughbred Earner In North America (January 2017): $14,752,650

CPSIA information can be obtained
at www.ICGtesting.com
Printed in the USA
BVHW041011040222
627985BV00015B/462